PLATO'S LAUGHTER

SUNY series in Ancient Greek Philosophy

Anthony Preus, editor

PLATO'S LAUGHTER

SOCRATES AS SATYR AND COMICAL HERO

Sonja Madeleine Tanner

SUNY PRESS

Cover image of Satyr and Dionysus by the potter Hieron used with permission by the antique collection of the State Museum of Berlin – Prussian cultural heritage (*Antikensammlung, Staatliche Museen zu Berlin – Preussischer Kulturbesitz*).

Published by State University of New York Press, Albany

Printed in the United States of America

For information, contact State University of New York Press, Albany, NY
www.sunypress.edu

Production, Ryan Morris
Marketing, Michael Campochiaro

Library of Congress Cataloging-in-Publication Data

Names: Tanner, Sonja, 1972-

Title: Plato's laughter : Socrates as satyr and comical hero / Sonja Madeleine Tanner.

Description: Albany, NY : State University of New York, 2017. | Series: SUNY series in ancient Greek philosophy | Includes bibliographical references and index.

Identifiers: LCCN 2016056708 (print) | LCCN 2017040526 (ebook) | ISBN 9781438467382 (e-book) | ISBN 9781438467375 (hardcover : alk. paper) | ISBN 9781438467368 (paperback : alk. paper)

Subjects: LCSH: Plato. | Laughter. | Comic, The. | Wit and humor. | Socrates.

Classification: LCC B398.C63 (ebook) | LCC B398.C63 T36 2017 (print) | DDC 184—dc23

LC record available at https://lccn.loc.gov/2016056708

10 9 8 7 6 5 4 3 2 1

Dedicated to

MARK, JACKSON, LIAM, and AUDREY,

and the many different kinds of laughter we share.

Contents

ACKNOWLEDGMENTS		ix
INTRODUCTION		xi
	The Superiority Theory of Laughter	xvii
	Playful and Consequential Laughter	xxi
	The Incongruity Theory of Laughter	xxii
	The Chapter Breakdown	xxiv
CHAPTER 1	The *Apology* of Socrates: Is Socrates a Comical Hero?	1
	The Comical Apology	4
	Socrates and the Homeric Hero	8
	Socrates and the Traits of Comical Heroes	15
	Humanity as Laughable and Self-Directed Laughter	18
CHAPTER 2	The *Laches's* Comical Structure and "The Refined Thinkers Who Are Really Poor"	23
	The *Laches's* Comical Structure	26
	Lysimachus as a Comical Figure	32
	Nicias as a Comical Figure	34
	Stesilaus as a Comical Figure	37
	Laches as a Comical Figure	39
	Courage, Laughter, and Self-Knowledge	45
	Conclusion	51
CHAPTER 3	Tumbling Down to Earth: Laughter, Limitation, and Self-Knowledge in Plato's *Charmides*	55
	Laughter on the Bench	58
	Tragic and Comic Laughter	59
	Socratic versus Critian *Sōphrosynē*: Theory and Practice	67
	Conclusion	77

CHAPTER 4 Naming the Nameless: Logos, Laughter, and Self-Forgetting 83

Laughter and Logos in the *Cratylus* 86
Laughter and False Speaking in the *Euthydemus* 92
Logos and the Satirical 102

CHAPTER 5 Bawdy Politics: Satyrical Laughter and Self-Knowledge in the Symposium 113

Aristophanes's Hiccups 118
Socrates as Satyr 127
Conclusion 145

CONCLUSION *Ponēria*, Self-Knowledge, and Comical, Platonic Optimism 151

NOTES 159

WORKS CONSULTED 195

INDEX 213

Acknowledgments

So many have helped to make this book better than it otherwise would have been, whether through direct support on the material or inspiring conversations. The remaining warts are entirely my own. May Logos itself enjoy the occasions for laughter that these shortcomings provide, evidence as they may be of the self-forgetting involved even in writing on self-forgetting. Particular thanks go to Andrew Kenyon; the SUNY Press, and its anonymous reviewers; the UCCS philosophy faculty and students, especially Raphael Sassower, Allison Postell, Mary Ann Cutter, Lorraine Arangno, and the Committee on Research and Creative Works for its support; Colorado College's philosophy faculty and students, Jonathon Lee, Bernie Freydberg, Rob Metcalf, Michael Naas, Shane Ewegen, Carolin Hahnemann, Naomi Reshotko, Arindam Chakribarty, Nalin Ranasinghe, Dmitri Nikulin, Monica Vilhauer, Edward Butler, Russell Ford; and the two gentlemen within earshot at a conference whose eyebrows shot way up when they overheard that I was working on comedy in Plato who, oddly, made me think that I might—just possibly—be on to something worthwhile.

More personally, I would like to thank Jackson, Liam, and Audrey, not only for being the lights of my life but, more specifically, for sleeping and thereby allowing me to write this; and August and Ava, my furry office companions, whose protective vigilance on two continents kept me safe from many a postal carrier and inquisitive squirrel while writing. Finally, my most heartfelt appreciation goes to Mark for offering support and inspiration in so many ways, including always being able to make me laugh, without which this would not have been possible. Thank you, my love.

An earlier version of the chapter 4 was originally published as "Comedy as Self-Forgetting: Implications of Sallis' Interpretation of Plato's Cratylus" in *Journal of Speculative Philosophy* 27, no. 2 (2013): 188-98.

Introduction

> [Plato] was so modest [aidemon] and well-regulated [kosmiois] that he was never once seen to laugh excessively [gelon huperagan . . . komikon].
>
> —*Diogenes Laertius, Lives of Eminent Philosophers*

Plato is funny. This single conviction immediately puts me and this book at odds with the bulk of almost two millennia of Platonic scholars and literature. It has, with some regularity, raised eyebrows. This book is, in a sense, a defense and explication of this conviction. I am not trying to make the reader laugh, nor am I suggesting that Plato was a comedian, especially not a comedian *instead of* a philosopher. What I am trying to suggest is that Plato frequently uses and incorporates the comic and laughter in his dialogues in philosophically meaningful ways that have thus far generated scant attention. What have we missed by neglecting these? What if we have simply failed to hear Plato's laughter?

There are a number of ways of answering this question. For one, I will argue that we have overlooked an exuberance in the dialogues that is not necessarily tied to ideological commitments, and that is often missing in how we read Plato and perhaps in our very comportment to philosophy itself. For another, I will argue we have missed all conceptions and uses of laughter other than the one type of laughter that is commonly thought to be recognized by "Plato": derisive or malicious laughter. In addition, we find instances of what we today might term *slapstick*, playful joking, farce, parody, plays on words, and satire.

Much has been written about Socratic irony, itself a kind of humor. Irony, however, tends to center on the rhetorical and the intellectual. Laughter can arise from a broader range of sources, including the physical, and itself constitutes a potentially corporeal, emotional, and intellectual reaction. It is not *eirōneia* (nor is it the Latinized irony) that describes the interlocutors' boisterous jostling of each other on the bench in the opening of the *Charmides*. And the reaction Socrates describes is not one of ironic detachment from the situation, a sort of laughter from above, but is instead situated, physical, and involving "much laughter" (*gelōta polun*) (*Charmides* 155c). Even if we do not go quite as far as Kierkegaard, who deems irony "infinite, absolute negativity," irony carries with it negative, empty, and destructive connotations that need not be associated with laughter.[1] Laughter is more robust and capable, as I will argue, of addressing a fuller range of gelastic occurrences in the Platonic dialogues than is generally recognized.

Laughter is an ambivalent force for the Greeks; powerful and life-affirming at times, but prone toward excesses and potentially devastating at others. Historically, it undergoes a philosophical change in Plato where Socrates suggests that being laughed at does not matter, whereas for many prior and contemporary tragic figures, the specter of being laughed at can be a fate worse than death.[2] Socrates actively defuses laughter's potency in this regard, and plays up its capacities to promote self-reflection and humility. What is to be feared, for Socrates, is not being laughed at, but lacking the self-knowledge that enables actions and beliefs that are ridiculous, or to be laughed at. Indeed, Socrates presents himself as a comic figure in a number of ways, participates in laughter, and repeatedly suggests himself (and others) to be, in some way, ridiculous. These are striking developments in the social function of laughter, but they are predicated on philosophical shifts in the meanings of laughter, meanings that elude us when we interpret the dialogues as strictly solemn.

The title of this book thus refers to occurrences—both actual and potential—of laughter in various forms in the dialogues. Actual occurrences of laughter in the dialogues are infrequent, but this is entirely consistent with laughter in Greek literature as a whole, where it is more often anticipated than actualized, and so an account of laughter must expand to accommodate this.[3] Indeed, laughter can be intensified by being left out, or implied, as I will suggest happens in the *Symposium*, when the ostentatious Aristophanes undertakes an assortment of "cures" for his hiccups while the speeches in praise of eros proceed. Laughter may also be the appropriate response of another set of participants in the dialogues—their readers, or audience.[4] This is where the concept of laughter becomes, perhaps, most difficult. How does one know what ought to induce laughter? Given cultural, social, and historical differences, how do we know what would have made a classical Greek laugh?

These are very challenging questions, to this day. Laughter is not reducible to theory, to what one knows, but remains intractable.[5] I cannot explain what is funny about something I laugh about by reference to an incongruity, or a sudden flash of feeling superior. Where actual laughter or explicit suggestions that something is ridiculous are omitted, the challenge is providing evidence that at least suggests, if not proves, laughter to be appropriate to the situation. I have taken a conservative approach to this challenge by using as a paradigm of laughter the slightly earlier, Attic literature written in large part to evoke just such a response: Old Comedy.[6]

Laughter in Aristophanes's eleven surviving plays, composing as they do the only intact works of Old Comedy left to posterity, occurs in a variety of forms. Parody, satire, vulgar examples, stock comic characters, bawdy events, puns, and jokes join ridicule in Aristophanes's various ways of eliciting laughter. When these occur in Platonic dialogues, such as Socrates's repeatedly playing the comic role of "elderly schoolboy" dedicating himself to study with such dubious figures as Euthydemus and Callicles, there is substantial reason to believe that these may be comical rather than simply "serious" (or, for that matter, merely "ironic") incidents. Just as we need not assume that anything comical that occurs in Aristophanes is a form of ridicule, we need not assume this in Platonic dialogues either.

Ridicule has been substituted for a larger whole in Platonic scholarship, and by focusing on ridicule (in what little literature that does so), we have missed examples of laughter that lie beyond its narrow scope. Laughter in this book, then, is intended as a broader construal that encompasses a greater variety of comic and humorous phenomena. It includes not just instances of actual laughter among direct participants in the dialogues, but also jokes, humorous incidents, situations, characterizations, and language, aimed at a broader audience including the dialogue's readers. Many of these occurrences do not provoke the dialogues' participants to laugh aloud, but are instead left for the reader to discern and, perhaps, to find funny. Doing so requires sensitivity to laughter beyond ridicule as well as sensitivity to the dramatic dimensions of the dialogues.

My proposal then is to cast a wider net, to search for many different sorts of laughter, not just in what is *said* in the dialogues, but also in what is *done* in them, in the argument as well as in the dramatic action. My goal is not to *prove* that such incidents or jokes are funny. Anyone who has ever tried to explain a joke knows what a mistake such an undertaking is. A naysayer could find dreariness even in the opening of the *Charmides*, in which men shove each other aside to make room for the handsome eponymous character next to themselves on a bench, thus sending those sitting on the far ends of the bench tumbling off to much laughter. But if I show that laughter in Plato amounts to more than ridicule, then a "serious" reexamination of Platonic dialogues and the use and meaning of laughter therein is necessary.

It might be objected at the outset that a gelastic reading of Plato appears a modern (over)interpretation of, and imposition on, antiquity. While the interpretation espoused here does indeed run counter to hundreds of years of agelastic, or even antigelastic, readings dating back as far as Neoplatonism, it is entirely consistent with several commentators from Greek and Latin antiquity, namely Aristotle, Cicero, and Quintilian, who appear to read Plato's Socratic *logoi* as comical. If this is the case, the antigelastic readings of Plato may originate from a later time.

Aristotle likens Plato's Socratic dialogues to Sophronic Mimes, a type of comical, dramatic production popular in the fifth century BCE that centered on the daily lives of the lower classes. Targeting types over individuals, much like New Comedy, the Mime involved little personal invective.[7] The Mime's purpose was to raise a laugh, and it apparently did so heartily. Cicero and Quintilian cite the *mimicus risus* as an example of excessive laughter to be avoided by the skillful orator.[8] The Mime thus exceeds the strictures of the liberal jest. It is striking, then, that Aristotle categorizes the Socratic logos as a type of mime, lamenting that: We have no common name for a mime (*mimous*) of Sophron or Xenarchus and a Socratic Conversation (*Sōkratikous logous*) . . .[9] The Socratic logos is akin to the Mimes of Sophron and Xenarchus.[10] Quintilian suggests a further connection anecdotally, "Grammar and the arts were once linked . . . and there were those who taught both, as Sophron shows, a writer of mimes indeed, but one of whom Plato so approved that it is believed that when he died he had his works beneath his pillow."[11] Diogenes Laertius claims that Plato was responsible for importing neglected works by Sophron into Athens.[12] While Aristotle's categorization might be written off as drawing on a likeness beyond the comical, perhaps in the eccentricity of Socrates's characterization, another source from Latin antiquity makes the connection between Plato and comedy explicit.[13]

Cicero suggests a gelastic reading of Platonic dialogues. A discussion of irony in the *De Oratore* lauds Socrates: ". . . my opinion is that Socrates far surpassed all others for accomplished wit in this strain of irony or assumed simplicity."[14] Socrates illustrates a paradigm of refined wit that is suitable to a gentleman. While we might be tempted to read this as another ancient testimony in support of what has come to be called Socratic Irony, Cicero's attribution of humor to Socrates extends past irony. In the *De Officiis*, Cicero writes, "There are, generally speaking, two sorts of jest: the one course [*illiberale*], rude, vicious, indecent [*obscenum*]; the other, refined [*elegans*], polite [*urbanium*], clever [*ingeniosum*], and witty [*facetum*] With this latter sort not only our own Plautus and the Old Comedy of Athens, but also the books of Socratic philosophy abound."[15] One might, at first blush, be startled to find in Cicero an advocate of Athenian Old Comedy as being refined and polite. But what is far more startling is that the "books of Socratic philosophy" are grouped together with Plautus and, by implication, Aristophanes, as exemplary of the recommended sort of laughter. If we can attribute the claims of his interlocutor to Cicero himself, Cicero read the "books of Socratic philosophy" as abounding with wit, humor, and laughter. And while the claim in *De Oratore* is specific to Socrates as an exemplary ironist, the phrasing of "books of Socratic philosophy" in *De Officiis* is broad enough to support reading this attribution to Plato and, inasmuch as some of his books constitute "Socratic philosophy," to Xenophon.

The suggestion with which I began—that Plato is funny—suddenly does not sound radical anymore. Rather than imposing a contemporary interpretation on works from antiquity, this project attempts a return to such ancient perspectives. It takes a "serious" look at laughter in the dialogues, but not in the sense of attempting to reduce all forms of laughter to a singular cause or theory, because laughter will ultimately exceed and evade any such reduction. Instead, I will attempt to elucidate some of the philosophical meanings and consequences of the multivalent uses of laughter in several Platonic dialogues and particularly in the comical portrayal of Socrates. I will suggest that laughter undergoes a historical shift in Plato, one that acknowledges its more positive and philosophical potential. Such potential is missed entirely when we attribute a superiority theory of laughter to Plato and believe laughter in the dialogues to be nonexistent, or at best, malicious. Important to this will be a linguistic argument distinguishing uses of the Greek *gelaō* ("to laugh") from compounded forms such as *katagelaō* ("to laugh at," "jeer," or "mock") and *epigelaō* ("to laugh approvingly"). While the compounded forms hold evaluative connotations, meaning laughing *at*, *down upon*, or *in support of* someone, the uncompounded *gelaō* supports a range of meanings that includes playful, inconsequential, and even benevolent types of laughter. The broader *gelaō* is essentially replaced by the more specific, negative, and compounded form *katagelaō* in claims that Plato holds, and that the dialogues reflect, a superiority theory of laughter.

What we will find is a far greater emphasis on the Dionysian in the dialogues than they are usually credited with. From the use of traditional comical techniques, forms, and characterizations to a more direct relationship between the stage and audience, Platonic dialogues contain within them the laughter that Plato has long been thought to be missing. Socrates himself, it will be shown, closely resembles a most Dionysian figure, a mischievous and comical hero at the service of the god of comedy, tragedy, and rejuvenation. Ewegen notes a critical difference: "comedy, unlike tragedy, is self-aware: it draws itself into the parodic critical space that it itself opens up."[16] Socrates acts as a yardstick against which we, the dialogues' audience, can measure ourselves, and what we will find is that we bear a closer resemblance to him, including in our laughability. Self-knowledge is thus not rendered impossible by what is comical; instead, the comical helps make possible self-knowledge.

The superiority theory figures prominently early on in this book, but largely so to move beyond focusing on it exclusively. If this attribution is indeed a false one, and laughter in Platonic dialogues is more than derisive ridicule, then we have misread or neglected at least some of Plato's laughter.[17] Turning to specific occurrences within Platonic dialogues, I will argue that laughter exposes incongruities within oneself as well as the hubristic pretensions to exceed such limitations, and thus that laughter can play a more positive role in regard to the Delphic imperative to "know thyself" than previously acknowledged. These incongruities are what I will call "performative contradictions," or contradictions between what one *says* and what one *does*, and they underscore the significance of action and *praxis* to dialectic. Knowing oneself is not accomplished discursively; acting in accordance with our beliefs is crucial to being the unified sort of person who strives toward the Delphic imperative at the heart of the philosophical enterprise. Laughter helps to curb overweening ambitions in this regard for the limits imposed by humanity mean that we remain, along with Socrates, always to some extent laughable.

The consequences of such an interpretation of laughter within the Platonic dialogues are far-reaching.[18] Substituting derisive ridicule with a more ambivalent laughter in the dialogues implies that we may have substituted self-importance for a certain humility and comic self-recognition that spring from this reading. Assigning to laughter a more substantial role simultaneously emphasizes ambiguity in the dialogues and stresses the challenge of interpretation. It indicates the need for revisiting at least some of what have calcified into "traditional" interpretations. It suggests that we have missed an exuberance in the dialogues, and perhaps, in our very comportment toward philosophy. Finally, what this ultimately points to is a revision of the relation of comedy and philosophy, one that recognizes some mutuality and cross-pollination among them rather than mutual exclusivity. Laughter may not be reducible to what is "serious," but neither are these incommensurable.

The Superiority Theory of Laughter

The case against the existence of laughter in Plato hinges on several passages in the dialogues in which laughter or comedy is explicitly discussed, and on the common attribution to Plato of what has come to be called the superiority theory of laughter. Morreall typifies this assessment of laughter in Plato: "As with so many topics, Western thought about humor and laughter begins with Plato. What we laugh at, in Plato's view, is vice, particularly self-ignorance, in people who are relatively powerless. Our amusement is a kind of malice towards such people, he thought, and this should make us wary of amusement . . . Plato singles out laughter as something to be avoided."[19] Morreall explicitly attributes a superiority theory to Plato, the "ancient critic of laughter,"[20] claiming that Plato thought that ". . . laughter is essentially derisive and that in being amused by someone we are finding that person inferior in some way."[21] For Plato, laughter is, in this account, antisocial, malicious, derisive, and "to be avoided." If Morreall is right, then laughter (*gelaō*) for Plato is nothing else than vicious ridicule (*katagelaō*). In our parlance, there is no "laughing with" in Plato, only "laughing at." Laughter, in other words, is an expression of a perceived superiority over the butt of the joke.

The attribution of the superiority theory to Plato is based on a discussion between Socrates and Protarchus in the *Philebus*, the longest explicit discussion of comedy, the ridiculous, and laughter in the Platonic dialogues. In a discussion about mixed pleasures, Socrates gives the example of one's "state of mind in comedy" (48a). When Protarchus is unable to see a mixture of pleasure and pain therein, Socrates gives the example of *phthonos*, or malice. He asks "will not the malicious person display pleasure at his neighbor's misfortunes?" (48b). Suggesting this to be a vice along with ignorance and stupidity, Socrates then says what one might conclude from this about the ridiculous (*to geloion*): "It is, in sum, a kind of vice that derives its name from a special disposition; it is, among all the vices, the one with a character that stands in direct opposition to the one recommended by the famous inscription in Delphi" (48c). There are three ways in which one can fail to know oneself: one can think oneself richer, more beautiful, or more virtuous than one really is; the third, according to Socrates, is by far the most common of them. Among the virtues, Socrates asks, "is it not especially to wisdom that the largest number of people lay claim, puffing themselves up with quarrels and false pretensions to would-be knowledge?" (49a). Those whom we call ridiculous are those who combine "this delusion with weakness and are unable to avenge themselves when they are laughed at," while those whom we call dangerous and hateful are those who "have the power and strength to take revenge" (49b–c). Such ignorance, in short, is ridiculous as long as it is harmless to others (49e).

Socrates then offers a broader claim that might imply he is offering a theory of laughter. He says, "in lamentations as well as in tragedies and comedies, not only on stage, but also in all of life's tragedies and comedies, pleasures are mixed with pains . . ." (50b). Things such as love, fear, and malice (*phthonos*), Socrates concludes, involve mixtures of pleasures and pain. Whether or not the generalization has been sufficiently argued for, Socrates is not claiming that *phthonos* is to be found in all comedy and tragedy, as Morreall implies. It is but an example of the kind of mixture he is suggesting. There is no "theory" of comedy in the *Philebus* passage. Read in its context, Socrates's claim supports the existence of malicious laughter, but does not support the claim that all comedy and laughter are malicious.

At first blush this passage may appear to substantiate Morreall's attribution of the superiority theory of laughter to Plato, but a closer look reveals two significant problems. The first is that of the *Philebus*'s context: the discussion of malicious laughter occurs within a discussion of mixed pleasures, and serves as an example of the latter, rather than a theory (let alone a comprehensive one) of the former. Malicious laughter is an example of pleasures mixed with pains. This is not a definition of laughter nor a theory of comedy more broadly. It is an example being used by Socrates to discuss an altogether different question. Socrates is suggesting that there is such a thing as malicious laughter; not that *phthonos*, or malice, is at the heart of all laughter. Indeed, we lack such an explicit definition from Plato altogether.

The second problem with the attribution is also derived from a neglect of dramatic context. It is the attribution to Plato of what Socrates (or other characters) says, and has been referred to as the "Plato says" fallacy. It is a fallacy because, aside from the letters, Plato nowhere speaks for and as himself in the extant works. To assume that Socrates stands in as Plato's mouthpiece demands a compelling argument on which this reduction can occur and such an argument has not yet been given satisfactorily. Such a claim, further, assumes that what Plato is up to in writing dialogues differs in no significant sense from the more contemporary tradition of writing treatises in which the author's thoughts are revealed and argued for. Such an assumption entirely dismisses the literary context and dialogical form of these writings. A great tragedy occurs when we reduce the meaning of literary dialogues to vehicles (and remarkably poorly chosen ones at that) for expressing the author's particular beliefs, akin to substituting such a meaning for a great poem. A good part of the beauty and meaning lies in the form, not just in the content.

We seem to be at an impasse. We have the *Philebus* passage, and a scattering of various overt comments about laughter, comedy, and related topics across a number of dialogues. This seems a scanty basis on which to assess the significance and role of laughter in the dialogues, and indeed it is. Perhaps this is why the topic has been left largely neglected, and the kind of reading Morreall offers, largely adopted. But there is a way out of the apparent impasse, and it lies in doing what too many Platonic scholars of the past several centuries have failed to do: taking the dialogues' literary and dramatic form "seriously." If we pay attention to dramatic form, much more laughter in the dialogues materializes: jokes, puns, humorous incidents, situations, and characterizations, many of which lie beyond any superiority theory. Assuming that these are not mere window-dressing, or poetic adornments in between the weightier, "logical" parts of the dialogues, we must then ask why these are included and what they mean, and we must reassess the view of laughter that is commonly attributed to Plato.

A closer look at the superiority theory is warranted. Hobbes supports this theory of laughter,[22] writing, in the Leviathan: "Sudden glory is the passion which maketh those grimaces called LAUGHTER, and is caused either by some sudden act of their own that pleaseth them or by the apprehension of some deformed thing in another by comparison whereof they suddenly applaud themselves."[23] Laughter, in other words, results either from something I do that pleases me immensely, or from a sudden feeling of superiority over the butt of the joke. In the first case, I take pleasure in my own perceived greatness. In the second, I take pleasure in seeing perceived inferiorities in others because it makes me think myself to be better comparatively. In both cases, the pleasure derives from perceiving greatness in oneself. Laughter is thus an expression of perceived superiority—either of oneself in general, or of oneself in relation to a specific butt who has been shown to be inferior. Hobbesian laughter is a function of *phthonos*, or malice, as Socrates describes it in the *Philebus*. Laughing is thus understood as vicious.

Freud also adopts the superiority theory but focuses on the psychological mechanisms by which it functions. He distinguishes between what he calls "tendentious" and "innocuous" jokes to do so. Freud writes, "Sometimes the joke is an end in itself and serves no purpose; at others, it does put itself in the service of such a purpose; it becomes tendentious."[24] Innocuous jokes, then, are those that do not serve a particular aim: "When a joke is not an end in itself, i.e., innocuous, it puts itself at the service of two tendencies only, which can themselves be merged into a single viewpoint; it is either a hostile joke (used for aggression, satire, defence) or it is an obscene joke (used to strip someone naked [Entblössung])."[25] Freud later adds cynical (critical or blasphemous) jokes to this category.[26]

The pleasure of laughter derives from "saving in effort spent on inhibition or suppression."[27] Jokes and humor are forms of economy in which we are able to satisfy instincts and save on the effort we must otherwise make to inhibit such instincts. What these instincts are depends on the type of joke or humor in play. In the case of innocuous jokes, Freud suggests that we take pleasure in the delight of child's play and economize on the effort of critical thinking. In the case of tendentious jokes, Freud suggests that we take pleasure in indulging lustful, aggressive, or cynical instincts from which we must at other times restrain ourselves. In both cases, the pleasure derives from the saving: in the first, in not having to think; in the second, in not having to keep our base impulses in check.

Playful and Consequential Laughter

Although Freud casts the distinction between innocuous and tendentious jokes in terms of how they economize on differing efforts, and ultimately uses this to support a version of the superiority theory of laughter, it is not entirely dissimilar from Stephen Halliwell's distinction between consequential and playful laughter. This distinction, which will become important later, already indicates a range of types of laughter that, when divorced from the Freudian account of laughter's pleasure, begins to tug at the coherence of the superiority theory of laughter. It is worth taking a brief look at now.

Halliwell distinguishes these types of laughter according to the agent's intention as well as the social function of the laughter itself. According to Halliwell, playful laughter is a "cooperative, reciprocally pleasurable form of behavior," a "badge and unifying agent of friendship" and occurs against a background of shared rules in a safe context.[28] It is laughter for its own sake. But Halliwell quickly notes the difficulties of circumscribing gelastic behavior in this way: "Much joking depends upon the appearance or pretence of insult . . . Accordingly, the dividing line between play and actual aggression . . . is thin."[29] Aristotle, likewise, seems aware of a fine line when he describes *eutrapelia* as "educated *hubris*."[30] Hence there is much concern in antiquity over how, when, and about what or whom laughter occurs.

Consequential laughter, for Halliwell, is "embedded in social processes of cause and effect."[31] On the far side of the continuum, its qualities are the reverse of those of playful laughter. Rather than being marked by mutuality, consequential laughter is one-sided. Instead of stemming from, and enhancing, friendship, consequential laughter operates on hierarchies of power and can disintegrate or prevent social connections. It is laughter that is put to the service of a particular aim. Ridicule and laughter aimed at expressing, establishing, or maintaining superiority generally fall into this category.

These two categories will be very useful in evaluating laughter in the Platonic dialogues. The problem is that the boundary between them is, as Halliwell suggests, porous, thus again challenging interpretation. It is easy to see how even laughter expressing superiority might be used in teasing, among friends, and thus be more fittingly described as playful. Similarly, what might be a genuinely consequential struggle could belie playful laughter. Discerning which side laughter falls into is a matter of carefully evaluating context. For now, however, if there is a form of laughter that is playful, and if its pleasure is not accounted for by economizing on one's efforts and thus making oneself feel superior over others in some way, then such a distinction may already anticipate the unraveling of the superiority theory of laughter as the exclusive laughter of the Platonic dialogues. Proponents of another influential theory of laughter—the incongruity theory—will help to tug at these loosening strings.

The Incongruity Theory of Laughter

A parallel argument against the superiority theory is offered by Francis Hutcheson, who promotes instead a version of the incongruity theory. Hutcheson responds by rejecting Hobbes's assumption that all human actions are motivated by "self-love." He acknowledges ridicule as but a specific kind of laughter, rather than the basis of all laughter itself.[32] Rejecting any attribution to Aristotle of a superiority theory on the basis of what is written in the *Poetics*, Hutcheson writes, "this [Aristotle] never intended as a general account of all sorts of Laughter."[33] Parody and burlesque attest to some of the many instances whereby laughter arises without any imagined superiority. The sort of laughter that arises among friends further precludes any perceived superiority, for among good friends "there is often an high mutual esteem."[34] Such exceptions, Hutcheson argues, undo Hobbes's rule as such, and point to ridicule being but a specific kind of laughter.

Hutcheson suggests instead a form of the incongruity theory: we laugh when "whimsical image(s) of opposite ideas" are joined together.[35] When an animal appears to be imitating typically human behavior, for instance, this may strike us as humorous, and it does so with no intonations of power differentials. Indeed, if superiority were the basis of all laughter, Hutcheson argues, then one ought to laugh in direct proportion to how superior one is made to feel, or how inferior the butt of the joke appears, and this, he claims, is not the case. This leads him to claim that "there must necessarily arise a great diversity in mens [*sic*] sentiments of the ridiculous in actions or characters, according as their ideas of dignity and wisdom are various."[36] Cultural and personal differences over what constitutes dignity and baseness preclude any single theory of laughter from specifying exactly what is funny in their conjunction. Laughter thus seems to arise from sources too diverse to be explained by only one.

Another proponent of the incongruity theory is Henri Bergson. Bergson specifies the incongruity in his version of the theory. It is when something lifelike is covered over by a certain rigidity that we laugh at the incongruity between these two. Say a person runs along, intent on a particular aim, then slips, tumbles, and falls to the ground. This is comic because of a certain mechanical behavior that is incongruous with the otherwise adaptable life form that is acting with artificial automation. The runner, so intent on achieving her goal, acted with rigidity and inflexibility instead of with the pliability characteristic of living humans. It is such encrustations of mechanization on the living that are comic, and they are laughable because of such incongruities.

Bergson's goal is very much in line with that of this book: ". . . we shall not aim at imprisoning the comic spirit within a definition. We regard it, above all, as a living thing."[37] To the extent that offering a theory of comedy can avoid "imprisoning the comic spirit," Bergson may be seen as successful. And indeed, the incongruity theory, especially given Hutcheson's accounting for cultural and personal conceptual variability, remains as open as theories of laughter can be. But the very theorization of something like comedy may become an example of Bergson's famous description of the laughable: "something mechanical encrusted on the living."[38]

While such theories are compelling and may shed light on the complex phenomena of laughter, there is no single theory adequate to explain what causes laughter in all contexts and across all historical and cultural differences. Incongruities of some sort may very well be present when something strikes one as laughable. That is not to say, however, that any correlation between the laughable and incongruities is necessarily causation. If it were causation, it would seem that any incongruity would be laughable, and that is not the case. Linguistic categories convey enough of a distinction between ancient Greek and contemporary English to render a unifying theory problematic, even among such closely related cultures. Anyone who has tried to translate a joke from one modern language into another realizes the fragility of laughter in this sense. Some, or even much, of what may have been funny to most Attic Greeks may not strike us as humorous at all. But there are enough common humorous standards—joke-telling, witticisms, puns, mimicry, to name a few—that we might recognize potentially comic moments and situations as such, even if we ourselves are not provoked to laughter by them.

The Chapter Breakdown

For the reasons alluded to above, I am skeptical as to both the explanatory power and the philosophical justifiability of either of these theories of comedy and laughter, and in fact, of the very project of theorizing laughter. Rather than selecting a theory of laughter and then approaching Platonic dialogues with it, I propose to begin with examples of laughter therein and ask what their philosophical significance might be. I am neither adopting nor attempting to forge a theory of laughter in doing so. There is nothing exhaustive or comprehensive about the selected moments of laughter I assess here. Indeed, much more research on different dialogues, jokes, and situations from perspectives other than mine is called for.

The objection might immediately be raised that drawing from multiple dialogues displays hermeneutic insensitivity, or even does violence, to the dialogues' various contexts and implies a unified, and perhaps even doctrinal, view of Plato's philosophy. This book does not, however, suggest that Plato's use of laughter is unified. Indeed, the aim here is to show how much messier the picture truly is: Plato does not appear to subscribe to a superiority theory of laughter, and to support this, I borrow from a number of dialogues and the characterization of Socrates therein to show the diversity of Plato's laughter over any unification thereof. Further, to whatever extent that claiming Socrates to be a sort of comical hero offers a unified view, we will see that his playing a comical hero allows for a great plurality of comical roles. Descaling the superiority theory of laughter from dominating interpretations of Plato's dialogues requires more than one dialogue in which other views and uses of laughter prevail. The result aimed at here is not to distill Plato's laughter, but rather to show how much more messy laughter in the dialogues is than has been assumed, and simultaneously, how philosophically fertile.

The chapters are arranged thematically with the intention of telling a story of Socrates as a type of comical hero, and do not follow any proposed chronological dating. I follow Howland in rejecting the possibility of accurately determining the chronological order of the dialogues' composition on the basis of stylometric analysis, "maturity of style," events internal to the dialogues, and other traditional considerations, and perhaps more importantly, of rejecting the hermeneutic significance of doing so.[39] A number of highly controversial assumptions go into establishing a chronological ordering, not the least of which is that Plato was developing his own doctrine through the dialogues, and that if we could only know when he wrote which dialogue, we could more precisely determine their meaning.[40] Choosing to write dialogues would have been a peculiarly ineffective choice, given such an intention, and the availability of earlier, treatise-like works by Anaxagoras and Democritus suggest what would have been a more appropriate medium in which to express one's personal convictions, if this had been their purpose. Instead, Plato develops philosophical dialogue, drawing from and developing several, earlier forms, including tragedy and, as we will see, various forms of comedy. Interpreting the dialogues *as* dialogues, and finding meaning in their literary and dramatic elements, as well as the philosophical arguments occurring therein, is thus how this book aims to proceed.[41]

There are several dangers to using various dialogues to support the claim that Plato uses laughter for philosophical purposes and that Socrates is something of a comical hero. The first is that, by jumping from one dialogue to another, one does violence to their unique dramatic situations, characters, scenes, and topic. Indeed, this book moves among very different sorts of dialogues and it is impossible to do full justice to the specifics of each, but neither is this the aim. Rather, the first aim is to show that laughter in the dialogues is ambivalent, taking examples from different types of dialogues as evidence.

The second aim—showing Socrates to be playing a comical hero—minimizes the second danger. The danger, affiliated with the first, is that cutting across various dialogues may seem to attribute to Plato something like a system, an attribution that would be very much at odds with the interpretation espoused here. But focusing on the characterization of Socrates as comical does not attribute to him particular consistency. Comical characters have little need for consistency. Indeed, as Plato portrays him, Socrates uses a broad array of types of laughter and comical devices—too broad for the constraints of a single theory or doctrine. Socrates qua comical character is versatile and defies tight restriction, sometimes playing a buffoon, at other times a venerable elder who laughs at himself, and at yet other times, a derisive provocateur. Describing Socrates's characterization as comical is no more doctrinal of a claim than describing him as a gadfly.

The story these dialogues tell is that of a revaluation of comical (as opposed to tragic) laughter and comical heroism. Unlike tragic laughter that is exclusively derisive and destroys the honor of the one laughed at, comical laughter includes a wide array of types, functions, and effects on the butt of the joke. Drawing from the laughter and heroism of Old Comedy, Plato's characterization of Socrates modifies both. Socrates is a more substantial and complex character (largely due to how much more developed his character is) than Aristophanes's protagonists, and the laughter this complexity makes possible is of a new form altogether. It is a laughter that turns logos on itself and exposes the limitations of the one laughing. It is self-reflective laughter.

The book begins with a look at what seems an unlikely comical dialogue, the account of Socrates's trial and conviction to death in the *Apology*. In his bold and comical defense, Socrates displays common traits and behaviors of the heroes of Old Comedy: *ponēria*, or comical roguery often exhibited in their use of *logoi*, turning the tables on their adversaries, being elderly, poor, somehow infirm, and ugly, displaying characteristics of beasts, humans, and the divine, and being rustic, rude, or base in manners. Drawing from an older tradition of the hero, rooted in Archilochus, and from an older tradition of laughter, rooted in Democritus, Plato's Socrates is a new sort of hero, one who is comical, but not *merely* comical, and one who is heroic, but only abstractly comparable to classical heroes, such as Achilles or Palamedes. Chapter 1 thus asks what sort of a hero is Plato's Socrates, and what sort of laughter is at play here.

In addition to its comical content, the focus in chapter 2 is on the *Laches*'s comical structure. The *Laches*, as has been suggested of other dialogues, draws heavily from comical precedents in its characterizations, puns, jokes, and, particular to the *Laches*, in its complex comical structure that ancient Greek audiences would have recognized as such. This structure addresses and implies the audience, involving interlocutors and readers in the action. But what may be yet more striking about the *Laches* is the suggestion that the very ability to recognize others as comical without seeing the comical in oneself, as Laches and Nicias do of each other, is true of humans generally. When Socrates then turns the laughter back on the interlocutors and its audience, as he does in the *Protagoras* and *Charmides*, the suggestion is that we too may have forgotten ourselves. We too may see the comical in these characters without recognizing that we ourselves may be laughable.

A look at the *Charmides* in chapter 3 shows why the superiority theory of laughter and comedy does not exclusively characterize the types of laughter found in the dialogues. Such a theory better characterizes the laughter of tragedy, wherein laughter appears to be exclusively negative and destructive. Plato's laughter is, instead, multivalent and diverse. The *Charmides* alone illustrates at least three types of laughter: it begins with an instance of what can anachronistically be called slapstick, it includes what appears to be an example of the laughter of superiority aimed at Critias, but it also includes a third form of laughter, namely the laughter that is turned back on interlocutors and audience. The superiority theory cannot stretch to accommodate these forms of laughter, and so a broader taxonomy of laughter in the dialogues may be required.

Chapter 4 addresses the performative contradictions of Hermogenes and the title character in the *Cratylus* to show that the self-forgetting of comedy suggested by the previous chapter extends to both a character's words and deeds. Akin to his role in the *Euthydemus*, Socrates, in the *Cratylus*, plays the fool in order to enact the absurdity of Hermogenes's and Cratylus's linguistic positions, in which the possibility of false speech is denied. The interlocutors, and the dialogue's readers, are thus placed in the position of either deeming Socrates's etymologies to be facetious and false, in which case false speech must be possible, or taking them at face value, in which case even the most ridiculous derivations, ones that even Socrates suggests to be absurd, must be accepted as true. At issue is the possibility of false speech, which Socrates indirectly affirms by comically and foolishly enacting the absurd consequences resulting from its denial.

Chapter 5 focuses on the *Symposium* and a discussion of eros, in which the body is, at times, completely forgotten to show how laughter exposes the interlocutors' hypocrisy. Aristophanes's hiccups remind us of this way in which speakers have forgotten their physical selves. The *Symposium*'s comedy of the forgotten body builds to a punch line in Alcibiades's promise to expose the hubris of Socrates, a claim that would have suggested physical violation, but ends up being an accusation that Socrates failed to violate him. Alcibiades builds up expectations of a dramatic revelation, which are then dashed by what is effectively a joke. Further, when Alcibiades demonstrates his love for Socrates based entirely on his internal goods, the symposiasts greet this with laughter. But if Alcibiades's disembodied love for Socrates is laughable, so too are the speeches that have venerated just such a love of psychic goods. Alcibiades's satyrical praise of Socrates, along with Aristophanes's hiccups, remind us of what is being left out of the accounts of eros, namely, the body. What will come to be called "Platonic love," or love devoid of any physical regard is here suggested instead to be a joke. The laughter of the *Symposium* is largely incongruous, much as Alcibiades's depiction of Socrates as a satyr, and it exposes philosophical incongruities in the interlocutors. It also presents us with an image that best answers the question the book begins with as to what sort of hero Socrates is.

If the arguments developed in the preceding chapters are accurate, their implications are extensive and need to be traced. First, the Conclusion sketches how reading the dialogues with an eye toward laughter and comic moments as philosophically meaningful affects how we read Plato. A different view of the self in Plato emerges from this discussion, and it is one that is more in keeping with Socratic Ignorance than generally acknowledged. The Delphic Imperative to "Know thyself"—at the heart of the philosophical undertaking for Socrates—is thus significantly impacted by considerations of laughter and comedy within the Platonic dialogues. So too are many assumptions that have become "traditional" about the relationship of comedy to philosophy, and laughter to what is serious. The book concludes with a reconsideration of these relationships and what this might mean for philosophy more broadly.

Although I believe the dialogues discussed here tell a particular story of the engagement and revision of laughter, there is a degree to which the selected dialogues are arbitrary. A similar project could be done with many others, including the *Protagoras*, *Gorgias*, *Hippias Major*, *Hippias Minor*, *Euthyphro*, *Ion*, *Meno*, *Laws*, *Menexenus*, *Lysis*, and more. These are merely some instances, examples, and functions of laughter in some dialogues. This book does not purport to be in any sense exhaustive in its treatment of laughter and comedy in the dialogues it has examined. Quite to the contrary, if its main theses are right, the literary dimensions of the dialogues—such as comedy, hold the dialogues open to a nearly inexhaustible array of interpretations. What it has attempted is a more extensive, but still partial, taxonomy of kinds of laughter in the dialogues, their possible functions, and philosophical meanings. The intention behind the book is thus to open up broader discussion of laughter and comedy in the dialogues, and in no sense to shut such discussion down with anything akin to authoritative pronouncement. Such a pronouncement would be as ridiculous and self-blind as Euthyphro, Hippias, or Dionysodorus.

As it is becoming increasingly more accepted that one ought to regard dramatic and literary dimensions in interpreting the dialogues, the next step is to turn attention to the employment of specific types of literary style, such as comedy and tragedy. Much more work on laughter and comedy in the dialogues needs to be done. A closer look at tragedy in the dialogues is also in order. Tragic dimensions and facets of the dialogues are receiving increasing attention in the literature, and deserve far more.[42] A comparable taxonomy of different ways in which tragedy is at work in the dialogues would be a fascinating study. I have paid very little attention in this book to irony. There is a considerable literature on irony already in existence and my intention was not to contribute to it, except by way of focusing on what is too often buried in it—laughter and comedy. Subsuming these elements under a heading of "irony" denies them proper recognition as such and prevents an evaluation of the philosophical meanings of laughter.

Although I have treated comedy and laughter as though they are separable from elements of tragedy for the sake of giving comedy its own hearing, they are more fundamentally intertwined than I suggest here. At the same time, I have also been very hesitant to designate any of the dialogues as "comedies" or "satyr plays," even on compelling evidence that Plato is making quite heavy use of such risible forms.[43] A label such as "comedy," if this book is right in its assessment, itself needs revision before it can more accurately describe the "serious," philosophically meaningful laughter of Plato's dialogues. It is not the aim of this book to undertake an explicit revision, so much as to suggest its need and, perhaps, to sketch some of the contours of what is needed. Plato, thus, may well be the elusive writer of both tragedy and comedy referred to at the end of the *Symposium*, as Clay claims, but, oddly, this makes him neither tragedian nor comedian nor ironist per se.[44] He is all of these, but not exclusively of one another.

It is in this spirit, then, that this book acknowledges but a few of its own many limitations. The book is but the shaggy hide of a satyr covering over what it clumsily hopes to reveal: a few golden treasures, due not to me, but to the alternatingly luminous, exuberant, perplexing, and philosophical dimensions of Plato's laughter.

1

The *Apology* of Socrates: Is Socrates a Comical Hero?

This chapter proposes that, contrary to what Socrates seems to suggest in the *Philebus*, comedy and laughter can not only contribute to self-knowledge, but they suggest the contours of what such knowledge might look like. Existing literature has largely focused on the self-reflexive character of the wisdom Socrates claims to have in the *Apology*, wherein he maintains only to know that he knows nothing, including of himself. Such lack of self-knowledge lies at the heart of what is laughable, but Socrates's awareness thereof distinguishes two forms therein. Parallel to the forms of wisdom Socrates articulates at *Apology* 20d, run two forms of what is laughable. Like the more-than-human wisdom, assuming oneself falsely in possession of self-knowledge renders one an appropriate object of derisive laughter. Akin to what Socrates deems human, wisdom is the recognition of oneself as lacking self-knowledge, and therefore as being laughable in a more playful and self-reflexive way. Socrates, I will propose, embodies precisely this self-knowledge in the *Apology*, revealing himself to be not identical, but remarkably similar to, a comical hero. His comical dramatization in the *Apology* indicates the contours of potential self-knowledge, including harmonizing one's words and deeds, recognizing both our limited selves as well as our tendency toward hubris, and that unless and until we achieve such self-knowledge, we remain fundamentally laughable.

Self-knowledge is presented as discrete from the laughable in the *Philebus.* Socrates suggests there that the "nature of the ridiculous [*to geloion*]" is "a kind of vice [*ponēria*] that derives its name from a special disposition; it is, among all the vices, the one with a character that stands in direct opposition to the one recommended by the famous inscription in Delphi" (*Philebus* 48c). While Socrates could easily be referring to the maxim "nothing in excess," for comedy and laughter are most certainly excessive, it is much more likely that he is referring to the maxim "Know thyself [*gnōthi seauton*]." What makes one laughable, it seems, is not knowing oneself.

And yet, Socrates, in the *Apology*, declares himself to lack such knowledge. Indeed, Socratic Wisdom appears to consist in precisely this awareness.

> Now perhaps I will seem to some of you to be joking [*paizein*] Know well, however, that I will tell you the whole truth. For I, men of Athens, have gotten this name through nothing but a certain wisdom. Just what sort of wisdom is this? That which is perhaps human wisdom [*anthropinē sophia*]; for probably I really am wise in this. But those of whom I just spoke might perhaps be wise in some wisdom greater than human, or else I cannot say what it is. For I, at least, do not have knowledge of it, but whoever asserts that I do lies and speaks in order to slander me. No please, men of Athens, do not make a disturbance, not even if I seem to you to be boasting somewhat. For "not mine is the story" that I will tell; rather, I will refer it to a speaker trustworthy to you. Of my wisdom, if indeed it is wisdom of any kind, and what sort of thing it is, I will offer for you as witness the god in Delphi. (*Apology* 20d–e)

Socrates's wisdom, he concludes, rests in his awareness of his own ignorance, or lack of knowledge, rather than in any positive, epistemic state. Comparing himself to the person who believes himself to be wise, but turns out not to know what he thinks he knows, Socrates says, "I *am* likely to be a little bit wiser than he in this very thing: that whatever I do not know, I do not even suppose I know" (*Apology* 21d). Socratic wisdom is cast in negative terms: it is constituted by *not* assuming his own knowledge. Put less awkwardly and more positively, it is an awareness of a lack of wisdom, a condition that allows Socrates to inquire further, but one that has consequences for how we see ourselves and for how we see Socrates.

The significance of this passage extends further. There is ambiguity as to which "god in Delphi" Socrates is referring. Apollo seems the more obvious one, but Dionysus, associated not only with wine but with drama and comedy, was also worshiped at Delphi for three months out of the year, in Apollo's absence. Could Socrates be playing on this ambiguity here? If the god in question is one associated with comedy, we may find a far more risible tone to the *Apology*, and perhaps, to the dialogues in general. The passage itself is deeply comical. At the very point where Socrates notes the jurors' outrage over his apparent boasting, he offers a yet more outrageous claim, namely that no mere mortal, but indeed, a god will provide witness in his favor. And this from a man on trial for impiety. Socrates claims to lack self-knowledge, but distinguishes the wisdom of being aware of this lack from ignorance of it. This awareness may enable inquiry into self-knowledge, but it also begins to sketch the content of human self-knowledge. If these types of wisdom are exhaustive, then we may participate more in the Dionysian and a bit less in the Apollonian than we flatter ourselves in believing. We may be, in other words, fundamentally laughable.

Under a tree sacred to Dionysus,[1] Socrates, in the *Phaedrus*, extends this lack of wisdom to self-knowledge, saying, "I'm not yet able, in accordance with the Delphic inscription, to know myself [*gnōnai emauton*], and it seems ridiculous [*geloia*] to me to investigate things that don't concern me while still lacking that knowledge" (*Phaedrus* 229e–230a). Two points emerge from this. The first is that self-knowledge is primary for Socrates, as suggested by various interlocutors who say that Socrates typically brings the discussion back around to the persons involved (*Laches* 188a). The second point is a broader one about humans generally. Laughable is anyone who investigates things without that knowledge, and yet we are hard-pressed to find anyone in the dialogues—including Socrates—who has such self-knowledge. Does Socrates's own, qualified lack of self-knowledge then not render him laughable? If Socrates himself lacks it, especially given his persistent pursuit of such knowledge, is there much hope for anyone else? And if not, does this not suggest that the majority of people—perhaps even all persons—are fundamentally laughable?

Just as Socrates suggests a distinction between his own and most others' wisdom, here too we find a significant difference. The difference between Socrates and those believing themselves to have greater-than-human-wisdom is not one of self-knowledge, for both appear to lack it. The difference lies in the stance each takes concerning whether one has it. Being aware of one's lack of self-knowledge enables seeing oneself as laughable. An ancient precedent for what Simon Critchley calls self-directed and other-directed laughter emerges from this.[2] Self-directed laughter acknowledges one's own remaining laughable, whereas other-directed laughter tends to assume otherwise. But are we reading Plato anachronistically in suggesting two seemingly modern conceptions of laughter as well as their applicability to humanity? This chapter concludes with a brief look at ancient precedents and antecedents for what might otherwise seem a decidedly modern view of comedy and laughter.

If Socrates is indeed some form of a comical hero, what follows from such a presentation? Socrates plays the comic hero to prove that laughter can and ought to be directed at oneself, and at remedying one's lack of self-knowledge. The laughter provoked by this is self-directed laughter, and it is through playing the comical hero that the character Socrates helps to establish such laughter. Plato's Socrates develops a novel, but not entirely unprecedented, conception of laughter in the process.

The Comical Apology

Plato's *Apology of Socrates*, although interrupted by dialogue, is as close to a Socratic monologue as we have in Plato's works. In it, Socrates draws frequent comparisons between himself and an assortment of Greek heroes in a grand and excessive defense that becomes, instead, offense.[3] Comparisons to heroes seem particularly ill-fitting given Socrates's outrageous behavior in the court room, including calling a god as his witness, insulting the jury, and suggesting, after being found guilty, that his punishment should be being treated like an Olympian victor. His provocations are met with outbursts from the jurors, noted in the dialogue. It is a very puzzling *apologia* if read straightforwardly, but a web of literary connections will help to contextualize some of the dialogue and offer support for Socrates as a hero. But this brings up a further puzzle: given Socrates's allusions to and comparisons with heroes, what kind of hero behaves as Socrates does in the *Apology*? In other words, what sort of hero is Socrates?

Jacob Howland claims that the *Apology* uses thematic and formal elements of tragedy to expose the political paradoxes in which the good of the whole is pitted against that of the individuals in it. Reading the *Apology* in line with classical tragedy allows us to see that it is the city itself that constitutes the true tragic figure because it is the city, and not Socrates, that acts in ignorance.[4] Howland's essay is illuminating and important in acknowledging the complex relationship between the literary and philosophical, but stops short of recognizing the comic elements at work in the *Apology*, elements that one might not expect, given the dialogue's serious topic. According to Howland, Socrates's speeches and deeds "do not fit the mold of comic drama."[5] It is Meletus, for Howland, rather than Socrates, who jests. However much the dialogue draws from tragedy, I wish to show here some of the many ways in which the *Apology* resembles comedy. Socrates's speeches and deeds do fit the mold of comic drama, Socrates does indeed jest, and Socrates himself resembles quite strongly the comic hero.

The *Apology* is exemplary in putting not just Socrates, but philosophy itself, on trial. As Sallis writes, "his defence speech will itself constitute an exemplification of that very practice against which the accusations have been brought."[6] That practice, as the *Apology* represents it, is infused with comedy. Greene writes that "The *Apology* is a comic justification of the life lived in the spirit of comedy—the exposure of pretension—at the behest of a god: surely this is piety! The unpopularity of Socrates arises from the fact that the public has no sense of humor . . ."[7] Socrates dramatically exposes the pretension of the jurors voting to convict, exposing their pretense to judge, rather than merely to react emotionally. He does this by giving them something to react to: a marvelous display of comic insolence and philosophical tenacity that is, in and of itself, shocking coming from someone whose life hangs in the balance. It is, however, a display perfectly consistent with the *modus operandi* of Socrates's life and practice as "lived in the spirit of comedy." Greene's claim is itself provocative: should the jurors have laughed at Socrates rather than sentence him to death? If so, is this the proper response to the *Apology* for us readers as well?

Laughter is one, but certainly not the only, appropriate response to the *Apology*. Socrates's comic antics have philosophical points. They are part of the dramatic critique and provocation toward philosophy that Socrates offers the jurors and the audience. Why does Socrates provoke the jury?

There are shorter and longer answers to this. The short answer is that he does so because he had always provoked the "men of Athens," and consistent with what he promises to do, he continues in the *Apology* his life work of provocation. What the *Apology* makes apparent is the extent (and the stakes) to which Socrates is willing to go to do this. In the *Euthydemus*, he puts on the line his reputation as a philosopher, and with it, possibly, his honor or glory. In the *Apology*, he is willing to sacrifice his life. What he shows is that none of these things—reputation, honor, glory, life, and even being laughed at—matter so much as does living the kind of life, and presumably, dying the kind of death, that is examined. In doing so, Socrates criticizes the fundamentals of the Homeric heroic code. And yet, in the *Apology*, he compares himself repeatedly to heroes who adhere to this code. The question then becomes why Socrates is willing to put all he has on the line, and it is a question that is at least partly resolved in the longer answer.

The longer answer to why Socrates provokes the jury is that he uses comic provocation to expose their pretensions to judge and thus tests the limits of logos and its persuasive power. On what basis can Socrates distinguish those who properly "judge" him from those who are mere "men of Athens"? Socrates does not so much argue his defense as he enacts it. Rather than trying to prove his own innocence, Socrates shows the ineptitude of those assigned to judge and the lack of logos in their judgment. He does this by playing into the types of persuasion that he expects to predominate so as to emphasize the type that ought, instead, to be employed. Turning to Aristotle offers some clarity on acknowledged modes of persuasion.

In discussing forensic rhetoric, or the type of persuasion used in the courtroom, Aristotle articulates the key modes: persuasion may be achieved by the use of argument (logos), by appealing to the audience's emotions (*pathos*), or by evincing a favorable persona (*ethos*).[8] Aristotle is clear about the persuasive power of the latter two: "Particularly in deliberative oratory, but also in lawsuits, it adds much to an orator's influence that his own character should look right and that he should be thought to entertain the right feelings towards his hearers; and also that his hearers should be in just the right frame of mind."[9] The person who lacks these "right feelings" runs punitive risk, according to Aristotle: "When people . . . feel friendly to the man who comes before them for judgment, they regard him as having done little wrong, if any; when they feel hostile, they take the opposite view.[10] These passages are helpful in striking the contrast between Aristotle's insight and Socrates's remarkable performance in the *Apology* to the contrary. Socrates makes explicit that he will not appeal to the audience's emotions, but in a way, he does just that. By evincing a persona so contrary to what the jury expects, Socrates evokes their anger. For Aristotle, the emotions of the jury or audience changes dependent on the orator's disposition: "our anger ceases toward those who humble themselves . . . We also feel calm towards those who are serious when we are serious . . ."[11] Instead of humbling himself, Socrates does the opposite. Rather than appreciating the gravity of his situation, Socrates makes light of it.

By demonstrating the effects of what are perceived as the wrong feelings by a majority of his audience, Socrates shows the extent to which emotions can override the faculty of judgment. Those voting for conviction are not judges for Socrates, as evidenced by his varying addresses to those who voted to convict him ("men of Athens") and those who voted to acquit (the more customary address of "judges").[12] They are emotional responders, convicting on the basis of perceived slights and their own anger, on *pathē* rather than on the basis of logos.

In the *Crito*, Socrates articulates clearly what is at issue concerning the trial. When Crito voices his concern about appearances, Socrates counters by stressing that the only concern he has is the basis on which he is persuaded to act. Recounting Socrates's behavior in the trial and Crito's own failure to prevent the conviction, Crito tells Socrates, "I am ashamed for you and for us, your companions, that the whole affair concerning you will seem to have been conducted with a certain lack of manliness [*anandria*] on our part" (*Crito* 45e). Crito deems the conviction and sentencing "ridiculous" (*katagelōs*, *Crito* 45e). Socrates responds by saying that he is persuaded (*peithesthai*) by nothing else but "that argument which appears best to me upon reasoning" [*tō logō hos an moi logizomenō beltistos phainētai*, *Crito* 46b]. Whether one appears to have acted without "manliness" or "courage" (*andreia*) is not the issue; how one is persuaded, and how one determines the right course of action is. Indeed, as we will see in the *Apology*, Socrates plays into the appearances that Crito comes to lament if only to stress their irrelevance. In doing so, Socrates takes a court case that might have been settled with some contrition and the offer of a reasonable fee, one that Crito intriguingly refers to as having been altogether avoidable in the first place (*Crito* 45e), and turns it into a capital conviction. The difference is made by his use of comedy.

To show this, the chapter analyzes Socrates's comically excessive performance in the *Apology*, contrasts it with a very different example of forensic rhetoric, and shows a number of ways in which Socrates's *apologia* borrows from comic heroes, comic use of language, comical strategies, and even from Aristophanes's critique of sophistic rhetoric. I will argue that Socrates uses comedy, here as he does elsewhere, not only to expose pretensions, but to test the limits of logos. Read in this way, the *Apology* reveals Socrates to be a hero in line with, if not exactly identical to, comic heroes, one who raises the stakes in his trial and uses his craftiness to turn the tables on the jurors. But the lack of identity persists, and prompts the question as to what sort of hero Socrates is.

Socrates and the Homeric Hero

Comparisons among Socrates and a variety of epic and tragic figures occur in the *Apology* both explicitly and implicitly, but one is particularly influential. Several scholars have shown a remarkable resemblance between Plato's *Apology of Socrates* and Gorgias's *Defense of Palamedes.*[13] Coulter describes the number of thematic, linguistic, and structural parallels as, "surprising and apparently more than accidental."[14] That Gorgias's *Palamedes* predates Plato's *Apology* is generally assumed and well supported by a number of scholars.[15] Among the correspondences, Gorgias's Palamedes and Plato's Socrates both claim not only to be innocent of all charges, but even to be benefactors (*euergetēs*) to their cities and accusers.[16] Palamedes and Socrates both proclaim that, rather than using lamentations, prayers, and other displays to move the jurors to pity, they will only *didaskein to alēthes.*[17] Both texts include an interruption of the *apologeisthai* by a *dialegesthai* with the accuser (in an *erōtēsis*, or interrogation of the plaintiff).[18] Thematically, both speeches claim that being condemned to die is not the issue (since all mortals effectively are); the issue is whether being killed off (*apothanein*, meaning to be killed or to die of laughter) happens justly.[19] Palamedes and Socrates both claim that the accusations against them arise from *phthonos.*[20] Even one of the most memorable passages of the *Apology*, Socrates's claim that the "unexamined life is not worth living" [*ho de anexetastos bios ou biōtos anthrōpō*], appears to be a modification of Palamedes's claim that "a life without trust is not worth living" [*bios de ou biōtos pisteōs esterēmenō*].[21]

Aside from raising interesting questions as to the historicity of the defense speech of Plato's Socrates and adding further support to the claim that Xenophon patterns his account of Socrates in the courtroom on Plato's, these striking parallels raise the question as to why Plato would have his Socrates respond so directly to Gorgias's *Palamedes*. Morr argues that Plato consciously alludes to Gorgias's *Palamedes* so as to set Socrates's death against a mythical context of another person who was unjustly convicted, and so to enlarge its meaning.[22] Calogero suggests the similarities to indicate that Gorgias was a source of philosophical inspiration for Socrates.[23] These readings assume that the similarities between the two indicate ways in which Plato is yoking his ideas to those of Gorgias, and thus pay little attention to what are quite significant differences between the two texts.

In stark contrast, Coulter emphasizes the rhetorical critique Plato's Socrates makes of Gorgias's Palamedes: "the *Apology* embodies a rejection in detail of the particular assumptions upon which the *Palamedes* is built."[24] For Coulter, the *Apology* could justly be called the *Anti-Palamedes*. Coulter argues that Gorgias's Palamedes acknowledges the difficulties of his situation, in which using persuasion (*peithō*), specifically in the form of arguments from probability, to cultivate the appearance (*doxa*) of truth (*alētheia*) in the jurors becomes more important than the truth itself, given that his life hangs in the balance. Rational instruction is thus less valuable in this case than persuasion, a position that Gorgias himself defended. Plato's Socrates, on the other hand, is fundamentally indifferent to the outcome of the trial, and so, does not feel constrained to employ rhetorical strategies of persuasion in addition to the truth itself. In the *Apology*, Coulter finds ". . . a portrait of a man who intends to let the truth speak for itself, and who is determined, for the most part, to avoid arguments based on probability."[25] But if Coulter is right, one would expect Socrates to offer a straightforward, perhaps even dry, rational account for why he is not guilty as charged, letting the truth itself defend him. Given that he does not do this, one is returned to the question as to why Socrates gives the excessive, incendiary speech that he does.

Beyond his philosophical correction of Palamedes's rhetorical defense and the overlapping notion of the wronged innocent, Plato changes the conception of the hero and his or her reception. For the two texts' remarkable overlap, their differences are illuminating. Socrates emphasizes heroic autonomy, whereas Palamedes presents himself as a hero very much dependent on his audience. In the claims as to whether a life is worth living without others' trust versus whether it is worth living without examination, Palamedes puts in the hands of the jurors the ability to trust him, and therefore render his life worth living. Socrates, on the other hand, denies the jurors this, and reformulates the claim so that his actions alone determine the value of his life, regardless of their reception.[26] The jurors' apparent lack of trust in Socrates need not affect the value of his life, which derives instead from his own choices and actions.

The comparisons between the texts also highlight the *Apology*'s more direct references. The dialogues teem with Socrates's agonistic encounters with sophists and those under their influence, from charlatans like Euthydemus to heavyweights like Protagoras. For instance, Socrates distinguishes himself from those who, like Gorgias, claim wisdom for themselves and who allegedly impart this for a fee (*Apology* 19d–20c).[27] Coulter points out that when he mentions wanting to converse with Palamedes in the afterlife and describes doing so as a great pastime, he uses the word *diatribē*, a word he uses elsewhere to describe refuting pretenders to wisdom.[28] Gorgias's Palamedes may be such a pretender.

For all they have in common, these figures' *apologiai* have at least one critical distinction that seems to have gone unnoticed: Gorgias's Palamedes presents himself as a likable figure to the jurors, while Plato's Socrates, in the *Apology*, does not. It is in this distinction that a substantive rhetorical critique of the former can be found, one that is interesting in its own right, but also in how it aligns itself topically with comedy. Quite unlike Palamedes, Socrates deliberately presents himself as excessive, comical, and inflammatory so as to jettison the third of Aristotle's noted modes of persuasion: that of persona (*ethos*). He makes every effort *not* to appeal to the jurors in the way they would expect and want. But he does not stop there: not only does Socrates fail to employ the persuasive force of a favorable persona, he works hard to present himself unfavorably. By neglecting to appeal to the jurors' pity, and by presenting an inflammatory and defiant persona, Socrates is testing the persuasive force of logos.

This distinction is apparent even in one of the commonalities the two *apologiai* share. Employing the ancient rhetorical strategy of mentioning that one will not mention something to call special attention to it, both Palamedes and Socrates claim that they will not appeal to the jurors' pity to seek acquittal, as already mentioned. Palamedes, however, mentions this so as to attest to his own nobility of character. Beyond Palamedes's own self-praise, he also flatters the jurors, saying, "Lamentations, prayers, and the petitions of friends are useful when judgment depends on the mob; but before you, the foremost of the Greeks, I need not use these devices, but only justice and truth."[29] Aside from being Greek citizens, the jurors would have nothing in particular to distinguish themselves above other Greek citizens, let alone to merit being "the foremost of the Greeks." This is sheer flattery on Palamedes's behalf. Socrates, on the other hand, sets up a direct and unflattering comparison between himself and the jurors, one designed to needle the jurors, and to make them feel shame and anger. Socrates predicts an emotional reaction and vote based on this, saying,

> Perhaps someone among you may be indignant when he recalls himself, if, in contesting a trial even smaller than this trial, he begged and supplicated the judges with many tears, bringing forward his own children and many others of his family and friends, so as to be pitied as much as possible, while I will do none of these things, although in this too I am risking, as I might seem, the extreme danger. Perhaps then someone thinking about this may be rather stubborn toward me, and, angered by this very thing, he may set down his vote in anger [*pros me schoiē kai orgistheis autois toutois theito an met' orgēs tēn psēphon*]. (34b–d)

Any juror likely to be angered by Socrates's lack of supplication is that much more likely to be enraged by Socrates's indication of as much and even more so by Socrates's comparison of his composure in a capital trial with their own indignity in a less consequential case.

Shortly thereafter, Socrates suggests why he has presented himself in so unfavorable of a light. In his final words to the jurors determining his innocence or guilt, Socrates instructs them as to the proper role a judge ought to play, saying ". . . it also does not seem to me to be just to beg the judge, nor to be acquitted by begging, but rather to teach and to persuade. For the judge is not seated to give away the just things as a gratification, but to judge them. For he has not sworn to gratify *whoever seems favorable* to him [*epi tō katacharidzesthai ta dikaia*] but to give judgment according to the laws" (35b–c, my emphasis). Once again, Socrates oversteps his conventional role as a defendant, audaciously taking it on himself to instruct the jurors as to their role. Socrates has made it clear that he is not playing to the crowd, but he also clarifies here that it is not the jurors' place to gratify or punish on the basis of a defendant's favorability.

By presenting himself as distinctly unfavorable (in personality if not in morality), unattractive, and even infuriating, Socrates has not only avoided using the mode of persuasion by persona in his *apologia*, he has gone in the opposite direction to make a point.

In this sense, then, it is possible to see that Socrates's defense is not a failure; his *apologia* is an offense against his reception by Athenians and jurors, who judge on the basis of their own *pathē* rather than logos, and who seem to demand the sort of flattery that Palamedes and some rhetoricians offer. Socrates deliberately subverts the process: instead of focusing strictly on a logical and persuasive defense against the charges, Socrates presents himself comically as so unbending and excessive a persona as to challenge the jurors not to yield to their emotional reactions to him, and instead to judge him on the basis of logos. More jurors than not fail to rise to the challenge. Socrates's response to his own conviction suggests that he is surprised that more did not fail the challenge: ". . . what has happened was not unexpected by me. But I wonder much more at the number of the votes on each side. For I at least did not suppose it would be by so little, but by much" (*Apology* 36a). He follows this up with a joke about how proportionately paltry the number of votes to convict is, given that he has three accusers.

Whereas Palamedes plays within and enforces the bounds of what is appropriate, customary, and acceptable in forensic rhetoric, Socrates goes beyond these, and even deliberately subverts such limits (here as well as in other matters, as we will see). By exceeding the bounds of appropriate and expected courtroom behavior, by playing, effectively, the comical hero, Socrates tests the persuasive power of logos. Without an appeal to pity and without a likable figure expressing appropriate contrition to whom jurors can grant favors, the jurors vote to convict. Socrates needs not and does not play by conventional rules of persuasion. Comedy affords Socrates the boundlessness necessary for this, as unlike the (arguably) more tragic Palamedes, Socrates need not constrain his behavior to fit within the bounds of acceptable behavior for a defendant. Socrates is in this sense, like comic heroes more generally, boundless.

Socrates's reception suggests further connections with comical heroes. For Aristotle, a tragic hero is determined in part by his or her reception. Assuming Socrates is right in suggesting that the jurors voting to convict him voted on the basis of their anger, he cannot be an Aristotelian tragic hero in part because his audience—or at least the majority of jurors, is not capable of feeling properly toward him. Socrates's comically insolent behavior assures this. As Aristotle writes, "And those who are neither moved by any courageous emotion such as anger or confidence, nor by a disposition to insolence, nor yet by great fear; only those feel pity who are between these two extremes."[30] Socrates stokes the audience's outrage, anger, and envy, rather than their pity and fear, and in this way, he is no Palamedes and no Aristotelian tragic hero. We thus are returned to the question as to what sort of hero does this.

The hero who provokes anger, outrage, as well as mirth, who subverts conventions, and flaunts this boundlessness is a comical hero. Several paradigmatic conceptions of the hero precede Socrates, including the classical opposition between Homer and Archilochus. Socrates plays a role more akin to an Archilochean hero than a Homeric hero, despite frequent comparisons to the latter. The tensions between such heroic conceptions are worth exploring briefly. Plutarch writes that Archilochus was expelled from Sparta because of his claim, substantiated by the new fragment, that it is better to discard one's shield than to be killed. For the proudly bellicose Spartans, whose mothers famously sent their sons off to war with the instruction to return "with your shield or on it," such a claim is particularly offensive. Plutarch writes that Archilochus was exiled for writing in verse that it is preferable to throw away one's shield than to be killed by the enemy.

> Shield that was mine, fair armour, now gladdens the heart
> of some Saian;
> Sorry I left it behind tangled in brush in my path;
> But for myself I escaped from the clutches of Death. Let perdition
> Take the old shield, for no worse surely I'll get the next time.[31]

The newly discovered fragment from Archilochus verifies Plutarch's attribution and extends Plutarch's quotation. The outrage over this claim, if it is to be taken as a straightforward declaration in the personal voice of Archilochus rather than a poetic persona, is not limited to the Spartans. Critias, admittedly a Spartan sympathizer, decries Archilochus as "especially revolting and disgraceful" for such a proclamation.[32] *Rhipsaspia*, or the abandonment of one's shield in battle, becomes a motif in Greek and Roman lyric poetry, with Anacreon, Alcaeus, and Horace including it in verse, but none so defiantly as Archilochus.

It is not only the heroic (or antiheroic) ideal associated with Archilochus that provokes anger; he is also held in contempt for his hateful mode of delivery. Pindar warns against adopting such a tone: "But I must flee the deep bite [*dakos*] of evil-speaking [*kakagorian*]. For though I am far, I have seen Archilochus, full of blame [*psogeron*], very much in want [*amaxaniai*], fattening himself on grimly worded hatreds."[33] The quote can also be read as an aesthetic rejection of derisive and vicious comedy. Whether it is Archilochus himself or the persona of his poetry, it is anger, in addition to laughter, that such comic heroes provoke.

The issue this raises, and particularly, the comparisons it generates between the classical, Homeric hero and the Archilochean comic hero, are taken up by authors favoring either side. Aristophanes has a boy quote the lines ironically at the end of *Peace*, to which Trygaeus responds that, while the speaker did indeed save his own life, he "shamed the parents who gave it."[34] Is it better to maintain one's military honor than to preserve one's life? Can virtue be maintained in retreat from battle? The questions are philosophically relevant, and they are also relevant in how they begin to delineate various forms of the hero. For a Lacedaemonian, the story of the three hundred Spartans holding off the Persian masses to their own imminent deaths makes it clear: there is no dignity in retreat and no value to a life spared at the cost of honor. The comic hero, for whom the triumph of life trumps that of nobility, may not have an objection to the solution Archilochus's pragmatic persona offers to having one's armor catch in the bushes while beating a hasty retreat from the enemy.

It is not surprising then to find Plato's characters joining in the debate. In the *Laches*, the title character espouses a conception of courage defined precisely by never yielding one's position. Socrates counters his definition by forcing Laches to admit that one might retain one's virtue in how one retreats from battle, perhaps using a retreat to confuse the enemy and spring on them an ambush, or that one might be virtuous in retreating when the gods support doing so. Whether Socrates himself is committed to such a view or whether he is countering Laches's definition to undercut Laches's confidence and expose his ignorance may be ambiguous, but the issue does not remain merely theoretical in the dialogues. In the *Symposium*, Alcibiades praises Socrates's courage, giving a vague example of how he saved Alcibiades's life and retrieved his shield, even though it was Alcibiades who received the medal for bravery (*Symposium* 220e). Alcibiades says that Socrates saved him and his shield, a shield that is described elsewhere as being made of gold and ivory and depicting Eros about to hurl one of Zeus's thunderbolts.[35] But Alcibiades then gives witness to Socrates's courage as exemplified by how

Socrates retreated from battle at Potidaea, quoting directly from Aristophanes to describe Socrates's comical withdrawal. Alcibiades's encomium presents Socrates as a hero, but there are clearly various models to choose from. Just what sort of hero is Plato's Socrates?

The implicit comparison between the dashing Alcibiades, fighting on horseback, and the ugly—even comical—Socrates on foot who saves him, echoes another fragment of Archilochus.

> I don't care for your tall general,
> with his long stride and long hair in locks
> and beard well trimmed. Show me a stocky man
> bandy-legged, sure of foot, full of heart.[36]

Socrates is this stout warrior to Alcibiades's dashing general. Like the comical hero, Socrates represents pragmatic over more strictly aesthetic values. As Alcibiades describes him, Socrates is the hero deserving recognition rather than Alcibiades himself. Socrates's courage in retreat enables him to save not only Alcibiades, but his beautiful shield as well, seemingly left behind to hasten a retreat, saving him both from the battlefield and the ensuing ill repute stemming from *rhipsaspia*. Unlike the Archilochean hero, Socrates not only keeps his own shield and his honor, he ensures that his beautiful, young friend does as well.

To the extent that a hero's reception determines what sort of hero she or he is, Socrates is akin to an Archilochean comical hero. He provokes emotions comparable to those elicited by Archilochus's hero, who abandons his shield, caught in the brush, to flee the battle with his life. Against conventional values, Socrates induces anger and outrage, and so appears comical. Because of this, and quite to the opposite effect, Socrates turns his into a capital trial and loses his life. One might take this to suggest that Socrates appears to be comical only in the perspective of the jurors voting to convict him, but it is not solely his reception that shows his resemblance to a comical hero in the *Apology*. He shares a great deal else in common with heroes of Old Comedy.

Socrates and the Traits of Comical Heroes

Socrates, as has become more apparent here and will be evident in chapters following, embodies the traits and behaviors of the heroes of Old Comedy.

With some qualification, Socrates can himself be seen to be a comical hero. He is not *only* a comical hero, however, interchangeable with a Strepsiades, a Lysistrata, or a Dikaiopolis, for, as Plato portrays him, Socrates is a far more nuanced and complex character. He is a philosophical hero, developed by Plato, but cut from the cloth of Old Comedy. So what are comical heroes like?

Cedric Whitman provides a thorough analysis of the comic hero, which will only be adumbrated here to underscore some of the ways in which Socrates is presented comically. Whitman describes Homer's Thersites as possessing several key characteristics of what will later become the comic hero. Thersites is a great talker (*ametroepēs*), he is ugly, poor, and he is an opponent of the government or authority figures.[37] He speaks truthfully but in a way designed to generate laughter. Where Thersites falls short of embodying a comic figure lies in his being ultimately pathetic, a weak and beaten figure who remains powerless, dejected, and laughed at by the soldiers. The comic hero, by comparison, may begin in such a state, but asserts himself by way of *ponēria*, in a Great Idea, to turn the tables and regain the upper hand. For Whitman, *ponēria*, despite its connotations of wickedness, is "the ability to get the advantage of somebody or some situation by virtue of an unscrupulous, but thoroughly enjoyable exercise of craft."[38] *Ponēria* could also be "a form of heroism," and often manifests itself in putting linguistic skills into play.[39] Wordplay and tricks of language are common to the comic hero, who will use these and anything else to achieve his ultimate end, catapulting himself well beyond what his humble origins and even reason itself would ordinarily allow.

The comical hero is permeated with ambiguities such as being "base," ugly, or otherwise vulgar, and yet triumphs over others who are none of these things. Whitman uses the notion of the grotesque to clarify these ambiguities. To Whitman, Thersites and other comical or proto-comical figures permeate several levels of being: they are subhuman, human, and superhuman simultaneously. The complex of beast-man-god can be exemplified in mixtures of form, such as in centaurs, satyrs, and silenoi, and in the god associated with the latter, namely Dionysus. Such figures indicate "a magical penetration of nature by the human consciousness."[40] They have contact with the "inner sources of power in the animal and vegetable world," thus suggesting ties to fertility rites and a greater link to mythology than often assumed.[41] But while they are akin to the comical, grotesque figures such as Chiron are not themselves comical.

Adding the driving force of *ponēria* to such a grotesque figure results in a creature that bears a striking resemblance to many heroes of Old Comedy. Aristophanes uses this grotesque beast-human-god structure in more direct and figurative ways. Peisthetaerus exhibits this structure quite literally at the end of the Birds, when he stands alongside his divine bride, having grown a set of wings, and is hailed as the new Zeus.[42] Peisthetaerus's *ponēria* is evident in the play's great plan: tired of Athenians arguing over laws, he proposes forming a new city. This marvelous city is built in the sky by birds, providing a splendid alternative city for the expatriated Athenians, but also intercedes human sacrifices to the Olympian gods. While proto-tragic and tragic heroes also share in this imagery, the comparisons in such cases are typically with more "noble" creatures. Achilles is frequently described as a lion and Odysseus is compared to a ram, but both descriptions elevate the powers associated with the hero.[43] Aristophanes also uses the structure in figurative ways. In the Knights, the oracle reveals that the lowliest person in the city—a sausage seller—will replace Cleon as head of the Athenian Council. When a sausage-seller passes by, he is hailed as a "savior" (*sōtēr*) and told of the prophecy.[44] In rhetorical competition with Cleon, the sausage-seller flatters shamelessly and offers the councilors free meals at the public's expense (an offer that Socrates will suggest as his own deserved punishment),[45] thus securing their vote. In the meantime, the sausage seller is imbued with supernatural power, rejuvenating the older Demos into a young and beautiful man by boiling him alive. Hailed at various points as immortal, superhuman, and most blessed, the sausage seller finally refers to himself as godlike.[46] He figuratively occupies multiple levels of being simultaneously—from brute or subhuman, to human, and divine.

Like the sausage seller, the comic hero can attempt to become divine by discharging her or his *ponēria* in a grand, oftentimes unscrupulous, but enjoyable plan. Socrates's *ponēria* is discharged in a scheme of putting the jurors on trial, and thereby flipping the trial on its head and testing the limits of logos. In this aim, tragic and comic heroes are again distinguished by Whitman: "the tragic hero tries it by the supreme moral sacrifice of *arête*, monolithic, grand, and pure of will, however tangled in his humanity. The comic hero has *poneria*, a far more resourceful weapon, and by craft, bravado, and a wholly dissociative imagination, he achieves the quest and climbs the brazen heaven."[47] In this way, the comic hero achieves a sort of transcendence.

The Aristophanean comic hero is a figure of salvation, a figure representing survival against the odds. The comic hero is a "desperate small fellow, inexcusably declaring himself for a social savior, an utterly self-centered rogue of *poneria*, representing a universal gesture of thumb-to-nose unto all the high and mighty . . ."[48] He represents ". . . the salvation of the self in all its individual waywardness, wickedness, and attachment to life. The result is a grotesque, appealing fellow, who extends one hand toward the blacker recesses of the psyche and the other toward the divine world of perfect supremacy and freedom."[49] Underneath the comic hero is a "heroic tenacity, which bespeaks the Greek, conquered and impoverished, but free in spirit."[50]

Socrates, as we have seen and will see, illustrates most of these traits, with one notable exception. Unlike the traditional, comical figure, Socrates is thoroughly unattached to life, as he demonstrates in the *Apology*. He is unattached in a way that Archilochus's hero, who abandons his shield with the aim of preserving his life, is not. He is unattached in a way that even Palamedes, who flatters and pleases to protect himself, is not. He is unattached in a way entirely consistent with his agnostic proclamation at the end of the *Apology* regarding the value of life as being known to no one but the god. He is a comical hero attached not to life itself, but to the logos that might enable the determination as to whether that life is worth living. He is a comical hero attached instead to philosophy.

Humanity as Laughable and Self-Directed Laughter

Like a comical hero, Socrates is laughable but in a novel way. For Socrates directs some of this laughter at himself, and in doing so, inaugurates a form of self-directed laughter that does not compromise his gravitas. He is laughable, but aware of this, and so does not venture into being ridiculous. Instead, his attention to his own laughability directs us to that in ourselves. We too can aspire to human wisdom and the attendant human laughability rather than remaining mired in our greater-than-human wisdom, and thus being ridiculous. Socrates, the comical hero, shows us the way.

While it may seem to be a dramatic step to read Plato's Socrates in the light of comedy and humanity as fundamentally laughable, neither view is entirely novel. Viewing humanity as risible and recognizing two different types of laughter both have ancient precedents. Nicknamed

"The Laughing Philosopher," Democritus appears to see humankind as fundamentally laughable and his Greek and Roman reception clearly identifies two different forms of laughter.[51] As with too many so-called Presocratics, the bulk of what little we know of Democritus comes through doxographical sources. According to Hippolytus, Democritus laughed at everything concerning mankind.[52] Horace ridicules Roman audiences' demands for spectacle and imagines that Democritus would laugh to see them: "Democritus would laugh whether a hybrid monstrosity, a cameleopard, or a white elephant made the gaping people stare; he'd look at them with full attention, not the stage, as a far more monstrous and entertaining sight."[53] The monstrosity of the audience Horace imagines as a more entertaining sight to Democritus than the theatrics on stage. Stranger yet than the "cameleopard" is the audience who demands such a spectacle. The true spectacle, gaping and staring, is unaware of itself as such. The audience has forgotten themselves. Democritus's response is laughter.

But what are we to make of his laughter? Two interpretations of Democritus's laughter follow: on the first, his laughter can be seen as sarcastic, dismissive, and misanthropic, while on the second, it is tolerant, humble, and humanistic. In his tenth Satire, Juvenal also asks what Democritus would think of Rome, and describes his imagined response as "the censure of merciless laughter" and "contemptuous mirth."[54] Also following this first possible characterization of Democritean laughter, Cynics see him as a misanthrope, but Gerhard claims that, according to the *testimonia*, Democritus's laughter was tolerant, not sarcastic.[55]

The laughter of Democritus is broadly—perhaps even universally—applicable. Juvenal lauds Democritean laughter (as well as Heraclitean tears), particularly when directed at the misguided beliefs and desires of the present day: "Democritus, long, ago, found ample occasion for laughter [*perpetuo risu*] no matter whom he met, and we can learn from his wisdom . . . He laughed at their [the people's] troubles, laughed at their joys and tears, and, if Fortune threatened, he told her 'Take a jump in the lake,' and pointed the way with his finger."[56] Democritus would laugh at the excesses of Juvenal's Rome, and Horace thinks the same. Juvenal goes on to discuss Democritus's "shrewdness" (*prudentia*) in this approach. Democritus's "contemptuous mirth" is justified and indeed constitutes a laudatory response to what might just as easily evoke tears: human excess, vanity, and self-ignorance.

From what very little that remains to posterity of Democritus's own writing and thinking, we might cull support for his humanistic and gelastic comportment. Democritus tells us that "A life without festival is like a long road without an inn to rest in."[57] In a fragment that expands on Chilon's, Democritus offers a humanistic sentiment: "Do not laugh at the misfortunes of men, but pity them."[58] Even for someone who finds the human condition inherently risible, there are limits, such as those already mentioned, including what is pitiful. Democritus is not singling out individuals who are laughable, but rather attributing being laughable to humanity generally. This is not the illiberal, "merciless laughter," Juvenal suggests, but rather a more liberal, humanistic form of laughter.

Two big questions arise from this: first, does self-knowledge turn out to be constituted by, or merely inclusive of, recognition of one's ignorance? And second, does Socrates's seeming lack of it (and ours) render him laughable? On the one hand, a lack of self-knowledge renders one (and pursuit of philosophical inquiry) ridiculous; on the other hand, recognition of being laughable and lacking self-knowledge encourages philosophical inquiry into the self. Does self-knowledge (or Socratic wisdom) necessarily include the ability to recognize oneself as laughable?

Drawing from the tradition of Democritus, Plato and Socrates develop a novel conception of laughter. This is self-directed laughter, and not the laughter of superiority. Knowledge that one is ignorant and thus laughable represents a very different way of looking at oneself as well as at one's relationship to laughter. This self-awareness distinguishes one from those who are self-blind, unaware of themselves, that they are ignorant, and that they are laughable. But it also distinguishes Socrates from most Aristophanean comic heroes in that he is aware of his being laughable. Socrates, we will see, uses laughter to prompt awareness of his and our own ignorance, and thus prompts greater self-knowledge.

The laughter Socrates uses draws from, but also modifies, older conceptions of laughter. In the dialogues, Socrates dramatizes a position similar to Democritus's that borrows from Aristophanes, but with a self-aware humility different from both. If Socrates sees himself and humans more broadly as inherently laughable, as they are for Democritus, one would expect, if not an outright statement, then behavior and dramatic clues to such effect. Socrates behaves as might Democritus, but using the literary machinations of a comical hero. We find this clearly in the dialogue in which Socrates directly defends his behavior and philosophical way of life—the *Apology*. In it, as has been shown, Socrates plays the part of Plato's master of comic ceremonies.[59]

If this is so, then there is indeed an ambiguity as to which god Socrates comically calls as his witness. For all his Apollonian intellectualizing, Socrates, seen as properly comical, expresses (rather than suppresses) his more base, Dionysian impulses. Such expression, however, has been argued here to be decisive in bringing about the tragic destruction of Socrates himself. Had Socrates defended himself as Gorgias's Palamedes does, or had he argued drily and rationally in his favor, he may well have been spared the death penalty. Instead, he presents himself as thoroughly unlikable, an Archilochean hero who turns the tables on and offends the "men of Athens" who "judge" him; one who angers and provokes instead of placates and pleases; and one who jests during his trial instead of taking it "seriously." By playing a comical hero, Socrates tests the limits of logos, but simultaneously, he brings about his own destruction.

The *Apology* may then strike us as a strange occasion for comedy, laughter, and the Dionysian. But the oddity may dissipate with the Dionysian belief that, like seasons do for the grapevine, destruction brings about regeneration. Seeing the Dionysian aspects in Plato's dialogues and in Socrates himself may point to a sort of rebirth. Far from representing tragic finality, then, the *Apology* may simultaneously be comical and philosophical.

2

The *Laches*'s Comical Structure and "The Refined Thinkers Who Are Really Poor"[1]

The first chapter suggested that applying Socrates's claims about wisdom in the *Apology* to self-knowledge accounts philosophically for two different forms of laughter. If lacking self-knowledge renders one laughable, and no one appears to have self-knowledge, then humans may all be fundamentally laughable. But this includes Socrates, who does differentiate his wisdom from that of others. What he says gives him an edge over others in that he is aware of his lack of self-knowledge, whereas others assume themselves to have it. Socrates may therefore be laughable in a different way than those who falsely assume themselves to be immune to laughter. If these claims are right, one should be able to support the existence of (at least) two different forms of laughter in the dialogues, and if humans are fundamentally laughable, one should see evidence that even the most earnest and dull characters in the dialogues are presented jocularly. Both are evident in the *Laches*.

Beyond this, what we will find in the *Laches* is a formal symmetry with Aristophanes's Old Comedy that underscores the significance of comedy and laughter to the dialogue's philosophical content. This comical form serves the purpose of addressing its readers directly, through the *parabasis*, and thus implicates its audience—us—in the inquiry. The influence of Aristophanes is significant, but what will also become apparent here is how the use of seemingly tragic figures for comical and philosophical purposes supports a historical shift in the use and valuation of laughter.

Laughter becomes something not to be feared, but rather, something to be used in the quest for self-knowledge and philosophical inquiry.

At first blush, a dialogue ostensibly concerning the virtue of *andreia* and featuring Socrates and two of Athens's celebrated generals—each of whom was historically slated soon to meet a tragic end—would, like the *Apology*, hardly appear the setting for comedic laughter. And indeed, the *Laches* is charged with a potent sense of looming tragedy, including several ominous references of what is to come. Thucydides tells of the battle at Mantinea in 418 BCE, where the commanders of the Argive coalition, including Laches, reluctantly yielded to the will of the soldiers, relinquishing a strong position on a hill before the arrival of reinforcements to fight the Spartans on the plain, where the Argives were defeated and Laches was killed in action.[2] Nicias too would face a violent end. After significant setbacks in what was an arguably hubristic military overreach in Syracuse, the Athenian army had an opportunity to escape, but Nicias, frightened by the portent of a full lunar eclipse, followed the advice of seers to delay the withdrawal. Because of this, the Athenian forces were then massacred or enslaved, and Nicias was taken hostage and killed.[3] Socrates's end is familiar to us. The tragedy is not limited to the individuals involved in conversation; the fates of Laches, Nicias, and Socrates are linked with that of Athens itself, for their demise also signals the decline of their *polis*, which was never again to achieve such military successes and imperial reach as it had before the Peloponnesian War. Inasmuch as Laches's and Nicias's failures in the dialogue foretell of their eventual historical failures, the dialogue takes on a tragic tone.[4]

Despite the dialogue's tragic dimensions, this chapter proposes that the *Laches* is to a significant extent comic both in content and in form. Why would Plato use laughter in his treatment of these seemingly somber historical characters and this solemn topic? However dark the future of its interlocutors, the *Laches* cannot ultimately be a tragedy because Laches and Nicias fail to recognize their own *hamartia* and self-blindness.[5] To put it in terms of the preceding chapter, they demonstrate more-than-human wisdom in not only lacking self-knowledge but being ignorant as to that. They fail to achieve what Socrates calls human wisdom—the awareness that they are ignorant, not because of a lack of opportunity or capability, but due to willful cowardice. It is precisely in this failure that the use of laughter and comedy can be found and precisely in such failures that the importance of *andreia* lies.

Laughter, in the *Laches*, aims at rectifying this self-blindness. Laches's and Nicias's failures to see themselves for whom they are may seal their tragic fates, but the disconcerting use of laughter with these otherwise tragic figures jars us to recognize that this need not be the case for ourselves. Even such imposing figures of martial valor as these generals can fail to understand and embody *andreia*, or courage. Even these accomplished figures are eligible for further education, if they can see themselves for who they are or, at least, that they lack such knowledge. The dialogue's laughter holds a mirror up to its interlocutors, into which Laches and Nicias ultimately dare not stare, but one in which we, the dialogue's audience, can see our own reflections, if only we summon the *andreia* with which to do so. The *Laches*'s laughter thus enables the fulfillment of the Delphic imperative to know oneself partly because its main characters miscarry in this crucial effort.

This chapter makes a somewhat bold and general interpretative claim about the dialogue. The *Laches* is about Laches and Nicias, Socrates, Lysimachus, and Melesias, as well as the dialogue's audience—ourselves, and not so much about a disembodied, abstract virtue of *andreia*. The focus on the definition of *andreia*, while essential to the dialogue, is, I imply, overemphasized in the literature and certainly not a question that can be abstracted from the characters discussing it and how they do so. More crucial is the application of *andreia*, or perhaps the failure to apply it, by the dialogue's interlocutors. Literary dimensions of the dialogue—from characterization to dramatic action to tone—thus bear philosophical content and demand philosophical attention. The surprisingly comical tone of the *Laches* is not incidental.

Comedy in the dialogue holds a mirror up for whoever embodies *andreia* enough to face themselves in it. But recognition of one's own failures and limitations is not enough, since otherwise Lysimachus's and Melesias's own acknowledged mediocrity would be an ideal. Even distinguished leaders, such as Laches and Nicias, fail to understand and fully embody virtues pivotal to their distinction, such as *andreia*, and these failures are grounded in a more fundamental one: they fail to see themselves as comical, and thus they cannot strive to remedy their own limitations. Socrates is the comical hero: he may be the teacher the interlocutors seek, and yet, at the dialogue's end, he too is caught up in the *aporia* concerning *andreia*, but he, unlike Nicias and Laches, pursues becoming a student. The teacher and the student are one and the same. Socrates is the aged schoolboy who can only learn what he teaches himself, but he can learn, since he does not presume to know already.

The *Laches*'s Comical Structure

The *Laches* contains a striking array of comical content, much of which would not strike the modern reader as particularly funny. Greek puns, for instance, are difficult to discern, even when precedented in Aristophanic comedy. As will be examined later, at 194a, Laches puns on Nicias's name in a way parallel to how Aristophanes does in the *Wasps*, but between translation and distance from such historical figures, neither is likely to trigger a laugh today. Political jokes may also fail to register for modern readers. When Socrates asks Lysimachus, "Do you intend to cast your vote for whatever position is approved by the majority of us?," Lysimachus, son of Aristides "The Just," a military and political leader of renowned civic virtue who was ostracized by new democratic forces in 482 BCE, responds—as though unable to remember what his father stood for—with a confounded "Why, what else could a person do, Socrates?" (184d).[6] But the *Laches*'s comedy is not limited to its content.

The *Laches*'s form is as peculiar as its content. Emlyn-Jones notes two notable elements of the *Laches*'s structure. The first is that what is deemed the introductory section takes up nearly half of the dialogue (178a-89d).[7] Second, the dialogue is unusual in the late entry of Socrates (181d1), and in having yet a further delay to his active participation in the dialogue (184d5).[8] Emlyn-Jones suggests that the postponement allows for a range of testimony to Socrates's bravery, intelligence, and familial respectability.[9] I propose an altogether different, structural interpretation here. Schmid suggests that, although less obvious to us today, the *Laches* "has the formal structure of Aristophanic comedy."[10] If he is right, and I believe he is, then not only does this suggest answers as to how to categorize the dialogue, it also suggests how deeply laughter and the comic are embedded in the *Laches*, and how central these are to its interpretation. The *Laches* should not be thought of as having a long "introductory" section, followed by the *elenchos* proper. If we look more closely at the dialogue, it reveals itself to follow quite closely the elaborate structure of a comic play. The *Laches*'s comical structure invites comparison between its two *agōnēs*, and suggests a greater thematic coherence between them. But the question then becomes one as to why this dialogue would be presented in comical form and what changes if we read it as comical.

Taking the comic dimensions of the dialogue "seriously," as though they might be philosophically meaningful as opposed to frivolous, reveals, I argue, two central themes in the dialogue: overcoming self-blindness and recognizing oneself as laughable. Courage is required for both. On this reading, comedy and laughter are far from being obstacles to achieving self-knowledge, as the passage in the *Philebus* may suggest. Indeed, comedy and laughter become vehicles by which such self-knowledge might be provoked, if one has the courage with which to pursue it.

While comic plays enjoyed a formal elasticity, and variations on, and exceptions to, comic structure abound, the basic format of a play in Old Comedy moves from a prologue, to a *parodos*, an *agon*, some dialogue scenes, *parabasis*, and finally, to an *exodos*.[11] Schmid suggests that the *Laches* follows this same pattern.[12] This chapter aims to develop Schmid's insight. If comedy is embedded even in the formal composition of Platonic dialogues such as the *Laches*, then it must be asked what has been neglected by more straight-laced interpretations. Comedy and laughter are deeply embedded within the structure of the *Laches*, specifically, because comedy and laughter are philosophically appropriate to the meaning of the dialogue itself. First, a closer look at how the *Laches* follows the formal structure typical of Attic Old Comedy, and particularly with relation to Aristophanes's *Clouds*.

The initial scene in Old Comedy is a prologue, wherein "the opening situation is expounded and the movement of the plot is begun."[13] In it, the fantastic idea is introduced. In the *Clouds*, this is Strepsiades's plan initially to send his son Pheidippides to Socrates's Thinkery to train in how to argue his way out of the debts he owes. When Pheidippides refuses, Strepsiades goes instead, becoming, in comic fashion, an aged schoolboy. In the *Laches*, the fantastic idea is Lysimachus's and Melesias's notion to turn their sons over to Stesilaus for training in virtue, pending the recommendation of Laches and Nicias (178a–80a). As we will see, in the *Laches*, as in the *Clouds*, fathers replace sons as students in need of education. Tessitore compares Lysimachus to Strepsiades, due to their shared forgetfulness, old age, and general dullness, which combine to prompt Aristophanes's Socrates to kick Strepsiades out of the Thinkery, after which Strepsiades compels his son to take his place.[14] Plato's Socrates takes the exposure of Laches's and Nicias's ignorance as reason why the plan to educate Lysimachus's and Melesias's sons should be enacted only after their fathers and everyone else in the dialogue are educated.

The *parodos* involves the entry of the chorus. In the *Clouds*, it is Socrates who summons the chorus of Clouds, who promptly appear. In the *Laches*, it is Laches who summons Socrates. Laches notices Socrates nearby and mentions his surprise that Socrates had not yet been invited to the discussion, appropriate as it is for him (180a–81d). Socrates, in the *Laches*'s first chorus, performs the function of the Chorus leader.[15] Just as the chorus of a comedy would sing, accompanied perhaps by an *aulos*, so here is Socrates the musical one, "singing" in the Dorian harmony indicated by Laches.

The *agōn* is a formal debate presided over by the chorus, in which each contestant offers a *rhēsis*, or a long set speech.[16] The *Clouds* has two *agōnēs*, the first of which is between the better and worse logoi (949–1104), and the second of which is the debate about father-beating between Strepsiades and Pheidippides (1345–451). The first speaker is typically the one to lose the competition. The *Laches* also has two *agōnēs*: in the first, Nicias and Laches offer competitive speeches concerning the sagacity of Lysimachus's pedagogical plan (181d–84c), and; in the second, Laches and Nicias compete to define *andreia* (189d–99e). In the first *agōn*, Nicias and Laches patently disagree about the plan, and each offers a speech to support his claim. In his speech, Nicias refers to their competition explicitly as an *agōnos* (182a3) in which he and Laches are contestants, and again deems their struggle a few lines later to be an *agōn* (182a4). In the second *agōn*, Socrates redirects the conversation toward an understanding of what they wish to cultivate through education, namely *andreia* (189d–99e). The first speaker of each *agōn* is usually the one to lose. In the first *agōn*, Nicias loses over advice regarding *hoplomachia*. In the second, Laches might be said to lose over the definition of *andreia*. If so, the question remains as to whether Nicias can be said to "win."

A succession of dialogue scenes tends to follow, often including a *parabasis*. The *parabasis* is an address by the chorus, often directly made to the play's audience that "introduces a protracted break in the action that effectively splits the play into two distinct movements, and requires a degree of closure at the end of the first and a new phase to be opened up in the second."[17] A key interpretative question then becomes what the relation is between these two halves. While tragedy never breaches "the fourth wall," comedy regularly does, whether by acknowledging the audience, making jokes about individual audience members, or referring to the actors' status as actors in the play.[18] In the *Clouds*, for instance, the Chorus leader, as though speaking for the playwright, begins the first *parabasis* with "Spectators, I will speak the truth to you frankly," and proceeds to argue why the *Clouds* ought to win the prize in comedy (518–62).[19] In the *Laches*, Socrates begins the first *parabasis* with, "Then what we ought to do," imploring Lysimachus not to let Laches and Nicias get away before being thoroughly questioned (186a–87b). If Socrates is speaking as a chorus leader in a *parabasis*, the "we" he refers to here extends not only to the interlocutors, but to the audience more generally, including its readers.[20] According to Schmid, the *Laches*'s second *agōn* is followed by a more compressed "*parabasis* in which Nicias and Laches join in addressing advice to the audience that includes Lysimachus and Melesias" (200b–d).[21] Although sound, their advice to cast aside thoughts of their teaching the boys themselves in favor of asking Socrates to do so, should he be willing, is met with a gentle demurral: Socrates claims to require further schooling himself. If the *Laches*'s middle section is a *parabasis*, then it seems the dialogue's audience is addressed and implicated directly, and a special distinction may be placed on this address.

The *exodos* usually involves the departure of the chorus and actors, and often takes the form of some sort of sexual union or feasting. "Feasting" on speeches is a metaphor employed in a number of Platonic dialogues, such as in the *Republic*, where Socrates, Glaucon, and Adeimantus are invited to a meal at Polemarchus's home, but feast on philosophical discourse instead (*Republic* 328a–b) and, more explicitly, in the *Symposium*, a drinking party where drinking is initially foresworn, and symposiasts are invited to enjoy *logoi* instead of wine (*Symposium* 176a–77d). The *Laches* has two *exodos* scenes; the first, calling for further discussion (187d) and the second, marking the end of the dialogue, calling again for further inquiry and the meeting of Socrates and Lysimachus on the following day for this purpose (200a–01c).[22] The framing of the dialogue thus returns to this motif when Socrates and Lysimachus promise to reconvene (even if there will be little to feast on).

Schmid extends the comparison with Old Comedy to the *Laches*'s functional structure.[23] Typically, a comic play opens with an initial situation wherein a fantastic idea is presented. In the *Laches*, as described for the prologue above, this is the proposal to send Lysimachus's and Melesias's sons to Stesilaus to educate them. Next is a phase of struggle in which the hero and his or her allies meet with difficulties in realizing the idea. In the case of Laches, Nicias, Lysimachus, and Melesias, these difficulties, as we will see, are largely internal. Then comes the realization of the idea. At last comes the final phase or consequences following from carrying out the idea. The *Laches* ends with a relinquishing of the plan to turn the boys over to Stesilaus for educational purposes. Lysimachus and Socrates agree that they are themselves in need of education, and so agree to meet on the following day to return to school themselves, thereby becoming the stock comical figure of the aged schoolboy. The *Laches*'s ending is classic Old Comedy.

The formal and functional resonance of Plato's *Laches* with Old Comedy plays such as Aristophanes's *Clouds* does not yet indicate exactly how we are to interpret such similarity. The form of the *Laches*, as Schmid outlines and as I develop here, follows a structure typical of Old Comedy, with a repetition of *agōn*, *parabasis*, and *exodos*. Instead of seeing the *Laches* as having a long introductory section followed by a relatively brief philosophical *elenchos*, recognizing its comic structure highlights the significance of its first half, as well as bringing into greater relief the tone of its *elenchos*. I will focus here on how the dialogue's formal structure invites comparison between its two sections, how this serves to define a middle to the dialogue, and what it means for the dialogue to address its audience directly. I will argue that, through these three elements, the *Laches* reveals a philosophical significance to its comedy, and extends this significance not just to its interlocutors, but to us, its audience. In doing so, the *Laches* simultaneously discloses a radical shift in the valuation and use of laughter from a tragic and negative construal to an ambivalent and dynamic force.

The *Laches*'s comical structure implicates its audience directly. Reading the *Laches* with an eye toward its comical structure, one that ancient Greeks would have recognized, places greater significance on the first *agōn* and brings it into comparison with the second. If the formally comical structure of the Laches contains the *elenchos* at 189c–d as an *agōn*, this brings into comparison the second, philosophical *agōn*, with the first on *hoplomachia*. Rather than reading the comic structure as a prelude to philosophical *elenchos*, in other words, the *elenchos* is contained within the greater comical structure and is therefore flavored by the comedy of the *Laches*. If the comparison holds, then dismissing the comical in the *Laches* can no more be done than dismissing the comical in the *Clouds*.

Laughter appears to be central to the dialogue and its interpretation, even if its meaning has yet to be further elucidated.

The use of two *agōnēs* invites their comparison. Although not recognizing the comical structure of the *Laches* as such, several thinkers point the way for this. Hoerber suggests that the predominant structural and dramatic clue to the dialogue's content is the use of pairs, contrast, and duality.[24] Hoerber lists as examples the appearance of characters in pairs, the use of contrast to distinguish, for instance, "the courage of Socrates at Delium" and the "failure of Stesilaus in combat," and the pervasive distinction between *logoi* and *erga*.[25] To use terms from the *Republic*, two aspects of soul are involved in courage: the *logistikon* and the *thumoeidēs*, represented by Nicias and Laches, respectively (*Republic* 435–42).[26] The courageous hero is the one who is able to harmonize both of these elements. If so, the doublets, pairs, and contrasts Hoerber focuses on indicate the distinct elements of virtue requiring harmonization. Lysimachus says explicitly that he will not be able to remember anything that follows the middle of the dialogue, and so shows that, at best, he represents only one note of the harmony. When compared, the two *agōnēs*, we will see, reveal how Nicias and Laches fail to achieve such a harmony.

The two *agōnēs* are separated further by the designation of the *Laches*'s middle. Lysimachus announces the middle of the dialogue, saying that Socrates can take his place in the argument, and that, because of his old age, he can remember neither the questions he wants to ask, nor the answers, and that he cannot remember new arguments if they arise "in the middle (*metaxu*)" (189c8).[27] This occurs at the very middle of the dialogue (counting Stephanus pages), where a new argument is initiated by Socrates, who shifts the question from the worthiness of *hoplomachia* to the question of *andreia*. Socrates's speech is central, occurring just after this (189d4–e8). Whatever importance is attributed to this speech and the elenctic *agōn* that follows, it is also important to remember that none of this is likely to resonate with Lysimachus. The focus must lie elsewhere. We will see that it lies on us.

Form and content reflect each other: it is entirely appropriate to shift the discussion to one of virtue at the exact middle of the dialogue, a placement associated with virtue itself (as it is for Aristotle) and with honor.[28] Drawing on this, Howland suggests that, "The center of a text is an appropriate place to . . . emphasize that which is especially important."[29] It is at the center of the dialogue that Socrates, the youngest of these interlocutors, replaces the old guard—Lysimachus. And it is at the center of the dialogue that a shift begins from the valuation of laughter as ridicule to a more genuine expression of the human condition itself. Each of its characters prove to be laughable, even its hero: Socrates. And if this section of the dialogue constitutes a *parabasis*, as already suggested, then we too are implicated.

Lysimachus as a Comical Figure

The *Laches* begins with Lysimachus and Melesias, both undistinguished sons of highly distinguished fathers. Lysimachus's introduction resonates with the old guard, Homeric, and aristocratic conception of virtue and honor in which these are linked to a family's social station and noble deeds.[30] Like Cephalus in the *Republic*, he represents an older generation largely out of touch with, and passive to, the present.[31] Lysimachus and Melesias claim to be raising their sons in the Spartan manner of having common meals (*syssitia*), after which they discuss great familial deeds for their sons to emulate. The comic problem lies herein, for Lysimachus now confesses that he and Melesias are ashamed of their own lack of noble deeds (*kala erga*) to tell about, and this they blame on their fathers for having spoiled them. Thus, they are appealing to Laches and Nicias for advice on whether *hoplomachia*, or fighting in armor, as they just witnessed Stesilaus demonstrate, is a noble course of study that might prevent their sons from turning out as poorly and undistinguished as Lysimachus and Melesias have. Lysimachus repeats the need for care (*epimeleia*) and nurture (*therapeia*) that is to help make their sons the best (*aristoi*) of men.[32]

The opening of the dialogue is lengthy and awkward, and initially "strikes the reader as singularly inept for a verbal artist of the calibre of Plato."[33] This holds only until we see the laughter in it. Emlyn-Jones describes the dialogue's opening by a long-winded, repetitive, and out-of-touch Lysimachus as a humorous parody of a formal address.[34] Lysimachus makes a "proem (179a1)" and presents an "exaggerated imitation of formal rhetoric (see esp. 180a1–5)."[35] The opening's laughter extends beyond parody, for it is the very character of Lysimachus (and Melesias) that is comical.

Lysimachus is presented as a comic foil to the truly courageous man, a counterpoint to the true embodiment of *andreia*, or manly courage. He is domesticated, apolitical, and even effeminate. Lysimachus and

Melesias are examples of a group whom Pericles, discussing the aristocratic ideal of *andreia* and the obstacles to it, refers to as *apragmones*, or "quietists," a significant set of affluent Athenians who take little or no part in the care (*epimeleia*) of political matters and leave behind no fine deeds as their legacy.[36] Literally, they are *idiōtēs*, or apolitical and private persons. One might then expect great things from Lysimachuas and Melesias in the private sphere, which sets Lysimachus up as a comic figure. While Lysimachus claims to focus his efforts on the *oikos* instead of the *polis*, he has failed terribly in the domestic circle as well. He and Melesias failed to raise their own children well and must now reach out very publically to amend this. Rather than reverse this course for themselves—and they are clearly ashamed of it—Lysimachus and Melesias wish to avoid it for their own children by procuring the proper *epimeleia* and *therapeia* for their sons. Announcing his intent to speak frankly, Lysimachus confesses his (and Melesias's) softness and effeminacy (*truphan*, 179d). He claims to spend most of his time at home (180d–e), and swears by Hera (181a) as the women he is surrounded by at home would do.[37] Lysimachus has forgotten himself as a man: he begins the dialogue confessing his own shame at his softness and effeminacy, and ends the dialogue arranging to return to school like a young boy.

Lysimachus is not being hyperbolic in his self-assessment.[38] As Nichols points out, "No one present ventures to suggest that Lysimachus and Melesias have in any way judged themselves too harshly."[39] Indeed, in conversation with Anytus in the *Meno*, Socrates uses Lysimachus and Melesias as examples of well-educated, but decidedly inferior sons of great men to suggest that virtue cannot be taught (*Meno* 94a–e). The problem seems to lie not in the quality of education, but in the very character of the one to be educated.

Lysimachus's inertia, idleness, and negligence are illustrated in his participation (and lack thereof) in the dialogue. He shirks any responsibility for his own actions, inattentiveness, and for the very quality of his character. Like Melesias, Lysimachus blames his father for his own idleness, looks to remedy the idleness of his own son by idly hiring someone else to teach him what Lysimachus has failed to convey, seems content passively to hand his son over to whomever is deemed fit to instruct by other interlocutors, and is utterly oblivious to the progression of the dialogue wherein no one, including Socrates, turns out to be fit to instruct. He asks Socrates to take his place in the conversation, blaming his old age for being unable to participate himself (189c–d). It is striking how inert Lysimachus's beliefs remain throughout the progression of the dialogue.[40] The inflexibility of Lysimachus's beliefs makes the dialogue's ending, in which he seeks to educate himself, as per Socrates's recommendation, both the more impossible and the more comical.

Nonetheless, Lysimachus's role as a comic foil does not relegate him to insignificance. Aside from introducing several central themes (the aristocratic virtue of manly courage, care for one's own, and the question as to whether virtue can be taught arise from his opening), as well as providing the occasion for the dialogue, Lysimachus represents a formal philosophical correctness in three regards. He is the only interlocutor (aside from Socrates) who is able genuinely, albeit comically, to acknowledge his ignorance. He is also the only interlocutor (aside from Socrates) who pursues further inquiry because of this acknowledged ignorance.[41] Like Melesias, he is rightly unconcerned with being ridiculed, a possibility mentioned by Lysimachus at the very outset (178a) and reiterated by Socrates at the closure of the dialogue (201b). Both occur comically. Lysimachus's *parrhēsia* at the dialogue's outset is a frank, shameful, and public confession of private failure (like Alcibiades's frank confession of failing to have privately seduced Socrates in the *Symposium*), and his returning to school at the dialogue's end, all the while stressing his senility, is comical both as a stock motif of Old Comedy and in the utter impossibility of its success. Lysimachus's character, and his refusal for any responsibility for it, prevent him from changing or learning, and so, prevents him from capitalizing on these crucial, but in his case, merely formally correct attributes. In this sense, Lysimachus is ridiculous but also ambivalent, as this book suggests is the case for laughter in Platonic dialogues more generally.

Nicias as a Comical Figure

Nicias is the head of Athenian government at the dramatic date of dialogue (197d), but by the likely time of the dialogue's writing, he has met his demise. The gap between these allows for a greater variety of possible representations. If Plato does present Nicias as at least partly a comic figure, this would have been well-precedented.[42] Nicias's historical reversal of fortune—from successful general negotiating a peace treaty with

Sparta to a prisoner of war facing a gruesome death at the hands of the Syracusans—did not prevent him from becoming the butt of comic jabs. Writers of Old Comedy ridicule Nicias for his tremendous wealth,[43] his military and financial schemes,[44] and the cautious nature for which he was renowned.[45] Phrynichus renders Nicias so timid as to walk "with a hangdog look [*hupotageis ebadidzen*]."[46] Aristophanes puns on Nicias's name and his timorous nature, to coin the word *mellonikian*, meaning to delay victory.[47] Plato appears to join Aristophanes in having Laches pun on Nicias's name at *Laches* 194a, where Laches describes his intense desire to win the competition with Nicias as *philonikian*, which translates to love of victory but literally means love of Nicias. Given his reputation, cultivated both in comical and historical texts, it would be more odd to cast Nicias as a "serious" exemplar of *andreia*, than to cast him comically.

The comical treatment of Nicias in the *Laches* resonates thematically with that of the historians. Plutarch and Thucydides are less critical of Nicias than the comedians, but echo aspects of his comic characterization. Plutarch notes his lack of courage and assurance as well as his preoccupation with divination.[48] Thucydides admits Nicias to have been "somewhat over-addicted to divination."[49] Such preoccupation with divination is referred to twice in the *Laches* (195e-96b, 198a-99a). Socrates seems to take a direct dig at Nicias's deferral to the seers regarding the retreat from Syracuse, saying that "the law decrees, not that the seer should command the general, but that the general should command the seer" (199a). Nicias's position as a military commander may suggest him to be an exemplar of the virtue of *andreia*, but some of his actions suggest otherwise.

Nicias's characterization in the *Laches* probes more deeply into the beliefs that inform such actions and tests the person responsible for both. The comical dimensions of this characterization are centered on a contradiction between Nicias's stated claims—his *logoi*, and his dialogical actions, or *erga*. Nicias makes bold claims regarding logos and his ability in logos (200b), and yet is unable to express what he believes to be *andreia*. He plays it safe, drawing on formulations of *andreia* he has "often heard [Socrates] say," and refusing to venture his own views for testing, despite Socrates's encouragement (194d).[50] O'Brien suggests that, in general, "Nicias represents *logos* in human affairs and Laches *ergon*."[51] While each of them is courageous in some regards, each fails to demonstrate *andreia* in his own realm. Neither can fully acknowledge his own ignorance, but each is comically forthcoming in highlighting the ignorance of the other.

Nicias's notion of courage as a scientific expertise, if possible, would render courageous action impossible. The knowledge Nicias describes would remove the uncertainty in the face of which courageous acts are deemed courageous.[52] Guaranteed success in an undertaking all but eliminates the possibility of acting courageously in it. Nor, given such knowledge, would courage seem necessary. His focus in defining courage is on forethought. As Nichols writes, "Nicias' deepest trait is anxiety about future events."[53] Rather than pursuing courageous action, "Nicias wants refuge from the dangerous uncertainties of the future. He seeks knowledge of future events as a substitute for courage."[54] The beliefs ventured by Nicias are effectively a denial of the problem.

Nicias's inability to face his own ignorance and eager willingness to expose that of Laches's render him comical. Nicias briefly admits to failing in the effort to define *andreia*, but immediately attacks Laches: "That's a fine attitude of yours, Laches, to think it no longer to be of any importance that you yourself were just now shown to be a person who knows nothing about courage. What interests you is *whether I will turn out to be* (*anaphanēsomai*) a person of the same kind . . ." (200a, my emphasis). By his own admission, he has already shown himself to be ignorant, and yet now suggests that this has yet to be determined (199e). Despite acknowledging his *aporia*, Nicias quickly bows out of the argument, saying that "enough has been said on the topic for the present" and that Damon would correct anything that had not been "covered sufficiently" (200b). He then even offers to teach Laches, once he feels "secure on these points" (200b). His accusation of Laches is equally true of himself. He no longer thinks it important that he has just proven himself ignorant of what *andreia* is, and yet in the same brief speech, he offers to instruct Laches on it, because Laches "seem[s] to me to be sadly in need of learning" (200c). In fourteen Stephanus lines, Nicias moves from agreeing with Socrates that he has failed to define *andreia* to suggesting his ignorance about this virtue to be still undetermined, and finally, having returned to unwarranted confidence in his own wisdom, to offering to instruct Laches on virtue. Unpleased with what he sees of himself in the mirror, he convinces himself of his own beauty and is quick to divert attention to Laches's flawed reflection instead.

This is a direct reversal of the purifying effects of elenctic refutation described in the *Sophist*: Nicias and, as we will see, Laches too, grow tame toward themselves and harsh toward others. In the *Sophist*, purification is brought about through the elenctic art, which questions "thoroughly about whatever anyone believes he's saying while saying nothing" (*Sophist* 230b). Elenctic refutation is the "greatest and most authoritative of purifications" (*Sophist* 230d). Its results are that, when brought to *aporia*, ". . . those who are being examined, on seeing this, are harsh [*chalepainousi*] on themselves and grow tame [*hēmerountai*] before everyone else, and in just this way they get rid of the great and stiff opinions which encase them . . ." (*Sophist* 230c). In the *Laches*, Nicias and Laches are harsh on each other and tame with themselves. Nicias says nothing, but pretends, quite to the contrary, that he has said enough not only to avoid becoming a student, alongside Lysimachus and Socrates, but to justify his instructing others. The second *agon* of the *Laches* is not genuine *elenchos*; it is a parody of philosophical inquiry rendered comical by the limitations and self-forgetting of its characters.

Far from recognizing his own limitations and taking the role of student, Nicias denies these and assumes the role of teacher. A comic reversal between teacher and student is affected here akin to that taking place in the *Symposium* between lover and beloved. Nicias shows himself to be quite opposite of Socrates in his willingness to teach. Nicias has been shown to be ignorant and yet, in the same brief speech, he offers to instruct Laches. Laches also proves himself ignorant of what *andreia* is, and yet neither he, nor Nicias, perseveres in the discussion, nor do they arrange to continue the inquiry the following day, as do Lysimachus and Socrates. The generals think they need no further schooling, and yet act like bickering schoolboys in the dialogue.[55] Socrates recognizes that he needs further schooling, and though this suggests the comical trope of the aged schoolboy, he is more courageous in part because he does not fear the potential ridicule this might incur. Instead, he properly fears lacking the self-knowledge that would render someone ridiculous, as Laches and Nicias are, at least partly, rendered. In this sense, it is not the aged schoolboy who is comical, but rather the adults who ought to understand and embody *andreia* more than they do.

Stesilaus as a Comical Figure

Laches counters Nicias's rhetorical defense of the study of *hoplomachia* with two humorous counterarguments. If *hoplomachia* were conducive to martial virtue, Laches argues, then the Spartans, who are more concerned with military virtue than anything else, would show interest in this putative study (182d–83c). But the Spartans disdain this sort of thing so much that the teachers of *hoplomachia* tiptoe around Sparta, fearful of being detected. Laches's second counterargument is that those who practice *hoplomachia* have never distinguished themselves in actual battle (183c). Far from it, Laches says that he himself has witnessed the same Stesilaus, whom the interlocutors had just been contemplating, make an utter fool out of himself in battle and in front of the enemy. Laches recounts witnessing Stesilaus demonstrate in battle the use of a weapon he himself invented—a scythe-spear—which promptly became entangled in the enemy ship's rigging: "So Stesilaus dragged at the weapon in an attempt to free it, but he could not, and meanwhile his ship was going by the other ship" (183d–e). Stesilaus ran along the edge of his own ship, desperate to save his thoroughly ineffective novelty, but finally lets go, as the scythe-spear threatens to drag him behind the enemy transport. This causes mutual laughter from friends and foes alike: "There was laughter [*gelōs*] and applause from the men on the transport at the sight of him, and when somebody hit the deck at his feet with a stone and he let go the shaft, then even the men on the trireme could no longer keep from laughing [*gelōta*] when they saw that remarkable scythe-spear dangling from the transport (183e–84a). Laches concludes from this that *hoplomachia* is not worth studying, because it has little value other than making the cowardly man overconfident, and so, more likely to act rashly, or making the courageous man more likely to be critiqued and ridiculed (*katagelastos*, 184c5) for any minor mistakes.

Laughter permeates the entirety of Laches's first *rhēsis*. Laches strategically and humorously counters Nicias's defense of *hoplomachia*, point by point.[56] In his *epideixis*, Laches introduces the possibility of being deceived (*exapatōsin*, 182e4) by practitioners of *hoplomachia*, and breaches the topic of pretending (*prospoēsis*, 184c) to greater knowledge than one has, as well as the dangers this incurs, including the possibility of becoming a laughingstock, ridiculed even by the enemy. Stesilaus is such a laughingstock and Stesilaus's *epideixis* serves to warn us against what we least wish to become.

Stesilaus is a buffoon, a suitable target for Laches's ridicule, and a mere facsimile of a man embodying *andreia*. Nails likens Stesilaus to a sophist: "Stesilaus is to the general as the sophist is to the philosopher: he puts on a display of how to fight in arms (178a), invents new weapons (183d–e), and teaches his skill to the young (179d–e). But Stesilaus cannot fight in a real battle, and his newfangled weapons don't work."[57] Stesilaus is all show, appearing to fight vigorously only when there is no real threat, and so, no need for courage, as Laches reveals. Despite his flashy peacetime performance, Stesilaus's value in combat is limited to providing comic relief. He is, per Laches's story, a clown. But he, like Lysimachus, also provides the occasion for the dialogue itself.

On one level, Laches's description of Stesilaus is pure slapstick and "perhaps the funniest passage in all of Plato."[58] Stesilaus, flaunting his spear-scythe, fails the test of practicality in an *epideixis* of preposterousness, ending up tangled and dangling in the rigging of another ship. He only lets go of the butt of his ineffectual weapon when he is frightened by a stone that lands near his feet. This is the man presented as a potential teacher of martial skill and bravery. The laughter of this scene is the laughter of ridicule. It is the laughter that erodes, or even destroys, honor. It is the laughter that a hero dreads more than death itself, like Medea, but in this case, it shows precisely that this is no hero. Stesilaus's pretenses to greater effectiveness and courage than he has are easily exposed through laughter for all to see. As is typical in Old Comedy, the second speaker in the *agōn* concerning *hoplomachia* wins. But as has been shown to be the case in other instances of laughter, the one laughing—in this case, Laches—quickly becomes the focus of laughter himself in the second *agōn*.

Laches as a Comical Figure

Laches sets up the criteria on which laughter will be turned on him by extolling the Dorian harmony in select persons. Laches declares himself to be a lover of *logoi* when the speaker's deeds (*erga*) harmonize with his words (*logoi*) (188d). That he is the one to articulate this standard enhances the comedy of his own, pending violation of it, and underscores what he will have forgotten in the process: himself. He says,

> Whenever I hear a man [*andros*] discussing virtue or some kind of wisdom, then, if he really is a man [*hōs alēthōs ontos andros*] and worthy of the words he utters, I am completely delighted to see the appropriateness and harmony existing between the speaker and his

> words. And such a man seems to me to be genuinely musical, producing the most beautiful harmony, not on the lyre or some other pleasurable instrument, but actually rendering his own life harmonious by fitting his deeds to his words in a truly Dorian mode, not in the Ionian, nor even, I think, in the Phrygian or Lydian, but in the only harmony that is genuinely Greek. (188c–e)

The truly musical man (here again, the Greek emphasizes his gender) is the one whose deeds and words harmonize in the Dorian mode. This is the only, genuinely Greek harmony, and it seems consistent with what Socrates says elsewhere, but as Schmid points out, Laches's principle of harmony is missing a critical Socratic element—being put to the test.[59] As Socrates says in the *Cratylus*, reinvestigating (*epanaskepsasthai*) what one says is necessary because "self-deception [*exapatasthai auton*] is the worst thing of all" (*Cratylus* 428d). Once Laches is tested, the belief in his own internal harmony must be jettisoned, unless he can return to self-deception.

That this harmony is Dorian is not incidental—the Dorian mode is linked with courage, moderation, and measure. In the *Republic*, Socrates associates the Dorian mode (*harmonia*) with bravery and warfare. The Dorian harmony is one of two left in the luxurious city, allowed to remain due to its ability to produce fine imitations of moderate (*sōphronōn*) and courageous (*andreiōn*) persons, and its ability to influence persons to avoid acting arrogantly (*huperēphanōs*), and instead to act moderately (*sōphronōs*) and in measure (*metriōs*) (*Republic* 399b–c). Aristotle also claims that harmony has an impact on character: "even in mere melodies there is an imitation of character, for the musical modes differ essentially from one another, and those who hear them are differently affected by each."[60] The "peculiar effect of the Dorian" harmony is that it "produces a moderate and settled temper [*mesōs de kai kathestēkotōs malista pros heteran*]."[61] The harmony of words and deeds lauded by Laches is thus one that is thought to contribute to moderation, measure, and courage, or to becoming a more virtuous person.

Because Laches is acquainted with Socrates's deeds, he suggests that Socrates is a viable candidate for achieving the true Dorian harmony of words and deeds, and is therefore to be allowed full freedom of speech (*parrhēsias*, 189a).[62] Hoerber claims this quality—his achieving the Dorian harmony between *logoi* and *erga*—is what renders Socrates the hero of the dialogue.[63] Socrates is superior to each contestant, "surpassing Laches in *ergon* and transcending Nicias in *logos*."[64] In this sense, Socrates is the truly musical man, exhibiting such a harmony, in distinction, perhaps, to Damon the music teacher. Socrates is a real military hero, acting with true courage, as opposed to Stesilaus the teacher of *hoplomachia*, who jumps at the drop of a stone. But Laches himself does not achieve the Dorian harmony he lauds, and because of this, laughter will be turned on him.

The historical Laches is a gruff and blunt man of action who was elected general (*stratēgos*) in 427/6 and commanded the Athenian fleet in Sicily. He hails from the deme of Aexone, whose citizens were known as aggressive speakers (to which Plato's Laches refers at 197c). His character in the eponymous dialogue is sensitive to the comical in others, offering two ridiculous stories about Stesilaus and other teachers of *hoplomachia*, but impervious to the comical in himself. Laches's notion of courage resonates with tragic laughter. As Nichols puts it, Laches's understanding of *andreia* "rests on preserving the opinion that ridicule and disgrace, above all for not bravely fighting for the city, are more terrible than the risk of death."[65] Laches is no verbal match for Nicias, and he beats a hasty, revealing retreat once his efforts to define *andreia* end in failure. Rather than mustering the courage to either continue these efforts or to recognize the significance of this failure, Laches withdraws from the inquiry, chalks his failure up to an inability to express what he still maintains that he knows, and remains largely silent except for several digs at his rival.

Laches's comical depiction, like Nicias's, is precedented in Attic Old Comedy and historically grounded. In 425 BCE, Laches was brought to trial on charges of misconduct by Cleon and acquitted.[66] Nails suggests this to have been political retaliation by the war-mongering Cleon against Laches for his efforts in establishing a peace treaty with Sparta.[67] Cleon charged Laches with embezzling funds in the Sicilian campaign (427–25 BCE).[68] Based on these historical events, Laches is depicted in thin disguise in Aristophanes's *Wasps*, a dramatic critique of Athenian litigiousness that was staged in 422. In the play, he appears as Labes ("grabber"), a dog from the deme Aexone (Laches's deme), who is brought to trial by a dog from Cydathenaeum (Cleon's deme) for stealing a Sicilian cheese and refusing to share it. Accused by a sophistic prosecutor, Labes is speechless in response. Nonetheless, the arbiter argues that Laches's inability to speak, his failure in logos, and his lack of musicality should not be grounds on which to convict him, and Labes, like the historical Laches, is acquitted. Aristophanes's play suggests Labes to have been a good dog for chasing wolves and guarding sheep, and for having stolen to help the people, whereas Cleon was a bad dog for taking the people's money for doing nothing.[69]

The historical Laches exemplifies *erga*, deeds and courage therein and, at least in an incomplete way, he is a courageous man of action.[70] But it is precisely in the realm of *erga* that Plato's Laches shows himself to lack the sort of courage in which he claims to believe. Laches makes fun of Stesilaus for making boastful claims that fall apart in battle, yielding to cowardice and ineptitude and yet Laches himself is guilty of what he mocks Stesilaus for—pretending to be more courageous than he is. For while Laches may embody courageous action in a military offensive, he fails to abide by his own notion of *andreia* as *phronimos karteria*, or wise endurance of the soul, in other realms of action.

Laches's view of *andreia* circumscribes it greatly. He seems not to see how courage could be applied to much more than a military offensive, including in military retreat. At 191a, after Socrates applies Laches's notion of courage to military withdrawal, Laches is perplexed, asking, "What do you mean, in retreat?" Historical references bear this out. Tessitore characterizes Laches as courageous in attacking, but cowardly in retreat.[71] Alcibiades's account of the retreat from Delium supports this (*Symposium* 221a–b). Alcibiades, on horseback, bids Socrates and Laches to be courageous (*tharrein*, 221a) but Laches is found wanting in relation to courage, whereas Socrates is the courageous hero whose keen self-possession (*emphrōn*) and bold—even comical[72]—swaggering help save Laches and Alcibiades.[73]

Laches also fails to see how *andreia* might be exemplified in philosophical inquiry. Dobbs offers a more generous reading of Laches, arguing that Laches's response to the experience of *aporia* demonstrates courage better than Nicias's because Laches acknowledges his own perplexity and attempts genuine inquiry to resolve it.[74] Particularly as opposed to Nicias's attempt to eliminate uncertainty in his ventured conception of courage as a form of knowledge, Dobbs argues that "Laches' belief in the need to persevere in the face of uncertainty is . . . essential to the conduct of genuine inquiry and prudential judgment."[75] Dobbs is right, and what Socrates suggests in the *Meno* supports this (86b–c). But Laches's belief in the need to persevere is undercut by his lack of perseverance in the inquiry.

Laches's performative contradiction—the contradiction between his words and deeds—invokes laughter from quite an unusual source. The contradiction itself is surprising coming from the very person who had earlier hailed a Dorian harmony between a speaker's words and deeds, but it serves to emphasize the performative contradiction. Laches suggests *andreia* to be first, endurance (*karteria*), and second, wise endurance (*phronimos karteria*), and yet, fails to exemplify such steadfastness or endurance in the inquiry itself. That he is exactly the person to lay stress on such a harmony both brings the performative contradiction to our attention and makes it funnier. Socrates plays on such a Dorian harmony when he asks Laches whether they ought to agree with their own logos. He then specifies, "With the one that commands us to endure [*karterein*]. If you are willing, let us hold our ground [*epimeinōmen*] in the search and let us endure [*karterēsōmen*], so that courage itself [*autē hē andreia*] won't make fun of us [*katagelasē*] for not searching for it [*autēn*] courageously [*andreiōs*]—if endurance [*karterēsis*] should perhaps be courage after all" (194a). Courage herself ridicules both Laches and Socrates for failing to search for her courageously.

Although such ridicule of the interlocutors by the logos in the *Protagoras*, or inquiry itself in the *Charmides* will be examined later, this is peculiar in a further regard. The gender of *andreia* is stressed here with the use of repeated feminine pronouns, making her ridicule all the more poignant.[76] Just as it is a young, beautiful, Thracian servant girl who laughs at Thales for his well-ward tumble, it is the gender of one who might be the object of erotic striving who laughs here. Similarly, Socrates in the *Symposium*, recounts some such mockery at the hands of Diotima, who makes fun of Socrates for taking categories to be exclusive, binary oppositions and for forgetting the middle, or what is in-between (*metaxu*, *Symposium* 202b and 204b) them. The derisive laughter of the feminine brings into relief the aspirations of manliness and presumption of manly courage in the one being laughed at in the *Laches*. *Andreia*, far from being attained or possessed, remains mockingly elusive.

As in these other examples, Socrates blunts the sting of being laughed at by a feminine personification of manly courage by including himself as a target. In the *Theaetetus*, he claims that this laughter is applicable to all who practice philosophy (*Theaetetus* 174a-b). Instead of touting his ability and bravado in the *Symposium*'s *agōn*, Socrates presents himself as a young and ridiculous student being "schooled" by—of all persons in patriarchal fifth century Athens—a woman. In the *Laches*, Socrates stresses that the ridicule is directed at himself *and* Laches, even though it is Laches whose performative contradiction is incurring laughter. Is it possible that Socrates's inclusion of himself in the ridicule is meant to suggest that laughter is not to be included in the category of what is terrible, or to be feared? Or is he emphasizing the importance of self-directed laughter, and inviting Laches into seeing himself as laughable?

While using laughter here to emphasize how *andreia* continues to elude the interlocutors, Socrates's inclusion of himself in those being mocked serves to dull the evocation of Laches's *thumos*. In the *Republic*, *andreia* is directly connected to the *thumos*: courage (*andreion*) is said to occur when the spirited part (*to thumoeidēs*) of one's soul preserves (*diasōdzē*) what is terrible (*deinon*) and what is not (442c). In the *Laws*, the involvement of *thumos* distinguishes liberal from illiberal laughter (*Laws* 935c–e). Oddly, the word *thumos* never occurs in the *Laches*.[77] Does this suggest that the laughter of the *Laches* is playful (*paidias*) and without rancor (*spoudē te ama kai thumoumenoisin mē exestō*), and thus the good sort of laughter that the Athenian in the *Laws* allows (*Laws* 936a)? While Laches and Nicias may personally be derisive toward each other (and Laches toward Stesilaus), Socrates extends the condition of being laughable to the interlocutors, and if comedy is a self-forgetting, Nicias, as we have seen, extends this yet further, to humans in general (200b). It is not a personal affront to Laches's *thumos*, but rather descriptive of the human condition.

As in the *Theaetetus* passage wherein the Thracian girl laughs at Thales, in the *Laches*, the ridiculer becomes the one ridiculed. Laches ridicules Stesilaus, Nicias, and Damon, but faces laughter in the same vein. Schmid claims that the image of *andreia* herself laughing at the interlocutors "is a charming pedagogical hook to pull Laches into further inquiry."[78] And yet, *andreia*'s laughter does not have that effect on Laches. Experiencing *aporia*, Laches quickly backs out of the inquiry, all the while proclaiming his willingness to continue (194a, 194c). Laches says he will endure in the inquiry, but aside from accusing Nicias of talking nonsense (195a, 195b, 196b), he effectively drops out of the conversation, with a meager, "I think perhaps I have asked enough" (196c). Indeed, his many jibes at Nicias prompt Socrates to suggest, "let's instruct [*didaskōmen*] him instead of making fun of him [*loidorōmen*]" (195a). But Laches has already recognized that he is in no position to instruct.

Laches fails to recognize his own ignorance, and instead, he blames logos. The problem for Laches, is not his own witlessness. Instead, it is courage's cunning ability to escape him in logos that is at fault: "I am really getting annoyed at being unable to express what I think in this fashion. I still think I know [*voein*] what courage is, but I can't understand how it has escaped me just now so that I can't pin it down in words [*sullabein tō logō*] and say what it is" (194b).[79] Like Aristophanes's Labes, Laches falls silent when pressed. He fails in logos. Socrates points this out in the *Laches*, saying: "Then I don't suppose, Laches, that according to your statement you and I are tuned to the Dorian mode, because our deeds are not harmonizing with our words. In deeds I don't think anyone would say that we partook of courage, but in words I don't suppose he would, if he were to listen to our present discussion" (193e). Laches, like Labes, is thoroughly unmusical, falling short himself of the Dorian harmony he so esteems.

Laches lives by the heroic code in which laughter and ridicule are imbued with the power to deny one the honor (*timē*) due.[80] Tragic laughter is almost entirely anticipated, rather than actualized, and it is the honor that it undermines that makes heroic action worthwhile.[80] Laches's fear, then, is fear of the malicious laughter that erodes honor. When Nicias distinguishes between courage and rashness to deny that animals can exhibit the former, Laches says, "You see, Socrates, how the man decks himself out in words and does it well in his own opinion. Those whom everyone agrees to be courageous he attempts to deprive of that distinction [*timēs*]" (197c). Nicias, perhaps sensing the gravity, quickly responds that he is not depriving Laches of such honor.

Courage, Laughter, and Self-Knowledge

If laughter holds up a mirror to its audience, courage is what makes possible an honest and considered look in it. And if this is the case, a radical revaluation of laughter and comedy occurs in the *Laches*. The *Laches*'s dramatic date is delimited on either side by internal references to the battle at Delium (181b, 188e–89b), which sets its earliest date as 424 BCE, and the presence of Laches, who died at Mantineia in 418 BCE (Thucydides 5.74.3). The date of its writing is more difficult to narrow down, but neither is such dating essential to its interpretation. Its authenticity is questioned by very few scholars, one of whom alleges inauthenticity due to the dialogue's "logical and dramatic defects."[81] The interpretation argued for here assumes no such grounds for claiming the dialogue's inauthenticity, and indeed suggests its logical and dramatic qualities to be far more sophisticated than sometimes assumed.

Several of the *Laches*'s main themes and its tone are introduced straightaway. The *Laches* begins with a direct reference to the man (the Greek emphasizes his gender) Stesilaus, a teacher of *hoplomachia*, or fighting in armor: "*tetheasthe men ton andra machomenon en hoplois*" (178a).[82] Lysimachus, the speaker, immediately proclaims his intention to be frank (*parrēsiadzesthai*) even though there are people who will laugh at (*katagelōsi*) such frankness. The question with which the dialogue begins is whether or not the study of *hoplomachia* is a beneficial course of study and "the sort of training that would make the best men" out of the sons of undistinguished fathers, such as Lysimachus and Melesias, themselves sons of very distinguished fathers (Aristides and the conservative politician Thucydides, respectively) (179b). Laches and Nicias had been invited to see Stesilaus display this method of fighting, and now Lysimachus and Melesias would like to know their opinions because they believe Laches and Nicias will speak frankly. Nicias defends *hoplomachia*, while Laches questions its value.

The *Laches* is framed by references to what is laughable. Frank speech (forms of *parrēsia* at 178a and 179c) and the comic motif of returning to school at an advanced age create a frame for the dialogue in which laughter and ridicule (*katagelōsi* at 178a and *katagelasetai* at 201b) are highlighted. In Lysimachus's frankness, he confesses his own and Melesias's softness or effeminacy (*truphan*, 179d), blames their famous fathers for this, and seeks to avoid the same for their sons by hiring a qualified teacher.[83] Its framing suggests, for Tessitore, that the dialogue is a "parody of philosophic inquiry."[84] Beginning with a form of *theaomai*, referring specifically to a philosophical gazing at or contemplation, the *Laches* is a paradigm of Socratic inquiry conducted with comical characters and "unlikely philosophers."[85] Lysimachus asks Socrates to speak for him due to his advanced age and consequent failing memory, which can retain neither questions, nor answers (189d). Lysimachus, Tessitore suggests, resembles Strepsiades of Aristophanes's *Clouds* in his old age, forgetfulness, and general insipidity.[86] He is the only one who responds correctly to the dialogue's *aporia* by expressing a willingness to continue the inquiry, but his bumbling passivity renders him least able to participate in philosophical inquiry. One wonders just what the conversation would be like on the following day, between Socrates and one who can retain neither question nor answer.

This comic frame brings the tone of the dialogue within it into question. Tessitore suggests the dialogue's comic elements to extend past its comic frame to the rest of the dialogue, which becomes particularly evident in light of testing one's arguments against one's way of life (188a-b).[87] Arieti reads the *Laches* as a comedy, citing several farcical elements: its pretext—two self-confessed failures asking two prominent generals for help in raising their sons, Stesilaus's making himself ridiculous, the distinguished generals' bickering ungraciously with each other, and its ending with old men returning to school with the boys.[88] He compares the plot to that of Terence's *Adelphoe*, wherein a father asks for advice on how to rear his son, but receives completely contradictory counsel.[89] Schmid views the *Laches* as neither a tragedy nor a comedy, but rather an exemplar of double philosophical irony, involving tragic and comic aspects, and "in which the uncertainty is turned back on the audience."[90] It is through this discomfiting goad that we, the dialogue's audience, can recognize our own need for philosophical inquiry.

Setting aside the question as to how best to categorize the *Laches*, what these scholars agree on is that it is heavily flavored with comical elements. It is not the aim of this book to settle the question of dramatic categorization. It is, however, an aim of the book to ask what philosophical meanings can be derived from comical elements such as those that predominate in the *Laches*. While the focus has thus far been the *Laches*'s form, it will now address more fully its comical content.

The notion of courage, or *andreia*, undergoes a dramatic expansion in Socrates's hands to include how one responds to philosophical difficulty, or *aporia*, as well as how one pursues philosophical inquiry.[91] This is paired in the *Laches*, as elsewhere, with a radical shift in the valuation of laughter. In the *Protagoras*, Socrates suggests a conception of courage akin to that offered by Nicias: "the knowledge of that which is and is not dangerous is courage [*andreian*], and is opposed to the ignorance of these things" (*Protagoras* 360c). Socrates follows this with an image similar to one he introduces in the *Laches*, saying: "For if the argument had a human voice, that voice would be heard laughing at [*katagelan*] us and saying: 'Protagoras and Socrates, you are strange [*atopoi*] beings . . .'" (*Protagoras* 361a). Logos laughs at them for having switched positions, and thereby contradicting themselves. Why does Socrates twice use ridicule and laughter in discussions of courage? I will suggest here that he does so to prompt the recognition that one ought not to fear ridicule and laughter as Laches does—that these are not, in the language of the *Protagoras*, dangerous. Rather, we ought to fear as dangerous the self-blindness that makes one an object of ridicule. Laughter, far from what the tragedians suggest, is not to be feared, but rather to be used both playfully and consequentially. The *Laches*'s laughter draws from both for—when such purposes exist—the sake of courageously recognizing and responding to *aporia*. We thus return to laughter's connection to the Delphic imperative: if one is ridiculous and laughable when one lacks knowledge, then laughable instances are opportunities to assess one's self-knowledge. Courage is required to face this self-blindness.

The question of courage comes up in the *Laches* for two reasons. The more apparent one is that *andreia* is the virtue most closely associated with *hoplomachia*, martial arts, and the distinguished careers of Laches and Nicias. A second reason is suggested in the *Meno*, where courage (*andreia*), *aporia*, and learning are explicitly linked. Courage is what one needs to properly respond to the experience of *aporia*: if one recognizes being at a loss, learning can take place if one has the courage to discover for oneself and not tire of the search (*Meno* 81d3–4). *Aporia* corrects for overconfidence when one does not know, but it is not itself enough to assure learning (*Meno* 84a5–c9). Courage is required to pursue learning, so the question as to how to educate the sons of Lysimachus and Melesias may turn out to be a question about what qualities of soul that the sons (and, as we will see, everyone else in the dialogue) need for them to learn. Socrates, in the *Meno*, says that, "I would contend at all costs both in word and deed as far as I could that we will be better men, braver [*andrikōteroi*] and less idle, if we believe that one must search for the things one does not know" (*Meno* 86b–c). In a state of *aporia*, one is best positioned to learn, if one is courageous, but this assumes the ability to recognize one's own ignorance.[92] While Laches and Nicias are undoubtedly courageous in some facets of their lives, their actions in the *Laches* belie a cowardly inability to acknowledge and accept their own ignorance. How they handle the experience of *aporia* will be the test indicating their courageousness.

The question as to how to educate Lysimachus's and Melesias's sons does not stay about the sons for long. It quickly becomes a test as to whether the interlocutors themselves know what they ought to, and how to proceed if they do not. Laches and Nicias are approached by Lysimachus as authorities, and yet the dialogue ends with the suggestion that all present would be better suited to return to school to learn what they have been shown not to know. This chapter examines the dialogue's prominent characters—Lysimachus, Stesilaus, Laches, and Nicias—as comical figures who fail, for varying reasons, to hit the mark of virtue, specifically *andreia*. Their failures hinge on pretension and self-deception. Each of them, in different ways, exhibits a self-blindness that renders them comical. Socrates too is laughable: although he is not self-blind, he includes himself in the laughter. This is crucial.

Laughter is an ambivalent force. It can be derisive and consequential in its infliction, exposing viciousness, but it is also appropriate for the man who most fully embodies *andreia*—Socrates. It can involve hubris and shame, but somewhere in between these lies the honor of the virtuous person, and laughter of varying sorts is applicable to the whole continuum. As will be the case for Aristotle, *andreia* seems here to occupy a middle position (*mesotēs*) between fear (*phobous*) and confidence (*tharrē*).[93] Laughter can jar us away from the extremities and toward the middle. It can help to curb overweening ambitions to exceed limitations and can remind us of our fundamental limitedness. The *Laches* ends with the suggestion that we are all in the position of being laughable, like the disguised Odysseus returning home, because like beggars at a banquet, we are all needy. Upon his return, Odysseus must learn humility and endure ridicule (in contrast to the hubris he displayed to Polyphemus) to find his way back to a virtuous middle. In this sense, laughter promotes humility, but not if it is used primarily as a tool to shame others. Critical is the recognition that it can also be turned back on oneself.

Laughter has been argued to be brought about by forgetting oneself, by laughing at others, but not seeing how one is laughable oneself. The Thracian servant girl's laughter at Thales's fall into the well exemplifies this: she laughs at him without recognizing that she herself is also laughable, as Socrates indicates (*Theaetetus* 174a–75e). While we might be tempted to see this example as but a narrow one, Nicias, in the *Laches*, extends its scope to humans generally. Nicias rebukes Laches, saying, "you seem to me to be acting in a thoroughly human fashion [*alēthōs anthrōpeion*] by noticing [*blepein*] everybody except yourself" (200b). It is "truly human" or, more literally (albeit awkwardly), "unforgettably human" to forget oneself and pay attention to others instead. If the comical in Platonic dialogues is self-forgetting, then the human condition, as Nicias presents it, appears to be inherently laughable.

If this claim is as important to the *Laches* as I take it to be, one would expect to find examples of it elsewhere in the dialogue. The dialogue's main characters provide several. Lysimachus and Melesias, although at least aware of themselves as undistinguished, nonetheless focus on the improvement and education of their sons, and given how they participate in the conversation, if at all, one wonders whether they are capable of escaping obscurity.[94] Nicias and Laches are both brought to *aporia* but, as distinguished generals, neither can face the implication that they are ignorant of the basic virtue of a common soldier. As Nicias points out, Laches notices the laughable in Nicias, and not in himself. But this is equally true of Nicias, who goes so far as to point this out, and yet does not see how it applies to himself, particularly in the passage at 200b, where he too experiences *aporia*, but in a brief passage, instead talks himself into offering to instruct Laches because, as he puts it, Laches sorely needs it.

A notable and sole counterexample is Socrates, who repeatedly turns the mirror back onto the interlocutors and himself. Nicias tells us that this is to be expected of Socrates: "whoever comes into close contact with Socrates and associates with him in conversation must necessarily, even if he began by conversing about something quite different in the first place, keep on being led about by the man's arguments until he submits to answering questions about himself concerning both his present manner of life and the life he has lived hitherto" (187e–88a). A bit further on, Nicias says, "I realized some time ago that the conversation would not be about the boys but about ourselves, if Socrates is present" (188c). But Socrates does not exempt himself from this investigation. When Laches advises Lysimachus and Melesias not to take himself and Nicias as teachers for their sons, but rather Socrates (200c), Socrates reminds him that "we were all in the same difficulty [*pantes en aporia egenometha*]. Why then should anybody choose one of us in preference to another?" (200e–01a). Socrates then exhorts Nicias and Laches to "join in searching for the best possible teacher, first for ourselves—we really need one [*deometha gar*]—and then for the young men . . ." (201a). They are all in need of a good teacher, says Socrates, and then as if to explain his comical turn as an aged schoolboy, Socrates quotes from Homer's *Odyssey*. Odysseus has returned to Ithaca at last, disguised as an aged and impoverished man. When Telemachus gives the disguised Odysseus food, he encourages him also to beg from the suitors, saying, "*aidō d'ouk agathēn phēs emmenai andri proiktē*."[95] Literally, the passage reads "reverence or respect is no virtue for a man who begs" (my translation). Like the disguised Odysseus, the interlocutors are old men in need of wisdom who are reduced to begging scraps from others, even if this incurs ridicule and mockery, much as it does for Odysseus. Comedy is so deeply embedded in the dialogue's structure because of how thoroughly this task is embedded in the *Laches* itself.

Conclusion

The significance of laughter and comedy to the question of *andreia* thus becomes more apparent. Inasmuch as laughter can expose our pretensions to knowledge when in fact we lack it, it can, at least potentially, play a significant role in piercing self-deception, and specifically the sort of self-blindness that each of the characters discussed here illustrates, and that may keep them from exemplifying *andreia*. And yet, it fails at exposing their self-blindness to any of them. This is particularly striking for the title character, because it is Laches who shows himself to be the most sensitive to the comical and to laughter. It is also Laches who is the most viable candidate of the characters discussed here, for embodying *andreia*, but he cannot face his own ignorance. The possible date of Plato's writing of the *Laches* would have rendered redemption too late for any of these characters. The audience of any lesson to be learned here is us. This underscores the relevance to the virtue in question of recognizing oneself as laughable, as possibly blind to oneself, and always potentially ignorant.

Courage only exists in the absence of certitude. This is, in a sense, what the historical Nicias denies. Fearing the portent of the lunar eclipse, he entrusts the seers, striving for a certitude that goes behind human knowledge. But the more certain he feels about this, the less courageous of an act it is to entrust the seers with determining the course of events. Socrates implies that the more knowledgeable one is as to achieving victory in battle or the wiser one is as to horsemanship in a cavalry attack, the less courageous one is in acting on this knowledge (193a–b). He then uses this to suggest that Laches's definition of courage—as wise endurance—leads to *andreia* turning out to be foolish endurance (193c–e). Laches illustrates this in his questioning Nicias as to whether a doctor who knows what is to be feared in terms of illnesses, or a farmer who knows what is to be feared in terms of farming, are courageous. Nicias denies that they are (195b–c). It is precisely in the absence of knowledge or certitude about the outcome of future events that courageous actions can take place. Courage may thus require some knowledge so that one does not slip into foolhardiness, but equally and remarkably, it requires ignorance as well. It is exactly because Socrates does not know whether he will survive the retreat at Delium that his actions are courageous. In this sense, courage demands a recognition of one's own ignorance, a recognition of always being laughable (even if not of always being ridiculous). But when we do muster the courage to look in the mirror, it is with some degree of uncertainty as to exactly what we will find.

Comic moments of the dialogues are not limited to content alone. This chapter has argued that the *Laches*'s form echoes that of comic drama and illustrates how the structure of the dialogue echoes those of traditional Old Comedies, such as those of Aristophanes. If the *Laches* does indeed have the formal structure of a comic play, the *Laches*'s laughter pervades its form and content. This implies that laughter has particular significance to the *Laches*'s philosophical meaning. It also suggests, particularly through the *parabasis*, that the dialogue's audience is addressed therein. We too become part of the comedy. While we may laugh at Lysimachus, Stesilaus, Nicias, and Laches, Socrates turns this laughter back on us, prompting the realization that we, the dialogue's audience, are also implicated. Like Laches and Nicias, we too may laugh too quickly at others without seeing the comical in ourselves.

The *Laches* shows dramatically—in both form and content—that ridicule is not to be feared. It is not an evil, as ending with Socrates and Lysimachus as aged schoolboys illustrates. If fear is the expectation of a future evil (198b), then ridicule need not be feared. Productive of some sorts of evil, lack of self-knowledge is to be feared. Laches and Nicias are both depicted comically by Aristophanes. While Plato may be drawing from this in his own characterizations of these figures, the focus in the *Laches* seems to shift to one on their self-blindness and the attendant discord between their *logoi* and *erga*. This is what makes them comical, rather than their wealth, gait, or difficulties with words, as are suggested by the comedians. Socrates does not just *say* that ridicule is not to be feared; in the *Laches*, he *shows* that this is the case by taking Laches and Nicias through *aporia* to show that mockery (of each other) does not diminish their honor. What does diminish their honor is their inability to face themselves, their turning away from the mirror he holds up.

The integral role of laughter in the dialogue's form and content suggests an answer as to why the dialogue is named after Laches. What makes Laches so central a figure is precisely the sensitivity to laughter he demonstrates. It is Laches who most closely embodies the values of tragic laughter that tie laughter to a loss of honor in the one laughed at, and to malice in the one laughing. If *andreia* involves knowing what is fearful, then the *Laches* seems to be an exhibition of how mistaken we are to fear laughter to the extent that many, such as Laches, do. The *Laches* concerns the attempted education of Laches, and the turning around of Laches from his love of honor and victory to a recognition that he lacks the self-knowledge he pretends to have and the lack of which he ridicules in others. That it fails for Laches presents a lesson for the dialogue's audience, a warning to recognize what Laches does not.

If this is the case, it becomes apparent the extent to which Socrates is reforming the valuation of laughter in antiquity. Laughter is not the proper object of fear; instead, we ought to fear the pretension, self-blindness, and lack of self-knowledge that make us objects of derisive laughter. At 186c, Socrates refers to his own poverty. As compared to the ridicule aimed at Socrates for his poverty in Old Comedy, poverty in the *Laches* becomes something closer to a virtue. It expresses the laughable human condition, for we are all effectively begging like the disguised Odysseus. Socrates, in this sense, appropriates the jab he attributes to comic poets who deem philosophers "the refined thinkers who are really poor" (*Republic* 607b). To be laughed at, as Socrates says to Euthyphro, "does not matter" (*Euthyphro* 3c). Fearful, rather, is it to be blind to how our words and actions fail each other, as Euthyphro demonstrates both in failing to recognize his own ignorance as to what piety is and in failing to recognize his own performative contradiction in esteeming piety and yet impiously proceeding with a lawsuit against his own father. Like Euthyphro, Laches, Nicias, Cratylus, Hermogenes, and Critias, to mention only a few, we may not be the tragic heroes we esteem ourselves to be. Instead, like Lysimachus, Stesilaus, Nicias, and Laches, we may be the humble characters of a comedy.

If there is such a statement as to the fundamental condition of humanity implied here, the question as to whom one ought to learn from comes to the fore once again. The refined thinkers have shown themselves to be poor, and the seemingly sagacious Socrates is heading back to school, wise only in knowing he has nothing to teach. Both are laughable, even if in different ways. Who, then, ought to teach the youth of Athens? This question is at the heart of the *Charmides*, to which the next chapter turns.

3

Tumbling Down to Earth: Laughter, Limitation, and Self-Knowledge in Plato's *Charmides*

Does being laughable, as each of the *Laches*'s characters are, preclude being virtuous? Is the teacher sought in the *Laches* even possible? This chapter focuses on two seemingly incongruent elements of the *Charmides*—laughter and *sōphrosynē*—to show that their relationship is closer than otherwise assumed. Their incongruence appears grounded in self-consciousness or, stated more strongly, in self-knowledge: laughter and what is comical seem to betray a lack of self-knowledge, whereas *sōphrosynē*, the virtue often translated as moderation, temperance, or self-control, instead, demands it. But if laughter and the comical figure can coexist with that agent's self-knowledge, the incongruence between laughter and *sōphrosynē* dissipates. Socrates is such a comical (and simultaneously virtuous) figure.

That the comical is somehow a function of self-perception is well-supported in existing literature on comedy.[1] The question is how? Does ignorance of oneself render one comical? Or, can a comical character possess self-knowledge? Hubbard distinguishes Hegel from Plato on this: "Unlike Plato . . . Hegel insists on a certain self-consciousness of the comic character . . ."[2] Like the *alazōn*, the comical person pursues trivial things in a serious way, but for Hegel, the comical figure must be both aware of this triviality, and so, not merely stupid, and yet unable or unwilling to behave otherwise.[3] Inasmuch as the *Philebus* passage is taken to represent a Platonic conception of what is comical, it is inferred, as Hubbard does, that the comical figure for Plato lacks self-knowledge. On this basis, Plato is generally thought to separate self-consciousness from the comical.

At least one of the characters of Plato's *Charmides*, however, suggests differently. While the lack of self-consciousness is indeed common to Charmides and Critias, it is not to Socrates, who is comical in a different way. It is Socrates who shows how comedy and *sōphrosynē* might be intertwined, because only he has the self-knowledge required for the latter. If Socrates is a comical character in Platonic dialogues as the previous chapters have suggested, then, I will suggest in this chapter, he defies the standard readings of what is comical in Plato because he, unlike characters such as Critias, is aware of himself as comical.

The self that is revealed comically, however, has unique and enigmatic features. Griswold has suggested the difficulty, or even impossibility, of full self-knowledge due both to the complexity and changeability of the subject.[4] Socrates himself is frustratingly complex, as Alcibiades describes him in the *Symposium*, an amalgam of irreconcilable opposites best likened to a satyr. The comic understanding of the self implies an intractable malleability, reversals, and change. In Aristophanes's works, for instance, the "man of the house" may suddenly find himself powerless (and in a woman's dress); the tyrant, reduced to a lowly sausage-seller; and the powerless (such as women and old men) may find themselves in control. Stability appears elusive, exposing instead what Hyland calls a "primordial incompleteness," or an "ontological aporia," which is "definitive of the erotic nature of the human soul."[5] Like Charmides and Critias, we may well still "fall." In this sense, a comical understanding of the self proves recalcitrant to full understanding.

Herein lies an answer to how laughter contributes to *sōphrosynē*. As "knowledge of what one knows and does not know," *sōphrosynē* requires awareness of one's limits. Laughter can bring about such an awareness. Ranging from tragic/consequential to comical/playful forms, laughter encourages the recognition of one's own limitations by presenting an external perspective on the self from which the self can be seen in light of its shortcomings. It is a perspective that laughs derisively, playfully, or mutually, but it is accompanied by Socrates's insistence that it is not truly fearful. It is a perspective that can belong to other persons, to ourselves, or even to personified notions. Whether one fears it as does Critias, accepts it, or even promotes it as a part of the human condition as does Socrates, such laughter thus enforces the Apollonian recognition of limitation through Dionysian means and contributes to a key aspect of *sōphrosynē*. Given its broad application by Socrates, what such laughter reveals is that being limited and laughable are not particular to any person, but are instead features of being human. But the comical notion of the self is one that remains recalcitrant to full and complete understanding. In the *Apology*, Socrates suggests that he knows himself better, even if only in one small respect, than his interlocutors do. Socrates, then, may not be merely ironic in claiming not to know anything, but rather, suggesting that he understands himself more fully as comical, and thus ultimately, as unknowable.

If Plato's Socrates shows us that laughter can include self-knowledge—however incomplete it may be—then laughter is not incommensurable with the Delphic imperative. I argue here that, instead of posing an obstacle to self-knowledge, laughter can enforce the Delphic imperative to know oneself in several different ways as will be examined more closely in this chapter. As shown in the *Charmides*, Socrates is a self-consciously comical hero, at least in part. The chapter begins with a look at comic tumbles, spills, and falls.

Falling down has been funny for a long time (perhaps for as long as humans have walked upright), and a comedic staple already in Attic Old Comedy.[6] A number of Aristophanes's characters are downright wobbly: the *Birds* opens with its characters stumbling about while searching for a better life, Trygaeus repeatedly fights falling off the giant dung beetle he is riding in *Peace*, and Lamachus, in the *Acharnians*, tumbles into a ditch, triggering a hyperbolic, absurd, and utterly false vision of his subsequent demise.[7] Figuratively, toppling may be yet more pervasive: the fall of the powerful (and conversely—the rise of the weak) is a recurrent trope in Aristophanes, in whose works men are coerced by women to end wars, men are subversively replaced by women in the Assembly, and generals are upstaged in their military efforts by peasant farmers independently negotiating peace treaties. To a considerably lesser extent, such falls occur even in the dialogues of Plato, a philosopher described by Nietzsche as "boring" and reported by Diogenes Laertius never to have laughed out loud.[8] I wish in this chapter to contend such views of Plato and to suggest that such falls—whether physical or metaphorical events—are funny in Platonic dialogues just as they are in Aristophanes's plays. But further, I would like to take such laughter "seriously"—not by reducing laughter to solemnity, because laughter will always exceed and escape such a reduction, but rather by asking what philosophical meaning might attend such laughter, philosophical meaning which we have decidedly neglected for as long as this antigelastic reading of Plato has prevailed.

Laughter on the Bench

Turning to the *Charmides*, we find evidence against such an antigelastic reading only a few lines in. At its beginning, Socrates, who has just returned from the fierce battle at Potidaea, asks about the state of Athenian youths. Critias tells him that there is one who is exceptional beyond all others—Charmides, who is beautiful in body and soul. As Charmides makes his way toward the many admirers awaiting him, hubbub ensues: ". . . his coming caused a lot of laughter [*epoiēse gelōta polun*], because every one of us who was already seated began pushing hard [*spoudē*] at his neighbor so as to make a place for him to sit down. The upshot of it was that we made the man sitting at one end get up, and the man at the other end was toppled off [*katebalomen*] sideways. In the end he came and sat down between me and Critias" (155c). Far from expressing superiority over an object of ridicule, this is an instance of what we would today call slapstick. It is physical, playful, funny, and apparently, Plato thought it somehow important enough to be included. Although this little episode can be easily passed up as insignificant—a humorous prelude before the "serious" business of philosophy begins—I would like to take the opposite tack and ask just what its significance might be. Why, given the above characterization of Plato and several of the explicit descriptions of comedy in his dialogues, would such a scene be included? And given its inclusion in the framing of the dialogue, what does the comic have to do with the dialogue's themes of *sōphrosynē* and self-knowledge?

The coveted spot on the bench is its stable middle, a position least threatened by the comical volatility of the extremities. This is where Charmides alights, between Socrates and Critias. The bench scene is a potent image for the dialogue: at its extremes lie excesses of self-certainty and self-ignorance, while the coveted central positions suggest a proper balance of these, as in *sōphrosynē*. Critias and Charmides will metaphorically tumble from its extremities. Socrates will not. Although Charmides is offered a position of honor, the question will be whether he deserves it. Charmides lacks the extreme self-certainty of Critias, but he shares with

Critias a coy reluctance to venture anything of his own. He does not have the courage to look in the mirror. As such, Charmides cannot overcome his self-ignorance, however deeply he may pretend to look into himself.

If laughter can expose pretense, then it plays a crucial role in being virtuous. Socrates participates in the rowdiness on the bench, along with Critias, and yet seems the very embodiment of *sōphrosynē*. Alcibiades attributes *sōphrosynē* and courage to Socrates explicitly in the *Symposium*, offering examples to support this (*Symposium* 216d, 219d), and Socrates has just returned from the battle at Potidaea at which he is said to have demonstrated these virtues. In administering the charm and remedy, Socrates claims to be under strict instruction from the Thracian physicians, to be "deaf to the entreaties of wealth, position, and personal beauty" (157c). It becomes more puzzling then, what to make of the passage in which Socrates recounts, in a rare glimpse into his personal and psychic state, his erotic response toward Charmides when he happens to glance inside his cloak. Socrates, it seems, is not immune to eros, but is, rather, *sōphrōn* enough not to be ruled by it. His response to peeking inside Charmides's cloak provides a practical display of his *sōphrosynē* in action. Indeed much of the dialogue that follows can be seen as an extended self-reflection by Socrates.

Tragic and Comic Laughter

The laughter of the bench scene is not the laughter of presuming oneself superior to others. It more closely resembles comic, rather than tragic, laughter. These types of laughter are distinct, and yet too often conflated. Halper, for instance, argues that Plato uses laughter to disarm ideas that the reader might otherwise dismiss, and instead, considers them without needing to approve or disapprove of them.[9] In this sense, laughter makes us think more carefully about things we believe ourselves already to know, and opens us up to doing philosophy. While this is a wise observation on the effects of textual humor on the dialogues' readers, it might be added that there are other forms of laughter operative in the dialogues for which this cannot be true. Laughter itself does not necessarily disarm; tragic laughter instead raises the hackles of its target. Laugher varies in its effects, in other words, depending on its kind. A quick turn to the difference between tragic and comic laughter will help to support this.

A brief look at the laughter of classical tragedy and comedy accentuates the radical departure Plato's Socrates makes from the laughter of tragedy and how much more akin Plato's laughter is to that of comedy.[10] Laughter's tendency toward excessiveness is clearly on display in the laughter of classical tragedy. Matthew Dillon argues that the laughter of tragedy is generically different from comic laughter, and there is much to support this view. Aside from a few instances, the laughter of tragedy is humorless, vindictive, and extraordinarily potent, whereas comic laughter, as presented by Aristophanes, shows a balance between derision and positive sources such as celebrations and festivals.[11] Laughter in tragedy threatens the hero's honor code and functions as an ethical sanction influencing behavior.[12] Two heroic examples from tragedy will suffice to make this point.

The potency of laughter and the threat it poses to one's honor are represented in extremes by Euripides's Medea and Sophocles's Ajax, for whom gruesome and violent deaths are preferable to the possibility of being laughed at. Clearly horrified at the prospect of killing her own children, Medea dreads the alternative, as she sees it, of being laughed at by Jason and his new bride as far worse.[13] She convinces herself to slaughter her children with six references to the alternative, ultimately concluding it is clear (*saph' isthi*) that ". . . the pain [*algos*] is profit, so long as [Jason] can't laugh ['*ggelas*]."[14] Laughter, here from *anagelaō*, meaning to laugh loudly, is worse than death and the murders she contemplates. This is the case for Sophocles's Ajax as well, who, after a humiliating loss of Achilles's armor to Odysseus, chooses suicide over anticipated laughter directed at him. That this laughter does not actually occur—Odysseus resists even Athena's encouragement to laugh in order to sympathize with Ajax instead—is not significant to its portrayal as unquestionably negative and vicious.[15]

Laughter, in tragedy, inevitably involves a loss of face, loss of sanity, hatred, or an ethical failure of grand proportions. As Dillon points out, there seems to be no distinction made in tragic usage between *gelaō*, *katagelaō*, and *epigelaō*.[16] Laughing—*gelaō*—is no different here from laughing derisively or maliciously—*katagelaō*. When we import this conflation and the derisive view of comedy into our readings of Plato, we are thus reading Platonic dialogues, and specifically the laughter therein, tragically. I will suggest instead that Plato's laughter has far more in common with comic laughter.

Comic laughter is, on the other hand, varied in its ethical characterization. Although comic laughter is regularly incited by shameful and abusive speech—*aischrologia* and the similar *loidoria*, *kakēgoria*, and *blasphēmia*, shameful situations, characterizations, and behavior, comic laughter is not as closely affiliated with strictly negative sources. Derisive laughter accounts for over half of the occurrences of laughter in Aristophanes's plays, according to Alan Sommerstein.[17] But beyond this there is greater variability in kinds of laughter. Sommerstein distinguishes three types of laughter in Aristophanes. The first, referred to as Type 1 laughter, is that of derision, or laughter that targets someone who does not wish to be laughed at and who has been exposed in some sort of folly, failure, or misfortune.[18] Type 2 laughter, marginally related to the first, is laughter arising from "language that is unintentionally amusing," such as Peisetairos's proposal in the *Birds* of sacrificing a gnat to honor the new wren-god.[19] We laugh at Peisetairos's impious and incongruous words, not at Peisetairos himself. Sommerstein's third type, however, is the most relevant for our purposes. Type 3 laughter is victimless and triggered by a pleasurable experience, but not one that comes at the pain or discomfiture of other persons.[20] It is a laughing *with*, not a laughing *at*, as suggested by the use of *gelaō*, *epigelaō*, *prosgelaō*, and *kachadzō*. This third type of laughter arises from shared pleasures at symposia or festivals (*Clouds* 621, 1073, *Birds* 733, *Ecclesiazusae* 849), sexual pleasure (*Clouds* 1078), escape from the threat of danger (*Peace* 335, 338–39, 539–40, *Wealth* 757–58), or from a reunion of separated persons (*Peace* 600, *Lysistrata* 512). Each of these instances involves a shared pleasure, a mutuality of laughter.[21] Sommerstein concludes from this that "the *telos* of comedy is shared pleasure."[22] Comic audiences, in other words, laugh *at* the characters, but also *with* them as participants sharing in a Dionysian experience. Comic laughter thus involves the audience in the performance directly.

If Sommerstein and Dillon are right, then comic laughter differs from tragic laughter in its multivalence and in its social and ethical characterization. Sommerstein writes: "The Dionysiac spirit, as it is presented in comedy, is the spirit of seeking enjoyment for oneself and others, as inclusively as possible . . . Its enemies are those who seek enjoyment for themselves at others' expense, or those who reject enjoyment for themselves and try to deprive others of it as well."[23] The strictly self-centered schemes of Strepsiades and Euelpides, writes Sommerstein, fail because they deny this *telos*.[24] In this regard, such laughter may well be generically different, as Dillon claims, from the laughter of tragedy. They also differ in their usages of the semantically broad *gelaō* and compounded forms such as *katagelaō*. Comic laughter distinguishes between these because comic laughter includes other types of laughter. Tragic laughter does not; if tragic laughter is invariably derisive, such a distinction is superfluous.

Common to tragic and comic laughter is the tendency toward immoderation. In a different sense than that at work in tragedy, laughter's tendency toward excessiveness is on display in comic laughter as well. Schlegel claims that a "freedom of all restraint" is the very environment in which comedy thrives.[25] Nonetheless, we find in classical philosophy, including Plato, a robust discussion and growing acceptance of boundaries for comedy and laughter. Laughter is increasingly seen as subject to the bounds of propriety, and through this, there is an emergent recognition of the distinction between what will come to be called by Aristotle the liberal and the illiberal jest. We see this already in Platonic dialogues.

Radically, though it revises the laughter of tragic and comic drama, Plato's laughter is much more akin to comic laughter than to tragic laughter. The laughter of the dialogues is multivalent, exemplifying a range of kinds of laughter, whether we divide these into three types, as does Sommerstein to laughter in Old Comedy, or into playful and consequential kinds of laughter, as does Halliwell. The categorizations, for our purposes, matter less than the point they share in common: comic laughter is not restricted to being malicious and derisive. Laughter for the Greeks is a much more diverse phenomenon than is oftentimes assumed, particularly if tragedy is our paradigm, and if that is the case, then Plato's laughter may have precedents and meanings we have generally overlooked. This provides a sketch of the rich background from which Plato is able to draw, and both of these types of laughter appear to be at play in the *Charmides*.

Laughter in the Platonic dialogues is multivalent and dynamic, ranging from joyful exuberance to a playful warning against thinking oneself superior to others. The *Charmides* illustrates this range, displaying (at least) three different types of laughter. There is the playful laughter of the bench scene at the dialogue's inception that we might anachronistically deem a form of slapstick. It is a mutual laughter, akin to Sommerstein's Type 3 laughter. There is the consequential laughter aimed at Critias's hubris, as displayed in his failed claim. While this might seem to be the laughter of superiority, illustrative of Sommerstein's Type 1 laughter, it is qualified by a third sort of laughter that then turns on the interlocutors and audience at large at the dialogue's end. Rather than feeling superior over the hubristic Critias, we are instead reminded that we have not done much better, and so, that we too are potentially ridiculous.[26] It would be simpler to focus on the laughter aimed at Critias as the most philosophically substantial laughter, and to dismiss the others as mere window-dressing, or setting the scene. Doing so, however, makes as assumption that we have made for all too long in philosophy, namely, that philosophy and comedy are fundamentally different, even oppositional, and that comedy should merely do the bidding of philosophy, its superior. I hope to bring this assumption into question here.

My focus will be not just on what is *said*, but also on what is *done* in the dialogue, on dramatic actions as much as on discursive speech. What may strike some as an overemphasis on the dramatic and literary dimensions of the dialogue here is, as I see it, instead an attempt at drawing clues from the often neglected or entirely overlooked aspects of literary composition to attempt a philosophical understanding of the dialogue's otherwise ambiguous content. Rosemary Desjardins writes that in Platonic dialogues, "words do not simply *mean*"; words must be interpreted and understood.[27] The same formulation for *sōphrosynē* that Charmides will offer—that it is "minding one's own business," and that Socrates will describe in the *Charmides* as incomprehensible as a puzzle (*ainigma*, 161c, 162b) is adopted by Socrates in the *Republic* as though it were a straightforward formulation (*Republic* 433a–b, 441d, 443d–e).[28] Truth, as Desjardins concludes from this, is not simply having true opinion, but tethering that opinion to causal reasoning that can lead to knowledge.[29] True opinion for Socrates, I would add, can also fail as such if not secured to one's actions. It is quite possible, in other words, to hold an opinion that happens to be true, but either not know what makes it true (per Desjardins), or to act in such a manner as to contradict the opinion.[30] Neither case reflects genuine understanding. Charmides and Critias will fail on both counts. Hence, I believe my emphasis on actions in relation to speech within the dialogue to be complementary (and substantial), rather than supplementary, to efforts at understanding the more strictly discursive claims made in the dialogues.

Since this chapter takes issue with the attribution to Plato of the superiority theory of laughter, clarification as to what that means is in order. If what is meant by attributing to Plato a superiority theory of laughter is a claim that *Plato* believes, as does Hobbes, that laughter is caused by, and is an expression of, feeling oneself to be superior to others (whether through one's personal greatness or another's inferiority), then this chapter ought to dispel that claim with evidence of other types of laughter that occur within the *Charmides*. A comparable example is deeming Plato a Psychological Egoist, based on Glaucon's recounting of the myth of Gyges in the *Republic*. This is the stronger claim. The weaker claim, inasmuch as it constitutes a claim at all, is not one I dispute. In it, attributing to Plato a superiority theory of laughter is simply, and to my knowledge, factually, claiming that what would later be termed the superiority theory of laughter was first alluded to by Socrates in a dialogue written by Plato. This is a decidedly different claim than the one that alleges the theory is Plato's *own*, exclusive belief about comedy and laughter. Similarly, suggesting that what would come to be called Psychological Egoism is first discussed in a dialogue by Plato is uncontroversial. To be clear, it is the stronger claim that I am contending here.

These three incidents in the *Charmides*, taken together, sketch a range of types of laughter, a range that cannot be subsumed under the superiority theory, and one that prompts us to consider the role laughter plays in *sōphrosynē* (and vice versa), as well as the significance laughter might hold for philosophy more broadly. This range—laughter in its playful exuberance, laughter exposing haughty disdain for (and yet a succumbing to) human limitations, and laughter that curbs the desire to think oneself immune to it—indicates a variety of ways in which laughter is involved in self-knowledge. On the one hand, a lack of self-knowledge may render us ridiculous and laughable, but on the other, a recognition of one's ongoing potential for being laughable informs any self-knowledge positively. Laughter, I argue, exposes our pretensions to be better than we really are and, as such, plays a critical role in the Delphic imperative to know ourselves. It exposes pretense by acknowledging what we oftentimes choose to ignore in ourselves, namely the incongruity between our words and our deeds. These incongruities between what we *say* and what we *do*, are what I will call performative contradictions.[31] The positive potential of laughter in regard to knowing oneself relies on one's capacity to admit and learn from such incongruities, rather than continue to paper over them, a capacity that Critias seems not to have. Nonetheless, laughter calls attention to performative contradictions in such a way as to incent us positively toward self-knowledge.

The situation may appear just the reverse: comedy might seem at odds with *sōphrosynē* and self-knowledge, as it is portrayed in the *Philebus*. The identification of comedy and vice is made explicit, where Socrates suggests the nature of the ridiculous (*to geloion ēntina phusin echei*) to be, ". . . a kind of vice [*ponēria*] that derives its name from a special disposition; it is, among all the vices, the one with a character that stands in direct opposition [*tounantion*] to the one recommended by the famous inscription at Delphi" (*Philebus* 48c). Comedy would seem, in other words, to obfuscate that most philosophical of imperatives, and the putative origin of Socrates's philosophical mission, to "know thyself." Of the three kinds of self-ignorance resulting—those of one's material goods, of one's bodily goods, and of one's psychic goods—Socrates goes on to say that ". . . an overwhelming number (of people) are mistaken about the third kind . . . and . . . believe that they are superior in virtue, although they are not" (*Philebus* 48e). This is especially true, Socrates claims, of the virtue of wisdom.

One can see how this passage in the *Philebus* might be used to support attribution to Plato of the superiority theory of comedy, or more broadly, of a negative view of comedy.[32] Where this sort of a reading goes wrong is that it does not pay attention to context. This discussion in the *Philebus* concerns mixed psychic pleasures, the main example of which is malice (*phthonos*). Comedy is brought up insofar as comedy can be malicious. This is not a discussion of comedy in general, but rather a specific and narrow form thereof, and this only within the context of discussing the sort of person who can derive pleasure from the humiliation of others. Socrates is acknowledging that malicious persons exist, but there is no indication of this constituting an all-encompassing theory of laughter. To the contrary, in the earlier passage, where Socrates does suggest something more general, namely what makes someone ridiculous, it is precisely the belief that one is superior when one is not. This is fundamentally at odds with the superiority theory. Further, it is not comedy and laughter that make knowing oneself impossible, but rather a lack of self-knowledge that makes someone a comic figure and laughable. In other words, it is not the reception of comedy that obfuscates the quest to know oneself. It is, instead, not knowing oneself that makes one into an object of ridicule. But this passage does not simply steer us afield.

Two significant points emerge from it: the ridiculous person, on this account, is one who is self-ignorant; one who thinks himself to be virtuous when in fact he is not,[33] and self-knowledge requires a precise measure of one's goods.[34] Socrates then modifies the first point according to whether the self-ignorant person has the power to affect others, or is harmless (49c). If she is powerful enough to stifle ridicule, it is fear and hatred that she inspires; if weak, she inspires malicious laughter. If Xenophon is to be believed, Critias fits the former bill: "For Critias was the most thievish, violent, and murderous of all in the oligarchy . . ."[35] As the leader of the ten tyrants ruling the Piraeus, Charmides would also have the power to affect others.[36] The ensuing discussion of Critias, a defense of Socrates against charges of corrupting youthful associates such as Critias and Alcibiades, centers on the virtue of *sōphrosynē*: whether it can be taught, and whether one who seems *sōphrōn* could become immoderate. At issue is Critias's immoderation and its source. Yet Critias, in the *Charmides*, assumes himself not only to know what *sōphrosynē* is, but also to be *sōphrōn*, and Charmides blushes modestly when given the opportunity to claim the virtue in himself, suggesting that he believes himself *sōphrōn* but would appear immodest in saying so (158c). Given their later history, which would have been well known at the time the *Charmides* was written, Critias and Charmides exemplify this dangerous combination of power and self-ignorance. Charmides and Critias, in other words, could have been merely ridiculous figures.[37] Given their political power, however, they become hated and feared instead. The *Charmides* begins comedically but ends, historically, as a tragedy.[38]

If the ridiculous person is one who is self-ignorant, then laughter, by drawing attention to what one would rather ignore, to the ways and degrees to which the measure has been exceeded, becomes a vehicle by means of which to know oneself. The Athenian Stranger in the *Laws* stresses the need for knowing the ridiculous. He tells Clinias: "Now anyone who means to acquire a discerning judgment [*tis phronimos*] will find it impossible to understand the serious side of things in isolation from their ridiculous aspect, or indeed appreciate anything at all except in light of its opposite" (*Laws* 816e–17a). To understand either, one must understand both. He then separates the serious from the comical and stresses the need to understand both: "But if we intend to acquire virtue, even on a small scale, we can't be serious and comic too [*poiein de ouk au dunaton amphotera*], and this is precisely why we must learn to recognize [*manthanein*] buffoonery, to avoid being trapped by our ignorance of it [*agnoian*] into doing or saying anything ridiculous [*geloia*] when there's no call for it [*mēden deon*] . . ." (*Laws* 817a).[39] It is important to the quest for becoming virtuous that we learn about (*manthanein*) buffoonery and the ridiculous. Ignorance of the possibility of being ridiculous may itself render one ridiculous. And yet, the Stranger claims that it is impossible to simultaneously be both comic and serious in the pursuit of becoming virtuous, a possibility that seems demonstrated in the *Charmides*'s bench scene, where the seated shove each other seriously (*spoudē*), thereby causing much laughter. Acquiring a discerning judgment (*tis phronimos*) about anything requires knowing its opposite, so to be a properly serious person, one must also understand the ridiculous.

Given that comic laughter is not exclusively derisive, other forms of laughter may relate differently to *sōphrosynē*. Socrates and Critias are both laughable, albeit in sharply divergent ways, and illustrate two distinct concepts of *sōphrosynē*. In what, then, does Socrates's *sōphrosynē* consist, and how does he differ from Critias?

Socratic versus Critian *Sōphrosynē*: Theory and Practice

The distinction between Socrates's and Critias's knowledge of self is illustrated in the search to define *sōphrosynē* in the *Charmides*. While Critias offers the first explicit definition of *sōphrosynē* as self-knowledge, his conception of this differs in several key respects from Socrates's. Whereas Socrates has insisted that the *sōphrōn*'s knowledge includes knowing of what one is ignorant (167a, 169b, 169e, 174d) and therefore of one's own limitations, Critias repeatedly drops this qualification (169e, 174e). Socratic (and, for that matter, Apollonian) self-knowledge consists in knowing oneself as limited and lacking, as is evidenced by Socrates's repeated disavowals to knowledge. A rare claim to knowledge does occur in the *Symposium* (177d), where Socrates claims to know the erotic arts, but as defined there, *eros* and the erotic are defined by deficiency, so the claim to know them again turns into a claim concerning one's limitations.

Socrates warns of the possibility of self-deception. When Critias accuses Socrates of trying to refute him, Socrates responds with what may be a surprising motivation, saying, "Oh come . . . how could you possibly think that even if I were to refute everything you say, I would be doing it for any other reasons than the one I would give for a thorough investigation of my own statements—the fear of unconsciously thinking

I know something [*phoboumenos mē pote lathō oiomenos men ti eidenai*] when I do not [*eidōs de mē*]" (166c–d). Philosophy yields dividends for the self, but also the common good: "And this is what I claim to be doing now, examining the argument for my own sake primarily, but perhaps also for the sake of my friends. Or don't you believe it to be for the common good, or for that of most men, that the state of each existing thing should become clear? (166c–e). It is significant to point out that what Socrates claims to fear is not being ridiculous, as the *Philebus* passage above presents it, but rather, he fears being self-ignorant or thinking he knows something when he does not. Socrates fears self-deception. Here already is a significant revision in what it is that one ought to fear: it is not laughter of others aimed at oneself, as Ajax and Medea consider most fearsome, it is pretentiousness and ignorance within. This is entirely consistent with his suggestion at *Apology* 29b that taking oneself to know what one does not is "reproachable" or "shameful" (*eponeidistos*). Socrates continues with: "Pluck up your courage [*tharrōn*] then, my friend, and answer the question as seems best to you, paying no attention to whether it is Critias or Socrates who is being refuted. Instead, give your attention to the argument [*tō logō*] itself to see what the result of its refutation will be" (166e–67a). The result of the refutation will be that the argument itself would laugh at the interlocutors, if it could. Laughter, as we will see, unsettles the kind of ossified self-certainty Critias typifies, and directs our attention to the continuing threat of self-deception. Rather than a thing to be feared, laughter in Socrates's hands, becomes in part a tool to help enable the doing of philosophy.

Critias does not stop at simply dropping Socrates's qualification that knowledge must include knowledge of limitations in his own understanding of *sōphrosynē*. Rather than exemplifying such moderation, Critias sets out a vision that is excessive, unjustifiable, and hubristic. But as Socrates will suggest (at 171b), *speaking* truly is not the only criterion for truth; so too is what is *done* correctly. Critias and his understanding of *sōphrosynē* fail on both counts. Extoling the virtue, Critias contradicts himself in practice. Laughter, in the *Charmides*, directs our attention to Critias's performative contradiction by encouraging the kind of self-reflection through which it would become apparent, even if Critias himself refuses such contemplation.[40] The errors and deception that Socrates will implicitly attribute to their inquiry underscore that Critias is not the mantic knower he may think he is, and that the Socratic understanding of self-knowledge, characterized by limitation, predominates.

Critias suggests the possibility of a self-knowledge that is absolute and has no epistemic limitations (174a). Socrates pushes Critias to specify what sort of person would possess this sort of knowledge of knowledge. This is a person who, as Socrates puts it, "knows everything that has been and is now and is ignorant of nothing" (174a). The life of such a person would be one free of deception and error, and filled with happiness (173b–c). Such a person would have no limits and no need to fear self-deception, as Socrates claims to do. The Critian *sōphrōn* has no epistemic limitations whereas Socrates's understanding of knowing oneself requires acknowledgment of limitations. The excessiveness of Critias's claim is in ironic contrast to the subject at hand, but Critias's immoderation is not limited to what he says: it also marks what he does, as we will see. The contrast between Socratic and Critian models of *sōphrosynē* is illustrated both in what each says as well as in what each does in the dialogue.

The Socratic model of *sōphrosynē* is one for which a lack of self-certainty is key. True *sōphrosynē*, for Socrates, is determined by true speech as well as correctness of action. The *sōphrōn* who inquires correctly while investigating the qualifications of the doctor, "will look into the manner of his words [*legomenois*] and actions [*prattomenois*] to see if what he says is truly spoken [*alēthē legetai*] and what he does is correctly done [*orthōs prattetai*]" (171b). It is an ongoing investigation into one's own beliefs as well as others' and includes a self-reflective dimension, for without reflection on, and critical investigation into, one's own beliefs, philosophical inquiry would stall. Socrates' professed ignorance provides the incentive for his ongoing investigations: "because of my own ignorance, I am continually investigating . . ." (165c). Socrates states this in other terms in the passage from 166d: it is the "fear of unconsciously thinking I know something when I do not" that motivates his inquiries into himself and others. Error and deception are unavoidable on this model, as becomes evident when Socrates later indicates the faulty turns and assumptions their conversation has taken. Such indication simultaneously *should* reveal to Critias that he is not an unlimited and unmistaken knower. Self-certainty would remove the incentive to philosophical investigation as well as eliminating the fear of being ridiculous. But as we will see, it is precisely Critias's overabundance of empty self-certainty that renders him ridiculous.

The Critian model of *sōphrosynē*, instead, relies on an unjustified and unjustifiable self-certainty, one that rests on little other than a hubristic overestimation of self. Critias explicitly equates knowledge of self with knowledge of what one knows and does not know (169e–70a), but when pushed, this claim crumbles comically. Asked by Socrates how it is that the *sōphrōn* knows *what* he knows, Critias admits, "He won't at all" (170c). Unable to know how he knows what he knows, Socrates clarifies, this person "won't know *what* he knows, but only *that* he knows" (170c), to which Critias agrees. *Sōphrosynē*, for Critias, is a matter of knowing *that* one knows, and not *what* one knows. If one cannot know *what* one knows, then neither can one know *how* or *why* one knows it. Justification for *what* one knows simultaneously becomes impossible. Knowing only *that* one knows appears to be bald self-certainty, a trait with which the dialogue reveals Critias to be amply supplied.

Critias's hubristic notion of the mantic knower can be taken to reflect his view of himself, given his actions in the dialogue. The criteria Socrates offers to designate true speech suggest that if we want to evaluate the truth of either's speech, we must pay attention to more than just what is *said*: we must also pay attention to what is *done* in the dialogue. Critias's excessiveness in deed punctuates the dialogue, matching his excessiveness in speech.

Self-reflection is left aside in Critias's model. For someone whose initial definition of *sōphrosynē* is knowing oneself, Critias is comically unwilling (or unable) to reflect on himself, to admit his limitations, and instead, he hubristically proposes the possibility of bypassing self-reflection and limitations altogether. Critias begins his participation in the conversation with a suitably moderate tone, saying, ". . . I would rather withdraw some of my statements, and would not be ashamed to admit I had made a mistake" than to have the conclusion Socrates draws out of his statements be true[41] (164d). He proceeds to suggest *sōphrosynē* to be knowing oneself, in accord with the Delphic imperative (or, as he interprets it, the Delphic salutation).[42] But what appear to be humility and moderation are short-lived. Critias proceeds quickly and comically to forget himself, refusing to admit mistakes and going so far as to postulate the existence of an infallible knower. A pivotal moment is narrated by Socrates.

> When Critias heard this and saw that I was in difficulties, then, just as in the case of people who start yawning when they see other people doing it, he seemed to be affected by my troubles [*hupo aporias*] and to be seized by difficulties himself. But since

> his consistently high reputation made him feel ashamed in the eyes of the company and he did not wish [*ēthelen*] to admit to me that he was incapable [*adunatos*] of dealing with the question I had asked him, he said nothing clear but concealed his predicament [*epikaluptōn tēn aporian*]. (169c–d)

Like a simulated yawn, Critias's *aporia* is not a true one, nor is it one that he can, or is willing to, face. Instead, he conceals (*epikaluptōn*) it. As Schmid puts it, Critias is here given the opportunity to demonstrate "the possibility of *sophrosune* after the Socratic model—the possibility of knowing that you do not know—but he turns away from this opportunity, choosing not to appropriate this insight into his own thought or to reveal it to others."[43] Instead of humility and recognition, he feels shame. Critias chooses to hold on to "his claim to knowledge and superiority, rather than choose truth and self-knowledge."[44] Socrates's response is to appeal to Critias's self-importance by granting, for the sake of the argument, the existence of a science of science, an assumption he will later allude to as unjustified and as having led the conversation astray (175b). Dodging the opportunity to reflect on himself and, perhaps, to know what it is he does not know, Critias instead seizes on this postulation.

Socrates, in word and in deed, demonstrates such self-reflection repeatedly, and in sharp distinction from his interlocutors. Socrates encourages self-reflection from Charmides, suggesting that he "look into [him]self" (160d). Socrates is doing more here than encouraging Charmides to speak up: as Socrates interprets the formulation of "minding one's business" elsewhere (*Republic* 443d–e), he is strongly suggesting to Charmides both that what is meant by "one's business" may be an internal (rather than external) state found within oneself, and he is imploring Charmides to put into practice the very minding of his own business that Charmides is claiming constitutes *sōphrosynē*. Although Charmides does indeed appear to "look [. . .] into himself very manfully" (160e), his understanding of *sōphrosynē* will prove to be heteronomously and superficially adopted from others, such as Critias. Charmides's youth softens these charges, as he might yet have had the opportunity to know himself. What we know of him historically, however, underscores the danger of moral heteronomy, especially in the hands of so handsome and charismatic of a figure.

At the very beginning of the dialogue, Socrates describes having physically reacted to Charmides's beauty, when he happens to glance under his cloak. His response—a philosophical inquiry into *sōphrosynē*—is an exemplification of itself. Self-reflection is a key component of his part of the inquiry. Socrates reflects on how his own ignorance impacts the conversation (165c, 166d); admits he is in difficulties (167c), and; assesses his competence in dealing with the "science of temperance" (169b). Socrates describes what he has said and the direction of the conversation as *atopos*, and questions whether the inquiry has been conducted correctly (172e). Socrates suggests he may have made himself ridiculous, but that it is more important to investigate as they are doing (173a). Socrates later confirms that his previously stated fears of being ridiculous were reasonable, that the inquiry has "made fun of the truth," and finally that he himself may be a "worthless inquirer" (176a) and a "babbler" (*lērōn*, 175a–76a). This latter self-accusation is particularly striking, as it is one of the frequent accusations made about philosophers by comic poets.[45]

But it is Critias at whom we are tempted to laugh. Critias's hubristic claims concerning knowledge without limits have been reduced comically to simply knowing *that* one knows, with no knowledge of what it is one knows or does not know. From the grandiose heights he discursively climbs to regarding the knowledge of knowledge as well as the unlimited knower, Critias has fallen. He has proven for himself *that* he (thinks he) knows, but not *what* it is that he allegedly knows. In other words, he has proven his own *hubris* and, if he cannot know what he knows, his own pretentiousness. As suggested by Socrates in the *Philebus*, there are many like Critias who believe themselves to be more virtuous than they really are.

Critias's metaphorical fall is not isolated in Platonic dialogues. Hubris in the form of claims to more-than-human-wisdom end with comical *aporia* for a number of other characters. Hippias, explaining his "godlike state of mind" declares it to be a reasonable one given that, "I have never met anyone superior [*kreittoni*] to me in anything" (*Hippias Minor* 364a). Euthyphro proclaims his confidence in his own wisdom concerning piety and impiety: "I should be of no use, Socrates, and Euthyphro would not be superior [*diapheroi*] to the majority of men, if I did not have accurate knowledge of all such things" (*Euthyphro* 4e–5a). Although this is a particularly insufferable claim given that Socrates has just left the courthouse where he was accused of impiety, Socrates immediately declares himself to be Euthyphro's pupil (*Euthyphro* 5a). Both Hippias's and Euthyphro's preposterous personal valuations and claims to wisdom are subsequently deflated by the Socratic *elenchus* in a comical manner. Like

Critias, however, neither Hippias nor Euthyphro appear likely to change because of this. Indeed, Euthyphro hurries off to pursue what was generally thought to be a most impious act—prosecuting his father—against which Euthyphro defended himself with his now-failed understanding of piety. Comical arrogance, in these cases, is impermeable and incorrigible.

A further connection can be made amongst these examples. Critias, Hippias, and Euthyphro all commit what might be called performative contradictions, or contradictions between what they *say* and what they *do* in the dialogues. Euthyphro proclaims his confidence in his own understanding of piety—one that promptly is revealed to be shallow and empty, and yet, he is about to prosecute his own father in a most impious manner. Hippias claims never to have met anyone superior to him at anything whatsoever, and yet proceeds to have his views on Homer decimated by a decidedly more competent Socrates.[46] Critias asserts *sōphrosynē* to be self-knowledge, and yet resists so much as even reflecting on his own claims, beliefs, and the ultimate failure of both in the *Charmides*. Laughter, in each case, exposes the pretense.

Laughter is only one means of deflating such ridiculous claims, and it is not the only one enlisted in these and other dialogues. But it is in play here, as is evidenced by repeated mentions of laughter, of the *atopos*, and of the ridiculous, Socrates's embracing—however ironic this may be—of the seemingly pejorative descriptions of philosophers made by comics,[47] the framing of the *Charmides* itself with instances (actual and potential) of laughter, and the use of rhetorical strategies typical of Old Comedy such as reducing lofty topics to the vulgar and banal, as we shall see exemplified shortly. If it is funny in Aristophanes, why do we read it so solemnly in Plato?

Reducing the lofty to the vulgar is a comical strategy routinely used by Aristophanes as well as by Socrates, and may have provoked laughter more readily among a more overtly aristocratic society. When the topic shifts to what benefit *sōphrosynē* could confer, Socrates proceeds in typical fashion to reduce Critias's lofty claims to vulgar and comical examples. Seeking clarification of what Critias means by doing something scientifically, Socrates asks whether this refers to the science of cutting shoes from leather (173e), to which Critias offers a shocked and emphatic denial (*ma di' ouk egōge*). Concerning the science that makes the temperate person happy, Socrates asks Critias whether this is the science of checker playing (174b). It is not at all surprising for Critias to remark, at 172e, "You certainly say some queer [*atopa*] things, Socrates," and indeed Socrates affirms that they seem *atopa* to him as well. *Atopa* literally means out of place (*atopos*), but can mean strange, eccentric (like *komisch* in German), and even disgusting or foul. This does not only describe what Socrates says; Socrates himself is *atopos*.

Socrates is *atopos* for more than saying comical things. What makes him *atopos*, particularly in the company of Critias and Charmides, may be his refusal to think that he knows when he does not. Schmid suggests this may be the missing benefit of *sōphrosynē*: not thinking one knows when one does not.[48] The benefit of *sōphrosynē*, in other words, may be not truly being ridiculous, even if the *sōphrōn* Socrates remains, like all of us, ultimately laughable (166d). If this is the case, Socrates is *atopos* in this sense, for he claims not to think that he knows. This allows him, as he admits explicitly, to pursue critical inquiry. Where Charmides refuses critical inquiry for himself because he assumes he can adopt beliefs from authoritative others, Critias refuses critical inquiry because he believes himself already to be in possession of a more-than-human wisdom, and thus not requiring further philosophical attention. Heteronomy and what Schmid terms the "over-inflation of one's self-concept," threaten morality as well as philosophical inquiry, which turn out to be closely linked.[49] Comic falls, such as that of Critias, can pop the overinflated bubble of self-estimation, assuming that one is willing to recognize this. Critias, like Euthyphro and Hippias, is not.

The distinction between appearances and reality does not, however, resolve the connection between comedy and philosophy, or the philosopher. Socrates refers to himself in this way toward the end of the *Charmides*: " 'I think I am making a fool [*lērein*] of myself,' I said, 'but all the same it is necessary to investigate what occurs to us and not to proceed at random, if we are going to have the least care for ourselves' " (173a). Caring for oneself involves sensitivity to becoming ridiculous. Philosophy and the philosopher do not merely *appear* ridiculous. Ridicule functions as a more important catalyst. At 175d, Socrates says the inquiry has failed to discover the truth, and instead has ridiculed it, and thus exposed the agreed-on definition as being of no benefit: "But in spite of the fact that the inquiry [*zētēsis*] has shown us to be both complacent and easy, it is not a whit more capable of discovering the truth. It has, in fact, made fun of [*katagelasen*] the truth [*alētheian*] to this extent, that it has very insolently [*hubristikōs*] exposed [*apophaine*] as useless [*anōphelēs*] the definition of temperance which we agreed upon and invented [*sumplattontes*] earlier" (175d). This is a different type of laughter from that resulting from the bench scene, one more in line with the laughter of superiority. Unlike the bench scene, where a form of *gelaō* (*gelasas*) is used, the word here is the compounded *katagelasen*. Where *gelaō* connotes laughter more generally, *katagelaō* is more specifically laughing at, laughing down, jeering, or deriding.[50] Here *katagelaō*, or ridicule, is said by Socrates to be capable of exposing falsity. As Schmid writes, "the logos, far from being tragic, embodies the spirit of comedy, as it laughs at our inabilities to see its and our own deficiencies, and complete them by importing the action to life."[51] It is human hubris that covers over our true limitations with pretensions to exceed them, and it is laughter that can reveal the pretense.

But, it might still be argued that, if we dismiss the bench scene as window dressing, itself meaningless to the discussion of *sōphrosynē*, the laughter provoked by Critias's arrogance is the laughter of superiority, the gratification of an audience who take ourselves to be better than, or at least not quite as pompous as, Critias. This is where Socrates interjects a very different and very curious form of laughter. Taken together with the bench scene at the dialogue's opening, and the laughter exposing Critias's hubris, this third incident of laughter bears on our reading of the first two. While laughter at Critias's expense may suggest the laughter of superiority, the inquiry's laughter at the dialogue's participants warns us against believing ourselves all too superior, since we are in the same predicament. The audience too is at a loss concerning *sōphrosynē*, and must critically reflect on what has been said, and what has not been, to reach a philosophically sound understanding of the virtue. The inquiry begins with the recognition of failure and *aporia*, an awareness of what we do not already know. While this may, in its nascent form, constitute but an awareness *that* we do not know, the crucial questions it indicates include *why* we do not know it and *how* we might overcome this limitation to know what we do not know.

We may be tempted to laugh at Critias, but Socrates regularly describes himself, and the philosopher generally, as laughable.[52] Insofar as the philosopher embodies the serious pursuit of becoming virtuous, she also typifies the comic. The philosopher is repeatedly described as, in some way, ridiculous (*geloios*). The one escaping from the cave in the *Republic* is said to return and become the "source of laughter" (*gelōt*) (*Republic* 517a). Alcibiades describes Socrates's arguments as at first showing themselves to be ridiculous (*geloioi*) (*Symposium* 221e). At *Gorgias* 485a-86c, Callicles claims that the person who spends too much time with philosophy, past the age of childhood, becomes a laughingstock (*katagelastos*) and ridiculous (*katagelaston*). And while Callicles's claim might be dismissed as that of an unsympathetic opponent, Socrates himself makes a similar claim in the *Theaetetus*, where he tells the story of Thales's fall into a well and the Thracian servant girl laughing at him for pondering the sky without knowing what was at his feet. The philosopher, at the very least, *appears* not to know herself, and thus *is perceived* as ridiculous.

Another interpretation of why the philosopher is repeatedly depicted as laughable in the dialogues becomes available to us. Rather than merely *appearing*—as opposed to *being*—ridiculous, the philosopher is aware of her own ignorance and so is aware of being potentially ridiculous. The philosopher, like Socrates, is self-conscious of his own being laughable if for no other reason than that he will never fully and completely know himself. Laughter at the philosopher, while more deserved in cases where the philosopher is ignorant of her own ignorance, is nonetheless merited in that human nature inescapably involves ignorance and limitation, and the philosopher is no exception.

A warning akin to that at the end of the *Charmides* is suggested by Socrates's aforementioned story about Thales in the *Theaetetus*. Socrates presents the story about Thales as an example of the absentminded philosopher, whose focus and priorities have shifted away from things that are of little account: ". . . Thales was studying the stars . . . and gazing aloft, when he fell into a well; and a witty [*emmelēs*] and amusing [*chariessa*] Thracian servant girl made fun of [*aposkōpsai*] him because, she said, he was wild to know about what was up in the sky but failed to see what was in front of him and under his feet. The same joke [*skōmma*] applies to all who spend their lives in philosophy" (174a-c). And just a bit later, he says, ". . . the philosopher is the object of general derision [*katagelatai*], partly for what men take to be his superior manner [*huperēphanōs*] and partly for his constant ignorance and lack of resources in dealing with the obvious" (175b). The philosopher, like everyone else, exemplifies a type of ignorance and as such, is laughable. Whether he truly *is* ridiculous may lie in whether he is aware of this.

Thales, however, is not the only butt of the joke. The philosopher's ignorance, caused by shifting from big questions to ordinary concerns, according to Socrates, ". . . causes great entertainment [*gelōta*], not only to Thracian servant-girls or any other uneducated [*apaideutō*] persons—they do not see what is going on [*ou gar aisthanontai*]—but to all men who have not been brought up like slaves" (175d). The Thracian maid laughs out of ignorance of these greater questions, and in this, she too becomes a butt of the joke. She is ridiculous for not understanding that the things Thales contemplates are of far greater account than those in which he is subsequently awkward and confused. Her laughter, perhaps of superiority, belies a lack of self-knowledge and suggests that she knows that of which she is actually ignorant.

Both butts might be said merely to *appear* ridiculous to the other: the philosopher for his clumsiness in ordinary affairs; the servant-girl for ignorantly thinking these ordinary affairs to be more important than what is distracting Thales. However, there is a warning implied by Socrates in the servant girl's laughter that the one haughtily mocking another may herself become a butt of the joke. In other words, the one who laughs as an expression of superiority, becomes the one laughed at. If laughter does provide positive insight into human nature as inherently limited, then we disregard this warning at our own peril, the peril of turning out to be the butt of another joke.

This warning brings us back to the focus of the *Charmides*, for it is the Thracian servant girl's lack of self-knowledge that turns the joke partly back onto her. The superiority theory is particularly ill-fitting for this reason. If laughter were always to be an expression of perceived superiority, our laughter would always be the laughter of the Thracian maid, haughtily misunderstanding circumstances and expressing instead our self-ignorance. But there is always the inquiry, the logos in the *Protagoras*, or Courage herself in the *Laches*, or some other personal or personified force to turn the laughter back on us, and to expose the pretense of our perceived superiority.[53] We could not be much farther from an endorsement of the laughter of superiority.

Conclusion

This chapter has illustrated several types of laughter occurring within the *Charmides* in an attempt to keep the superiority theory from dominating our understanding of laughter in Platonic dialogues. It has also begun to sketch some of the philosophical implications of reading these occurrences as laughter, rather than simply as expressions of power relations. Not only can laughter contribute positively toward virtues such as *sōphrosynē*, it will be shown to advance a philosophical agenda by way of exposing tensions between our beliefs and, to use Desjardin's wording, what it is to which we tether these beliefs—our actions. While the next chapter will indirectly further the claim made in the second—namely, that the joke at the heart of the *Cratylus* too lies beyond the superiority theory of comedy, the fourth chapter will focus on what is brought to light through the joke: the performative contradiction between what is *said* and what is *done* by Hermogenes and Cratylus in the dialogue, and the way in which humans' inextricable bond with logos further underscores our limitation.

If self-consciousness is part of the comical figure of Socrates, then Plato is revising laughter significantly. While drawing more from the framework of comical, rather than tragic, laughter, Plato revises this to support a philosophical program. Laughter, severed from tragedy's strict ties to honor, superiority, and shame, can help prevent or remedy self-deception and ignorance. Socrates, as we have seen in this chapter, stresses self-deception and ignorance as genuinely fearful, rather than being laughed at. Implicit in laughter directed at the self, as Socrates employs, is the recognition of one's own limits. Inasmuch as this brings about a knowledge of what one does not know, laughter thus provides a critical contribution to *sōphrosynē*. The Apollonian characterization of *sōphrosynē* is thus infused, in the *Charmides*, with the Dionysian.

A further consequence follows from this. Despite intriguing anecdotal evidence to the contrary, Plato has been supposed to be concerned primarily with his contemporary, fourth-century Middle Comedy, rather than the Old Comedy of Aristophanes.[54] If the comical thus involves self-knowledge in Platonic dialogues, these have more in common with, and reflect more influence from, the Old Comedy works of Aristophanes.[55] The following chapters will further develop this relationship.

But the sort of laughter generated by personified concepts, such as Courage herself, or the Inquiry itself, or Logos, is of a novel kind. The laughter Socrates introduces into the *Charmides* is a self-reflective laughter. It is a laughter that recognizes the limitations of the one laughing. Instead of the laughter of superiority and arrogance, self-reflective laughter is a laughter of (at least some) humility, one that equalizes more than it stratifies. It is a laughter that necessitates self-consciousness, something that could not seem much further from traditional readings of the *Philebus* passage discussed earlier. If we revisit the *Philebus* passage, this chapter's ensuing discussion may now shed light on to how else one might translate one of the terms key to the undue influence of an antigelastic reading of Plato. In that passage, Socrates suggests the nature of the ridiculous (*to geloion*) to be, ". . . a kind of vice [*ponēria*]" (*Philebus* 48c). Translated as "vice," as Dorothea Frede does here, *ponēria* implies moral condemnation, a sentiment that should, at this point, seem unsuitable for a Socratic view of the ridiculous. When not taken in a moral sense, however, *ponēria* may also be translated as a form of roguery or knavishness and is a key feature of the comic hero and the comical plot as discussed earlier. We will see further support for how Socrates employs such roguery in turning to the *Cratylus* and *Euthydemus*.

A puzzle we are left with at the *Charmides*'s end suggests the appropriateness of laughter to us more generally. Reviewing where the conversation went awry, Socrates suggests that they have overlooked "the impossibility that a person should in some fashion know what he does not know at all—because our agreement amounts to saying he knows things he does not know." And yet, "there is nothing more irrational than this" (175c–d). Critias does not know what he thought he knew. He is not this omniscient person. Nietzsche writes that "Socratic culture is rooted in an optimism which believes itself omnipotent."[56] While such delusions of omnipotence may be attributable to Critias, they do not apply to Socrates. Further, as will be shown in the next chapter, our necessary connection to logos is a sign of how limited we are as humans. Critias has assumed that he understood what Socrates meant by "knowing what one knows and does not know," and indeed, this is one of the questions the inquiry leaves us with: what does it mean to know what one does not know?

We have in Socrates's demeanor a possible indication of an answer to this question. Socrates repeatedly describes himself, and the philosopher more generally, in comic terms. If laughing *at* oneself includes a recognition of one's limitations, then one can be said to "know" (if not in a strictly epistemic sense) what one does not know. This is not a claim to know the content of what one does not know since doing so would be ultimately to recognize no limitations at all. Such a person is Critias's omniscient knower. Rather, the one who recognizes herself as comical, who is aware of herself as limited and flawed, understands her limitations without necessarily overcoming them. This state—being aware of one's limitations without being able to overcome them—is where laughter of various forms thrives. It is a self-consciously comical state, or self-reflective laughter, and if the argument of this chapter holds, this is a state that properly acknowledges the human condition.

The bench scene at the dialogue's beginning is thus a potent image for the dialogue. The image exposes the playful struggle for a stable central position—one that avoids the volatile extremes and one associated with honor and virtue.[57] The comic struggle results in Charmides's sitting down between Critias and Socrates. Significantly less confident than Critias, Charmides nonetheless refuses to venture his own beliefs in the inquiry, and so, remains stuck in his own ignorance. Socrates, on the other hand, professes fear of the kind of pretense and self-deception of which Critias and Charmides may both be guilty.

If Socrates exemplifies the virtue of *sōphosynē*, his participation in the ribaldry on the bench suggests that the *sōphrōn* is not immune to laughter, any more than to being erotically drawn to Charmides. The *sōphrōn*, however, needs not succumb to either eros or laughter, both being forces prone to excessiveness. Such excessiveness is shown, as it is on the bench, to be vulnerable. *Sōphrosynē* and laughter must both be curbed by limitations, and the *sōphrōn* may be the one who is able to avoid truly being ridiculous, despite realizing that human limitations render us irrevocably laughable. Finally, the *sōphrōn* who laughs may have taken the warning to heart, and realizes that it remains possible to turn the laughter of superiority back on the one laughing.

Sōphrosynē, according to Socrates, fundamentally involves a self-knowledge that includes knowing one's own limitations. Comedy offers the possibility of recognizing these limitations by exposing the pretensions we construct to obscure them and by offering vantage points from which they might be funny. Laughter may thus be important to *sōphrosynē*, but *sōphrosynē* is also vital to laughter. The very limitations with which Socrates is concerned throughout the discussion, and that Critias ignores, are requisite to curb the excessiveness to which laughter is prone. If Socrates is indeed *sōphrōn*, then his participation in the bench scene at the beginning of the dialogue should indicate the compatibility of laughter with *sōphrosynē*. Laughter is in this way entangled with *sōphrosynē*, and perhaps in a more significant way than we ordinarily think, with philosophy itself.

Here I join other scholars in calling for a revision of the theory of comedy commonly ascribed to Plato.[58] What is now called the superiority theory does not encompass the manifold types of comic occurrences within the dialogues, as evidenced by the bench scene and underscored by the inquiry's laughing at the dialogue's participants and audience at its aporetic end, nor does the passage in the *Philebus* support the superiority theory's depiction as "Plato's" umbrella theory of comedy.[59] Laughter plays a much more diverse role within the dialogues than generally believed, and, if this is true, more and much more research is required on the matter.

Given this, a revision of the role played by laughter within the Platonic dialogues is necessary. Far from being a boor, Plato may actually be funny at times, and reading the dialogues with this possibility in mind opens up both new hermeneutic challenges and potential, old misreadings. Ascribing to Plato a sense of humor makes interpreting the dialogues thornier, and further obscures the notion that we are getting at Plato's true views when we do. Instead, the dialogues invite us, like Charmides and Critias, to look within ourselves, and to ask, along with Socrates (166d), whether we are not simply pretending that we are more virtuous, or in other ways better, than we really are. They ask us, in other words, whether we might not ourselves be ridiculous. If we take the laughter of Platonic dialogues to be that of superiority, as we look down on the preposterously arrogant Hippias and Euthydemus, the haughty Critias, or even the absentminded Thales, we lose the realization that we may not know much better. The joke, in other words, may just be on us.

4

Naming the Nameless: Logos, Laughter, and Self-Forgetting

Unlike the Socrates of the *Laches*, the Socrates of the *Cratylus* and the *Euthydemus* is a sucker. He takes logos and those who build their professions on the use of logos at face value. Socrates's playing the fool warns us away from doing the same but it also invites the audience into doing philosophy for ourselves. At issue in these dialogues, as in the *Laches*, is the question of who is to teach the youth. Where to look for an answer may be implied by the satirical forms of the dialogues themselves. For while the audience is warned away from uncritically accepting logos as offering an understanding of reality or from uncritically accepting sophistic charlatans as teachers of what is most important, the importance of doing philosophy for oneself is underscored. Socrates's buffoonish performance—and it *is* performance—exposes ambiguities and philosophical questions for our examination and critique. Through his performative critique of etymology and protreptic, Socrates thus offers a cautious and critical protreptic of his own, one that provokes us into philosophizing while urging caution.

Put otherwise, less pejoratively, and more specifically, Socrates of the *Cratylus* and the *Euthydemus* plays a comic hero for philosophical effect. Like the comic heroes of Old Comedy, Socrates in the *Euthydemus* is mocked and derided as the aged schoolboy, only to end up rejuvenated and triumphant. But he is triumphant only with the critical involvement of the audience, who recognize what remains implicit and what Crito has but a vague sense of—that Socrates has tripped the brothers up with his performance. Nor does Socrates let down his comical guard in the *Cratylus* where, despite ongoing commentary questioning their legitimacy, Socrates is relentless in offering admittedly questionable etymologies.

But unlike many, if not all, heroes of Old Comedy, the sort of laughter Socrates prompts from his audience is of a different sort. It is self-reflective. The previous chapters have shown that Socrates includes himself in the laughter, rather than merely using laughter to mock others. It is not just Socrates who is able to laugh at himself. Socrates is *atopos*—he is strange and laughable, and his comical traits might easily be chalked up to his unique character. But such self-reflective laughter is not limited to Socrates. Philosophy itself is presented in a comical light, as subject to self-reflective laughter as will become apparent in the *Cratylus*, and even more pointedly, in the *Euthydemus*.

The *Euthydemus* offers a caricature of philosophy and philosophers at which we are invited to laugh. In this way, it provides an example of laughter as reflective of philosophy. In the dialogue, Socrates acts the buffoon, which even his friend Crito describes as shameful (305a), quite opposed to the high esteem in which he is regarded in the *Laches*. In the *Apology*, Socrates presents the accusations against him as including "making the weaker speech the stronger, and by teaching others these same things," both of which these brothers can be seen doing in the *Euthydemus* (*Apology* 19b–c). The brothers exemplify these accusations against Socrates, and yet are deemed to be philosophers. If this is the case, Plato does what Aristophanes is accused of doing in the *Apology*, namely, offering a comical and historically questionable image of self-proclaimed philosophers. If this is the case, then Socrates may not be pointing his finger so much at Aristophanes and comedy, as he is at Aristophanes's and comedy's reception.

Laughter emphasizes the role of the audience in a unique way. Not only can an audience expect from Old Comedy to be addressed directly in the *parabasis*, as discussed in the previous chapters, comedy pierces the fourth wall more broadly. What characters may not find funny—perhaps because it is at their expense, or perhaps because they are otherwise unable to see, the audience might. The shortcomings of characters are highlighted to the audience more so than to interlocutors.[1] In its address of the audience, laughter threatens to expose the dramatic illusion. Socrates, in the *Cratylus*, does as much at several points when he describes his own etymologizing as comical or reveals the mechanisms that make him appear to have all of the etymological answers.

It is in its effect on the audience that laughter poses the greatest danger as well as conferring a potential philosophical benefit. A great danger of comedy is that comic portraits can be mistaken for accurate portrayals of reality. Socrates suggests this in the *Apology*, where he twice mentions his own comic portrayals as contributing to slanderous conceptions of who he is and what he does (*Apology* 18d, 19c). These comedians are among Socrates's self-described "dangerous accusers" (*hoi deinoi . . . mou katēgoroi*) who got hold of Socrates's jurors when they were young and "most trusting" (*malista episteusate*, *Apology* 18c). It is that trust—naively believing that an image accurately reflects its original—which renders otherwise-harmless comedy and laughter dangerous. And it is that trust, combined with Socrates's provocative and comical *apologia*, that leads to Socrates's conviction and execution. We are indirectly warned against placing such trust in the comical character of Socrates.

Such laughter emphasizes the role of the audience, and it does so with two different functions. Laughter may have a protreptic function in the dialogues, disarming the ideas presented for an audience as Halper argues and appealing to the audience to seek a more just life for themselves, but it also has an apotreptic function, which sets the audience on its guard, effectively "arming" us, and rendering us more cautious and alert, and thus counteracting the naïve trust that enhances comedy's danger.[2] The audience is crucial because, in a sense, we are all in the position of Crito in the *Euthydemus*, needing to distinguish the true philosopher from the false. The stakes include not only the education of our children, and of ourselves, but also the consistency of our *logoi* and actions, and the very life of Socrates. Keeping the audience on its toes is particularly important given the dual nature of logos.

Socrates's etymologies in the *Cratylus* and the eristics of the *Euthydemus*'s sophistic brothers demonstrate in action the inherent ambivalence of logos. Logos can be true or false: it can be used to conceal as well as to reveal Being (*Cratylus* 408c).[3] Logos cannot be measured by human will, as Socrates appears to do in his "inspired" etymologies and as Protagoras's famous maxim implies.[4] Nor can logos be used entirely to comprehend logos itself. The very project of the *Cratylus*, as a logos on logos, implies its philosophical limitation. And yet, there is no alternative to using logos in inquiry. However, by critically arming and agitating its audience through self-reflective laughter, Socrates makes a genuine, philosophical response more possible, one that recognizes what Socrates's fool does not: that logos must appeal beyond itself so as to be possible.[5] And it must be recognized in its duplicity. It is comedy and comic logos that most accurately reflects this.

Plato's laughter—in the form of actual and implied risibility—holds both protreptic and apotreptic functions. It arms *and* disarms, and thus facilitates self-reflection. Put briefly, its protreptic function is to disarm its audience and lure them into the discussion.[6] Its apotreptic function renders its audience more cautious, alert to discrepancy, hypocrisy, and deception. It is laughter's apotreptic function that helps to guard against its own danger, namely the danger of being received uncritically, the danger of mistaking a comic portrait for an accurate portrayal of reality. In this sense, Plato's laughter stimulates and demands philosophical thinking from interlocutors as well as from the dialogues' audiences. We will see that the mirror such laughter holds up for us reflects a familiar figure.

Laughter and Logos in the *Cratylus*

Socrates plays the sucker in the *Cratylus*, mocking loose etymologizing by appearing gullibly and enthusiastically to advocate it. He takes seriously what one ought not to. His performance prompts questions for the audience as to what is wrong with his doing so. By recognizing the absurdity of the etymologies and laughing at them, we immediately become participants in an ancient philosophical debate. Laughter disarms ideas for an audience while simultaneously drawing us into contemplation of those ideas. In this way, the *Cratylus* is an example of protreptic laughter, which disarms Socrates's etymologizing, as though it were "only" a joke, but nonetheless asks philosophical questions and invites the audience into doing philosophy.

A prime example of this occurs in a joke apart from the etymologies that is threaded through the *Cratylus*. Cratylus's joke as to Hermogenes's true name underscores the philosophical significance and function of laughter in the dialogues. The performative contradiction involved in the joke exposes the interlocutors' pretenses and, in so doing, reveals a larger semantic issue at the heart of the dialogue: the preconditions for speaking, or employing logos, sensibly. Socrates counters the interlocutors' denial of these preconditions, akin to the brothers' denial of these in the *Euthydemus*, with comic logos, playing the fool so as to prompt recognition of the logical commitments we make when we speak. The chapter argues that laughter punctuates the surpassing of limits and measure (*metron*) and so indicates not only human limitations that bind us to logos, but also suggests the limitations by which our use of *logoi* is restricted.[7]

The *Cratylus* is a dialogue concerned with *onoma*, translated to its primary meaning as "name," but a closer look at the finer shading of this word is in order. Where the English "name" tends to imply proper names, the Greek *onoma* is not limited in this way, referring to nouns, verbs, adjectives, and pronouns in the *Cratylus* in a way that Sallis suggests brings it close to the English "word."[8] Although a secondary implication, *onoma* also suggests a name in opposition to the real person, thing, or reality it represents, a "mere" name, reputation, or even a false name or pretense.[9] Euripides's Helen claims that she herself never went to Troy; it was, instead her *onoma*.[10] It is opposed to *ergon*, work or deed, as in Heraclitus, whose fragment reads "the bow [*biós*] is called life [*onoma bíos*] but its work [*ergon*] is death."[11] The name *onoma* itself and, as Heraclitus here suggests, its assonance, thus already carry suggestions of the word's own potential inaccuracy, pretext, or facade. This is in stark contrast to, and direct criticism of, the reliability of names to convey reality that is presumed by the poets.

The power of *onoma* approaches near-magical heights in Greek poetry, as is evident from two instances of refusals to name. Odysseus famously outwits Polyphemus by denying him the power of his real name, telling him his name is, instead, "Nobody."[12] Arguably, the remainder of his brutal homeward detention is due to his reversing course and, once safe at sea, shouting his true name to the Cyclops, son of Poseidon whose wrath (*odusao*, a play on Odysseus's name) will detain him because it can now meet its intended target. Euripides's Orestes resorts to euphemism rather than naming the Furies, saying, "I do not want to name [*onomazein*] them," lest doing so invoke their anger further.[13] Concurrent with such power, *onoma* is imbued with trustworthiness, for the poets.[14]

Such accuracy in conveying reality is under fire already amongst the Presocratics, as even a cursory look at two Presocratic philosophers will show. As Heraclitus suggests in the above fragment, things contain their own opposites within them, and so a name such as that for "bow" (*biós*) can, at best, only convey half of its being.[15] A thing's *onoma* and its *ergon* may be in a state of strife with one another, a state belied by the thing's seemingly static name. Names are thus arbitrary, conveying but a partial and conventional view of the world. Names are equally unreliable for conveying what is (*esti*) for Parmenides, because they fragment what is whole and unified. The section of his poem describing the way of opinion (*doxa*) thus begins with instruction to attend to the deceptive ordering conveyed by the youth's use of words, and pins the problem on mortals' insistence on naming (*onomazein*) two forms, of which they can properly only name one.[16] Contrary to Heraclitus, words for Parmenides's speaker suggest opposition, fragmentation, and change in the realm of being that cannot properly be ascribed to the unchanging unity of what is. In this way, names are conventional and convey the misguided opinion of mortals, rather than accurate descriptions of reality. Although for different reasons, both perspectives are agreed on the impossibility of deriving an accurate understanding of reality from *onomata*.

The question as to the possibility of deriving an understanding of reality from *onomata* is in play in the *Cratylus*. It may not be surprising, then, to find several of the dialogue's interpreters reading the debate between Cratylus and Hermogenes as one paralleling Heraclitean and Parmenidean positions. Cratylus is known as a dedicated Heraclitean, and, according to Diogenes Laertius, Hermogenes is a follower of Parmenides.[17] Arieti concludes from this biographical information that the *Cratylus* is a confrontation between followers of each, and thus also of their positions.[18] Sprague sees a Platonic critique of Eleaticism as central to both the *Euthydemus* and the *Cratylus*, and of the Heracliteans in the latter dialogue.[19] A brief look at their positions, however, calls the relationship claimed into question and suggests a different contention.

Although Cratylus and Hermogenes appear to represent Heraclitean and Parmenidean positions, respectively, they differ in two key respects from their philosophical influences. First, both Cratylus and Hermogenes assume that names are correct (*orthōs*): their disagreement concerns the source of that correctness (*orthotēs*). Cratylus's and Hermogenes's question is whether names are correct by nature (*phusis*) or by convention (*nomos*) and custom (*ethos*). Heraclitus's and Parmenides's question is whether names can be correct at all. For Hermogenes and Cratylus, there is no falsity of names, whereas Heraclitus and Parmenides imply the opposite. For Cratylus, what one might call a "false" name—one that does not access the thing's nature—ceases to be a name at all, amounting to nothing more than pointless noise (*Cratylus* 430a). Since any name one uses, according to Hermogenes, is a correct name, it becomes impossible to name falsely (*Cratylus* 385d), although Hermogenes says otherwise (*Cratylus* 387b, 408c). A second marker distinguishing the debate of Cratylus and Hermogenes from that of Heraclitus and Parmenides is that the former's debate involves an assumption as to whether one can derive knowledge about reality from *onomata*. Heraclitus and Parmenides deny that such a move is ever possible because *onomata* are, by their very function, false accounts of reality. Cratylus and Hermogenes are thus, at the very least, not particularly orthodox followers of Heraclitus and Parmenides, respectively.

If this is true, the *Cratylus* does not seem to illustrate a confrontation between Heraclitean and Parmenidean positions, as Sprague and Arieti suggest. Given the significant difference between Cratylus's and Hermogenes's (and, for that matter, Heraclitus's and Parmenides's) positions, it may be counterintuitive to align them here, but if the *Cratylus* is concerned with the question as to the correctness of names, and if we take "seriously" the dialogue's laughter, Cratylus and Hermogenes will turn out to have more in common with each other than either does with his Presocratic predecessor. Corresponding to the two differences above, there are two issues that emerge from comparing Cratylus's and Hermogenes's positions vis-à-vis their predecessors: that concerning the truth (*orthotēs*) or falsity of *onomata*; and the relationship between *onomata*, knowledge, and reality. A few remarks are in order on each of these two points in turn.

At stake in the *Cratylus* is a question larger than that concerning the source of the correctness of *onomata*. The confrontation in the *Cratylus* is not one of Heraclitus against Parmenides. Rather, it is a confrontation that pits Heraclitus and Parmenides against Hermogenes and Cratylus on whether *onomata* can ever be correct. Heraclitus and Parmenides, on very different grounds, imply the impossibility of naming correctly. All names are to some extent false. Hermogenes and Cratylus differ as to the source of correctness, but both assume names to be correct and deny the possibility of false naming. This may seem but a minor semantic debate, but I will argue it to be an investigation into the very prerequisites for naming and, more broadly, speaking correctly. Naming is a part of logos, and to use logos correctly, concepts of truth, falsity, difference, and contradiction are necessary. Denying any of these, as all four of these figures do in various ways, leads to the inability to use logos correctly, an inability that is key to the performative contradiction and the laughter in the *Cratylus*.

The importance in asking for the source of the correctness of *onomata* recedes in the presence of the larger and older question as to the correct order of things, *onomata*, and logos more broadly. Sprague suggests that the stance one takes on the source of the correctness of *onomata*—whether this is derived from nature or convention—matters very little. Both positions "lead equally to the obliteration of the distinction between truth and falsity."[20] What is important is establishing the correct order of things: first we attend to *ta onta*, and only then to names and language.[21] Naming and language cannot determine their own correctness.

Attention to the use of *onomata* and of logos correlates with the relationship between *onomata*, knowledge, and reality. At question in the *Cratylus* is whether one can derive knowledge about reality from *onomata*, or vice versa—from an understanding of reality to *onomata*. Bringing Heraclitus and Parmenides to bear on this question highlights a historical shift in emphasis on this relationship. Around the middle of the fifth century BCE, the focus of intellectual debate shifts away from asking about language as a corollary study to nature and turns to the use of language, its functions, and the effects these have on the audience.[22] For instance, Gorgias, denying the possibility of speaking accurately, focuses instead on language's ability to captivate and enthrall audience.[23] To put it into Austin's terminology, the focus shifts from language's ostensible meaning to one concerning language's illocutionary and perlocutionary force, the intended social significance and the actual effect (such as persuasion, being warned, or feeling enthralled) the locutionary act—uttering whatever was said—has on its audience. While such terminology is certainly anachronistic, this chapter suggests that a strong parallel in linguistic development is exemplified in Platonic dialogues such as the *Cratylus*. We miss much of the significance of Platonic dialogues when we read them as straightforward descriptions of what some thinkers (Socrates, Plato, or others) believe to be the case about reality. While appearing to answer the question as to whether one can derive knowledge of reality from *onomata* negatively, the debate in the *Cratylus* signals its readers to look elsewhere, to turn to the social significance and the effects of language, to ascertain its meanings. We will see that such signals are located not merely in what is *said* in the dialogue, but in what is *done* in it—in the effects that what is said has on interlocutors and readers. And we will find through this that laughter plays a much more substantial role in the dialogue than is usually attributed to it.

Reading the *Cratylus* and its etymologies with an eye on comedy is precedented. More frequently than most other dialogues, the comic spirit of the *Cratylus* has been recognized in the literature.[24] Targeting etymology for comical purposes was already precedented in Plato's time. Aristophanes had already made comical hay of etymology in the *Clouds* where his Socrates claims that thunder (*brontē*) is none other than cosmic flatulence (*pepordas*), as is apparent from their names (*tōnomat'*).[25] The Greeks may not have expected all etymology to be in earnest, but the questions remain as to whether comedy in the *Cratylus* extends past its etymologies, and what, if anything, the laughter of the dialogue means philosophically.

Laughter in the *Cratylus*, far from being superficial, prompts us to consider the logical presuppositions necessary for speaking sensibly. The *Cratylus*'s audience is put in a precarious position. Without recourse to a conception of truth and falsity in naming (*onomazein*), neither interlocutors nor readers can reject Socrates's ridiculous etymologies as such. Comic play here forces us either to recognize our own position within the questions at stake or then to take the absurd at face value. We are invited by the dialogue, in other words, to do philosophy and, if we cannot arrive at a better answer, to recognize our own limitations in doing so. This will be seen to be the case both in relation to the joke about Hermogenes "correct" name, and in relation to Socrates's etymologies.

Socrates, in the *Cratylus* and the *Euthydemus*, acts out the absurd consequences that follow from a denial of truth, falsity, contradiction, and difference. In the *Cratylus*, he enacts an extensive set of comical etymologies, all the while presenting the etymologies as questionable and his proliferation of them as devious. His doing so places his audience in the curious state of judging the etymologies, and thus interlocutors and readers are prompted to employ the very concepts that are at issue: truth, falsity, contradiction, and difference. Even if we read the etymologies as straightforwardly as does David Sedley, who judges them to be something of an unfortunate, historical mistake on Plato's part, notions of truth and falsity are in play. The real absurdity of the etymologies may thus stem not from their being comical, but rather from the inability to deem them comical without participating in the philosophical debate at the heart of the *Cratylus* as well as in the *Euthydemus*. Like Hermogenes and Cratylus, we may well contradict our own positions in the process of doing so. By laughing, in other words, we are inaugurated into doing philosophy for ourselves.

Laughter and False Speaking in the *Euthydemus*

This connection between denying the possibility of false speaking and the failure to use *logoi*, or speak, sensibly in the *Cratylus* is illustrated in a comparable fashion in the *Euthydemus*. At issue in the *Euthydemus*, as I have argued is at issue in the *Cratylus*, is the very possibility of speaking and thinking correctly, of using logos sensibly. Interlocutors in both dialogues deny these conditions for logos—conceptions of truth and falsity in logos, difference, and contradiction—and in both cases, Socrates enacts comically the consequences of such a denial. Both pairs of interlocutors—Hermogenes and Cratylus, and Euthydemus and Dionysodurus—contradict their own positions performatively, in what they *do* in the dialogue. In the *Cratylus*, this is most clearly illustrated in the joke as to Hermogenes's "correct" name. In the *Euthydemus*, this is apparent in the claims by the sophistic brothers that, applied to themselves, deny the brothers the ability to speak sensibly. The consequences of both sets of contradictions are acted out comically by Socrates, who invites us through laughter to recognize the philosophical gravity of what is at stake. The comical and illogical moments of these dialogues, far from being marginal or "merely" dramatic, play philosophically significant roles, indicating both a duality in logos and in ourselves.

The *Cratylus* and *Euthydemus* have been associated with each other with some regularity in secondary literature, but a primary connection between them can be forged through a figure of some importance to both: Protagoras. Socrates tells us that Protagoras is infamous for saying (*elegen legōn*) humans to be the measure (*metron*) of all things, but humans and logos turn out to be themselves rather limited: humans are limited by logos, and logos is limited to the preconditions of its own use (*Cratylus* 385e). Protagoras is mentioned six times in the *Cratylus* as an influence, however much Hermogenes denies this, on Hermogenes's linguistic position. Protagoras looms as a forerunner in each dialogue due both to the content of his teaching, and the rhetorical strategies he uses to teach. According to Diogenes Laertius, Protagoras confused his rhetorical opponents by focusing on their *onomata* to the exclusion of what they meant: ". . . in his dialectic he neglected the meaning [*dianoian*] in favour of verbal quibbling [*pros tounoma*] and he was the father of the whole tribe of eristical disputants now so much in evidence . . ."[26] The reality of something is thus disregarded in favor of the *onoma* used to discuss it. In the *Euthydemus*, Socrates cites Protagoras as a clear rhetorical influence on Dionysodorus and Euthydemus, particularly in their common denial of falsity (*Euthydemus* 286c). The sophistic brothers are part of this eristical tribe.

Protagoras, Dionysodorus, and Euthydemus are further linked in the *Euthydemus*. Socrates, after hearing Dionysodorus suggest that contradiction does not exist, claims to be amazed by the argument, although simultaneously disclaiming its originality and efficacy: "The followers of Protagoras made considerable use of it . . . It always seems to me to have a wonderful way of upsetting [*anatrepōn*][27] not just other arguments, but itself as well . . . The argument amounts to claiming that there is no such thing as false speaking, doesn't it?" (*Euthydemus* 286c). Diogenes Laertius attributes to Protagoras the argument that "everything is true [*pant' einai alēthē*]."[28] The denial of false speech, or positively, the claim that everything said is true can be seen to "upset itself" by undermining the very spirit in which a claim is put forward. If everything is true, then its converse—that everything is false—must be equally true. If that is the case, then there is nothing to recommend the original statement over any other, and the argument has upset all *logoi*, including itself.

Socrates proceeds to show in the *Euthydemus* how, in denying false speaking or in claiming all speech to be true, one effectively denies oneself the ability to speak, to use *logoi*: ". . . you do in fact completely stitch up [*surraptete*] men's mouths [*ta stomata tōn anthrōpōn*], as you say. But since you would appear to stitch up your own as well, you are behaving in a charming fashion [*charien*] and the harshness of your words [*epachtheis tōn logōn*] is quite removed [*aphaireitai*] (303e). Their *logoi* are denied of the heaviness, grievousness, and annoyance (*epachtheis*) they would otherwise present, if they were not applicable to themselves. The sophists' words must be held up against what they are doing by saying them. They may render others speechless, but the brothers deny themselves the power of logos simultaneously. What *logoi* the sophists present deny them of sensibility because they violate the very preconditions of sensible logos.

Socrates enacts the consequences of what the sophistic brothers deny. Recognizing the possibility of false speech, and denying that all speech is equally true, are two preconditions for speaking sensibly. The *Euthydemus* suggests two others: conceptions of difference and of contradiction. Leading to the claim that falsity in speech does not exist, Dionysodorus suggests that contradiction (*antilegoi*) cannot exist either (286a–b). There is either speaking the truth, or being silent. It follows then that there cannot be false opinion (286d), ignorance (286d), refutation (286e), or mistakes (287a). Socrates proceeds to contradict all four of these by acting the fool, allowing himself to be trapped by the brothers' questions concerning sense in what is said. Socrates says, "I made a mistake on account of being so stupid" (287e), and in one act, demonstrates the possibility of false opinions, mistakes, ignorance, and contradiction. To the extent that he is successful in refuting the brothers with this, he even contradicts the impossibility of refutation. Socrates is aware of this, asking whether the brothers think this to have been a mistake: "Because if I did not make one you will not refute me no matter how wise you are, and you will be 'helpless in dealing with the argument' [*oude echeis hoti chrē tō logō*] And if I did make one, you said the wrong thing when you claimed it was impossible to make mistakes . . ." (287e–88a). The brothers' helplessness in dealing with the argument is literally that they "bring nothing that is necessary [*chrē*] for the *logos.*" Put otherwise, they fail to satisfy the conditions necessary for logos. Socrates is playing the fool for a philosophical purpose. Their logos may knock down the *logoi* of others, but in the process, says Socrates, it falls down (*katabalōn*) itself (288a). While the brothers may not recognize how their arguments undo themselves, Crito, Ctesippus, Clinias, and the dialogue's readers are invited to do so. Indeed, the dialogue's protreptic power depends on its audience's doing so.

Euthydemus follows suit, contradicting his own position and suggesting that Dionysodorus has done the same by upbraiding his brother for "utterly destroying" (*diaphtheireis*) the logos (297a). Socrates asks Dionysodorus where he learned that the good are unjust, to which Dionysodurus misguidedly responds, "Nowhere" (297a). Euthydemus chides his brother, anticipating the faulty direction in which the argument can now turn: "this fellow here [Socrates] will turn out to be knowing, and then he will be knowing and not knowing at the same time." Dionysodorus blushes. Socrates is quick to move on this, asking Euthydemus, "Your all-knowing brother doesn't appear to be making a mistake, does he?" (297b). Although Dionysodorus is equally quick in changing the topic, even interrupting to do so, the moment is revealing. Dionysodorus has indeed "utterly destroyed" logos, but his brother is guilty of doing the same. Euthydemus's reprimand wholly violates what the brothers have claimed throughout the dialogue, namely that there exists no false speaking, no ignorance, no mistakes, no contradiction, and no refutation. Contrary to his claim as to the impossibility of mistakes, Dionysodorus has made one, and Euthydemus's action—pointing out his brother's error and the logically ensuing incongruity—contradicts his own speech. Both have enacted performative contradictions. In recognizing these as laughable, something we are prompted to do at many different points, the dialogue's audience effectively participates in the philosophical issue in question by recognizing these limits. If the brothers are right, there is only either true logos or silence.[29] By laughing, the audience acknowledges the existence of something in between these, a logos which can be true or false. And so it remains for each of us to turn inward, to look inside oneself, as Socrates encourages Charmides to do in the eponymous dialogue, to discover what is already there within us.

The tone of the *Euthydemus* is very much in question within the dialogue. While Socrates plays a sucker, marveling at the brothers as though they were gods, he simultaneously calls into question how the dialogue is to be read. Socrates refers to the seriousness or playfulness of the brothers' eristic eleven times.[30] He deems what has taken place to have been a joke (*paisai pros se* 278d), akin to pulling a chair out from underneath someone about to sit down or tripping them up (*huposkelizōn kai anatrepōn*) with words, but anticipates something serious and wonderful to come (278c–e). When Ctesippus describes the eristic as complete nonsense (*paralērēin*), Socrates again suggests that it is only because the sophists are offering conjuring tricks (*goēteuonte*) in imitation (*mimeisthon*) of the Egyptian sophist, Proteus, and deny them a serious exposition (*epideixasthai spoudazonte*, 288b–c). Socrates exhorts the brothers to be earnest (*spoudasēton*, 288d), and later claims suddenly to realize that they are indeed (*spoudazeton*, 294b). Nonetheless, at the dialogue's end, he implores Crito, at a loss as to how to educate his sons, to think the matter over for himself. The ambiguity of tone may encourage Crito to make up his own mind, rather than taking his cue simply from Socrates.

Socrates never seems to let down his nonetheless-dubious play of admiration for the sophistic charlatans. While this presents a significant danger of being misunderstood, and indeed of his being indistinguishable from them, there is enough textual evidence to support their distinction. A significant passage suggesting such a distinction comes from Socrates's elucidating the problematic ambiguity in the sophists' use of *manthanein* (277e–78e). Although credit for explicitly naming the fallacy of equivocation may go to Aristotle, Socrates is here offering an implicit statement of the problem. According to Socrates, to avoid becoming confused by such a fallacy, one needs to know the correct uses of *onomatōn* (277e).

And yet, Socrates uses *onomata* ambiguously as well. At several points in the dialogue, Socrates uses *thaumazein*, as potentially suggesting either a positive note of approval or as something that brings one to perplexity. What distinguishes Socrates's protreptic from that of the sophistic brothers? What distinguishes Socrates's use of ambiguity from that of Dionysodorus and Euthydemus? Socrates offers a hint when he characterizes his own tone in handling the sophists, describing it as what Sprague translates as "dead earnest," but is more literally "wonderfully serious" (*thaumastōs spoudazoimen*) (*Euthydemus* 283c2). He had just deemed the brothers' logos as "wonderful, in a way" (*thaumaston gar tina*, 283b). The verb *thaumazō* and its cognates appear sixteen times, the bulk of which are used to describe the brothers' logical tricks.[31] Michelini takes this to evoke the magician, or *thaumatopoios*—a "wonder-worker"—a figure already used by Isocrates to denounce eristic tricksters and "admired only by children and foolish adults."[32] By appearing to fall for the illusions displayed, Socrates plays a sucker, a fool, an idiot. He appears tricked by the wonders of the magicians.

Socrates has earlier warned that his own protreptic would be "unprofessional," or *idiōtikōs* (a qualifier he will repeat in describing his own approach), as well as laughable (*geloios*) (*Euthydemus* 278d). He does, however, promise to give his own ". . . example [*paradeigma*] of what I want a hortatory argument to be [*epithumō tōn protreptikōn logōn einai*], though amateurish [*idiōtikon isos*] perhaps, and expressed at length and with some difficulty" (*Euthydemus* 282d). Beyond a substantial distinction in self-assessment, a considerable difference lies in their outcomes. While the brothers' eristic brings about a number of reactions in Clinias, it is Socrates's protreptic that turns Clinias toward philosophy.[33] At 279d, Socrates describes this effect on Clinias, "*kai hos ethaumasen.*" Clinias has been provoked to wonder. And as Socrates tells us in the *Theaetetus*, that is where philosophy begins (with *thaumazein*, 155d). Clinias has been turned toward doing philosophy.

How does Socrates turn Clinias toward philosophy? By clarifying the use of ambiguity in the brothers' question about learning (*manthanein*)—by effectively exposing the magician's deception—Socrates inspires wonder in Clinias, and thus prompts Clinias toward asking questions for himself. And yet, by his own use of ambiguity, Socrates brings himself and philosophy into direct relation with the manipulators of ambiguity, namely Dionysodorus and Euthydemus.[34] Eristics is shown to be the "paradigm of otherness," and a grotesque comic image of dialectic.[35] The test lies in Clinias's (and our) ability to see the image as such.

A further difference can be noted: while both the brothers' and Socrates's performances are laughable, the laughter they generate is dissimilar. The brothers' laughter is that of superiority, of showing themselves to be more linguistically adept than the unfortunate Clinias. The laughter of Socrates's performance, rather than flattering his ego, flirts with making a fool of himself, instead of Clinias. Socrates generates self-reflective laughter.

This does not prevent Socrates from poking fun at the sophists. Socrates gives the brothers a small taste of their own medicine, punning on the meaning of anatreptic, or "turning over," when he describes the brothers as overturning their opponents as though they were wrestlers. Socrates says that a person who knows only the "frivolous parts of study [*paidia estin*]," rather than knowing matters themselves, ". . . would only be able to make fun [*prospaizein*] of people, tripping them up and overturning [*huposkelizōn kai anatrepōn*] them by means of the distinctions in words [*tōn onomatōn*] (*Euthydemus* 278b–c). Such persons would be inconsequential jokesters: "just like the people who pull the chair out from under a man who is going to sit down and then laugh [*chairousi kai gelōsin*] gleefully when they see him sprawling on his back [*huption anatetrammenon*] (278b–d). The anatreptic the brothers offer is tripping others for sport, turning them onto their backs rather than toward thinking through a better life. This is child's play, frivolous, and the laughter resulting from it is derisive. Although humbling, it does little toward inspiring genuine, philosophical questioning, and indeed may even suppress such an impulse. The brothers offer anatreptic, but not protrepic.

Part of the problem lies in what to make of such seemingly frivolous play. Socrates again begs the brothers, even if only out of pity for his earnest efforts, to be earnest themselves (*spoudazonta kai autō spoudasēton*) at 288d. And then he shifts to claiming that the brothers are very serious indeed, exclaiming "how marvelous" (*hōs thaumaston,* 294a), and saying: "By the gods, Dionysodorus, I said—for I realize that you are both now in earnest [*spoudazeton*], although I have provoked you to it [*proukalesamēn spoudazein*] with some difficulty—do you two really know everything [*onti panta epistasthon*]?" (*Euthydemus* 294b). Why Socrates shifts his assessment appears left to the audience to determine. Have the brothers changed their tone, or has Socrates suddenly realized the gravity of their seemingly inconsequential play? Are they kidding? Are they serious? And if they are joking, does that not immediately undermine their denial of false speech? The difficulty of assessing the tone is heightened if we read Socrates's performance as comical, as is its danger.

Relying on the discerning judgment of his audience, Socrates's comical performance is dangerous both for himself and for philosophy. As Crito indicates, Socrates's reputation is at stake. And if Socrates's testimony in the *Apology* can be brought to bear on this, the reception of comedy as straightforward reality is one of the factors affecting Socrates's conviction and execution. As self-proclaimed "philosophers," the brothers and their eristics pose a further threat, namely that to philosophy. This is evident in Crito's response. Crito says to Socrates that the brothers had been "chattering and making a worthless fuss about matters of no consequence" (*Euthydemus* 304e). Then Crito concludes from this that philosophy is "of no value whatsoever" (*Euthydemus* 305a). Without the ability to distinguish true from false proponents of philosophy, philosophy and philosophers are endangered.

Clinias too faces such difficulty. When Clinias laughs at Ctesippus's sophistic retort to Euthydemus, Socrates asks him, "why are you laughing at such serious [*spoudaiois*] and beautiful things [*pragmasin kai kalois*]" (300e). What remains serious is what is at issue, the *pragma*, but what is laughable are most of this art's practitioners including, as we are invited to determine for ourselves, Euthydemus and Dionysodorus. Socrates advises Crito that serious persons are "few and beyond price," whereas laughable (*katagelastous*) practitioners (*epitēdeumati*) of an art are many (307a). His final words to Crito in the dialogue, are "pay no attention to the practitioners [*epitēdeuontas*] of philosophy, whether good or bad. Rather give serious consideration to the thing itself [*to pragma*]: if it seems to you negligible, then turn everyone from it, not just your sons. But if it seems to you to be what I think it is, then take heart, pursue it, practice it [*tharrōn diōke kai askei*], both you and yours [*ta paidia*], as the proverb says" (307b–c).

The dialogue's last words echo what is at stake in the dialogue—*ta paidia*. At stake in the *Euthydemus* may be the youth, but the hero of the dialogue is a comically old man.

Socrates's fool is a comical archetype. Intergenerational conflict plays a key role in the *Euthydemus*, one that Socrates plays up dramatically. Socrates plays what had already become a comic archetype of the old man attempting in some capacity to rejuvenate himself or, more specifically, the elderly schoolboy.[36] Age-related comments and jokes aimed at Socrates come from all sides. When Socrates tells Crito that he is considering offering himself to the sophistic brothers as a student, Crito responds, "Aren't you afraid that, at your age, you are already too old [*hēlikian*]" (272b–c). The sophistic brothers are malicious about Socrates's age. Dionysodorus refers to him as "such an old Cronus" (287b), and Euthydemus says to Socrates, "you keep talking nonsense [*phluareis*] and are practically senile [*archaioteros*] (295c–d).[37] *Phluareis*, from *phluareō*, also means playing the fool. Socrates does exactly this, emphasizing his age and inability to learn by discussing his music teacher's frustration with him. He himself remarks on his age, and claims to seek rejuvenation through the sophists, saying, "being elderly [*presbutēs*] . . . I surrender myself [*paradounai emauton*] to Dionysodurus here just as I might to Medea of Colchis" (285c). Medea, who had rejuvenated Aeson, demonstrates her technique to Pelias's daughters, cutting up an old ram, boiling the parts, and pulling out a young lamb in the ram's stead. The daughters, in imitation, cut up and cook their father Pelias to disastrous results. Dionysodorus's suggestion, itself a play on ambiguity in the Greek, that it is appropriate to cut up and boil (for) the cook, is another reference to this rejuvenation (301c–e). Aristophanes's Demos already received this treatment; now it is Socrates's turn.[38]

Like Aristophanes's Strepsiades, Socrates attempts a spiritual rejuvenation by "handing himself over" to be educated by the younger practitioners of "philosophy."[39] The question is whether Crito will do the same to his sons. To whom ought we hand ourselves, or our children, over? Will they destroy or rejuvenate us? The mythical reference to Medea warns him not to entrust his sons to the "grotesque" (307a) practitioners of what might pass as "philosophy," lest the education these imitators offer yield similarly disastrous results. We find that Socrates here appears to enjoy a comical rejuvenation. By playing a fool, he displays in action the mistakes and ignorance the brothers claim to be impossible, and thereby, he shows precisely what is serious about the brothers' play.

Eristics is helped by the assumption that nothing serious results from their playfulness, but something significant does.[40] The brothers' logic-chopping is presented as mere amusement, harmless play, or inconsequential laughter. It is not inconsequential. Eristics assumes the impossibility of a stable correspondence between word and object.[41] The brothers' insistence on the impossibility of error, false speech, contradiction, and ignorance is evidence of the disruption of any consistent relationship between word and object. At stake is the very possibility of logos, and with that, the very possibility of philosophy itself.

Eristics and sophistry use the assumption that the playful cannot be serious, but Socrates here shows why this is false. If the brothers are right, there is no distinction between true and false logos, no error, and no ignorance. Socrates has shown how the brothers themselves demonstrate this to be false, and further illustrates its falsity by playing the error-prone fool. Socrates recognizes the gravity of the brothers' eristics, its subversion of logos. His play has philosophical consequences as much as the brothers' does.

If we apply this to the *Cratylus*, we can see why Socrates's etymologizing cannot be dismissed as frivolous and inconsequential play, nor can it be seen as straightforward and solemn. A significant claim emerges from the laughter of the *Euthydemus*, namely, that taking the brothers seriously, as potential teachers of the youth, means to accept their assumption that logos does not correspond regularly to anything. This renders the brothers' speech something akin to pointless noise, or, as Cratylus would put it, to banging on a pot. It puts the audience into a contradictory predicament, for we grant them a truth claim when their very position entails that such truth claims are impossible. Taking the brothers playfully, on the other hand, also reduces their speech to mere silliness and takes them out of contention for becoming the teachers of Crito's son, any more than Stesilaus might teach military fighting to Athenian youth.

Given this, one might wonder what, if anything, sets Socrates's jesting in the *Cratylus* apart from Euthydemus's and Dionysodorus's jesting in the *Euthydemus*? Socrates's "seriousness" is comic and laughable, but without undermining the possibility of objective standards while the brothers' playfulness undermines such standards. Sheer frivolity, or child's play, is what does *not* lead or contribute to better understanding. This leaves open a wide space for what can be deemed "serious play." Plato's laughter operates within that space.

The use of laughter and comedy within a philosophical dialogue inserts a distance and an ambiguity between audience and characters. Incorporating comedy into a serious discussion, ". . . threatens to shatter the enthrallment of the audience in the dramatic illusion."[42] Much like what Socrates does for Clinias in clarifying the mechanisms on the basis of which the magicians are able to bring about their "wonders," the incorporation of comedy in the dialogue itself keeps the dialogue's audience from enthrallment in illusion. Far from numbing minds, the incorporation of comedy prods and provokes the audience. It renders the audience "more alert and cautious . . ."[43] It acts, effectively, as does a gadfly. Comedy stings.

Without letting his comic guard down in the *Euthydemus*, Socrates can present what is repellant or appealing. Denying the audience the authority of his own pronouncements on the matter forces us to render our own.[44] While Michelini focuses on how Socrates's comical performance presses us—the external audience—to be more cautious, Halper argues that it acts instead to disarm ideas presented, and thus encourages the audience to entertain possibilities we might otherwise immediately dismiss.[45] Michelini's and Halper's positions may be reconciled, for it is entirely possible that Plato's laughter includes both apotreptic (per Michelini) and protreptic (per Halper) effects.[46] The brothers are the measure of a type of ugliness that has an apotreptic function on the audience. Crito senses this too: they are offputting.

The danger lies in conflating such a caricature or stage mask with what is real. If even friends of Socrates, such as Crito, cannot tell the difference between a Euthydemus or a Dionysodorus and a philosopher, then we cannot laugh at these charlatans without reflecting on how we might appear just like them, and yet how philosophers may be different. It is not in laughing at the comical representation: witness Socrates not only present in the audience but also laughing at his own Aristophanic representation. If this is so, then the blame Socrates casts on comedy in the *Apology*, as having provided the earliest prejudices against him, can now be better understood. Socrates may not be blaming Aristophanes so much as he is blaming his uncritical reception, and it is through Plato's use of laughter in the dialogues, that the audience is incited to provide the critical reception that was, perhaps, lacking in that of Aristophanes's audiences.

Laughter calls into question what is otherwise assumed by opening or exposing a gap between two things. Self-reflective laughter opens such a distance within the self, from which one can observe and view oneself critically, even philosophically. Laughter regarding logos in the *Euthydemus* and *Cratylus* exposes a gap between a speaker's words and actions, and between those words and logos. Laughter thus reveals complexities in what one might take to be simple. And this applies even to playfulness for the sophistic brothers, for as much as they present it to be merely laughable and nothing "serious," it seems precisely Socrates's point that it is no such thing. The brothers' play makes bold philosophical claims—claims that laughter itself exposes as indefensible. Amid all the *Euthydemus*'s laughter, Socrates urges a "serious" turn to the *pragma*, and away from the eristic plays on language. The necessity of words and speech generally to *pragma*, or more broadly, toward *ta esti*, is what Socrates's comical performance in the *Euthydemus* suggests. We find a comparable suggestion at the heart of the *Cratylus*.

Logos and the Satirical

Comedy in the *Cratylus* reveals not only humanity's inextricable bond to logos, as Sallis contends, but, as I argue here, it also exposes hubristic pretensions to exceed such limits. Hermogenes and Cratylus both present hubristic philosophical positions that render them incapable of dialogue with each other, and hence, they require Socrates's mediation. It is by depicting a distinct lack of measure, as is evident in Hermogenes and Cratylus, that comedy enables us to know ourselves as beings who are necessarily limited to logos, to inaccuracy, and to error. The self-knowledge that comedy makes possible, in other words, prompts us to recognize our own ignorance and shortcomings, and scale our claims back accordingly. The humility resulting from this stems from the recognition that, to some extent, we always remain the papered-over incongruity, the lack of self-identical presence, because names and, more broadly, logos, however arbitrary and inaccurate, are all that we have. We are, in other words, laughable.

We are thus limited to logos, but logos itself, or at least our use of it, is subject to its own limits, its own *metron*. At issue in the *Cratylus* and the *Euthydemus* are these limits, the semantic preconditions for using *logoi* sensibly. As we have seen in the *Euthydemus*, these preconditions include notions of truth, falsity, difference, error, contradiction, without which we fail to use logos sensibly, and instead fall into the sorts of performative contradictions of which Euthydemus and Dionysodorus are guilty. As I will suggest, such prerequisites are at issue in the *Cratylus* and, as has been shown in the *Euthydemus*, it is comic logos that exposes the limitations in question. In both dialogues, Socrates enacts a comic logos so as to expose limitations in logos and its usage. The dialogues' audiences are invited to laugh because, in so doing, we recognize the insensible use of *logoi* as such, and so participate in the philosophical debate in question.

A brief look at another approach to the *Cratylus* may help differentiate just what is so unique about a comic reading of it. According to David Sedley, the enigmatic character of the *Cratylus* is due to the lengthy series of far-fetched etymologies that comprises a considerable portion of the dialogue.[47] The main response to these today is to treat them as some form of satire on someone or something.[48] Sedley thus wants to challenge the "fundamental but unargued assumption" underlying this reading of the *Cratylus*: "that Plato must think the etymologies as ridiculous as we do."[49] He assumes the etymologies to be sound because "the dialogue as a whole never calls that soundness into question, thus leaving us no exploitable gap on the matter between speaker and author."[50] Citing Proclus's reading of the *Cratylus*, Sedley claims that there is no hint of reading this dialogue as satire by the ancients: "If Plato was joking, the joke flopped."[51] Indeed, Proclus's reading does not suggest a great appreciation of Platonic humor, but the assumption as to the correctness of the historical reading of Plato as humorless is precisely what is in question.

To turn the tables here, Sedley's argument for the seriousness of the *Cratylus*'s etymologies relies on a fundamental and unargued assumption itself, one that a comic reading already calls into question, namely, the mutual exclusivity of seriousness and comedy in Plato. Further, a comic reading such as I am attempting to offer here of the *Cratylus* opens up precisely the kind of "exploitable gap" that Sedley finds elusive, although the gap illustrated is one between the speak*er* and the speak*ing*, rather than between speaker and author.[52] It illustrates a split between the form and content of the dialogue, one that is not only "exploitable," but also has profound consequences. Finally, regarding the historical "flop" made by Plato's *Cratylus*, as suggested earlier, the humor of the dialogues was indeed recognized by ancient commentators, even if not by Proclus, as discussed in the Introduction. While my intent is not to engage in an extended polemic with Sedley, the contrast with a comic reading is fruitful. Comedy is a self-forgetting of just the kind that covers over such chasms, and it is through recognizing comedy and comic moments within the dialogues that such contradictions can be brought to light.[53] Comedy can thus support philosophical inquiry.[54]

A turn to the *Cratylus* will show how comedy and laughter might hold this function. Hermogenes's and Cratylus's positions on the correctness of names appear to be stark opposites, and yet Socrates reveals them to be in some sense the same by performing the comedy of the *Cratylus*.[55] In what sense can what we today call conventionalism and naturalism be identified? A closer look at both positions will show the basis of this identity in their shared lack of measure (*metron*) and how comedy illuminates it. Hermogenes states his initial position at 384d–e: ". . . any name [*onoma*] you give a thing is its correct name. If you change its name and give it another, the new one is as correct as the old. For example, when we give names to our domestic slaves, the new ones are as correct as the old." He then elaborates as to how names derive their veracity: "No name belongs to a particular thing by nature [*phusei*], but only because of the rules and usage [*sunthēkē kai homologia*] of those who establish the usage and call it by that name." A name, in other words, is correct if there is general agreement that it is the name for a particular referent. This form of conventionalism may not strike us as particularly extreme, but Hermogenes then posits a stronger version of this, claiming that such agreement need not occur among any group of people, but might obtain for any given individual and differ depending on when and in what context (private or public) a name is used. As Socrates restates this position, "whatever each person says is the name of something, for him, that is its name" (385d1–2). Referred to in the literature as the Humpty Dumpty theory of language, Hermogenes's position is far more extreme than it appears at first blush.[56]

Contrary to his admissions at 385b2–6 and again at 387c14–d1, Hermogenes is denying that any standard exists in naming and so is claiming that falsehood cannot exist therein. The example of renaming one's slave already suggests the arbitrariness of names, but human mastery over language extends beyond the master-slave relationship. Changing something's name depends entirely on the will of any person. Since there is no standard for naming correctly apart from that individual's whim, one can never be mistaken in naming. In the absence of false names, all names are thus correct. Hermogenes may claim willingness to listen to anyone, but his position does not allow for a standard by which any other might be judged false.

Cratylus denies the possibility of falsehood explicitly: "In my view, one can neither speak nor say anything falsely [*pseudē*]" (429e2). His is a naturalist position that claims there to be a natural fitness of names to their referents, but just what this special relationship of names to things consists in is not revealed. In using a name, on this theory, one either accesses the essence of the intended referent or one does not. There is no false naming, then, because one either names things according to their natural essence or then speaks nonsense. One who mistakenly calls Cratylus "Hermogenes," for example, is not speaking falsely; he is, as Cratylus puts it, "just making noise and acting pointlessly, as if he were banging a brass pot" (430a3–4).

Hermogenes and Cratylus each articulate a position that they then contradict in deed. The joke as to the correctness of Hermogenes's name illuminates this. At the dialogue's beginning, Hermogenes objects that Cratylus denies "Hermogenes" to be Hermogenes's true name, but refuses to explain why not, and the joke is returned to at multiple points in the dialogue (383b, 384c, 408b). Hermogenes cannot refute Cratylus, because on his own relativistic conventionalism, whatever name (or lack thereof) with which Cratylus wants to baptize Hermogenes *is* actually Hermogenes's name. Despite this, Hermogenes protests Cratylus's joke and demands an explanation, something as unnecessary for Cratylus to offer as it would be for the slave owner (383b). Cratylus cannot consistently call it a "false" name; he instead denies that it is Hermogenes's name altogether, rendering Hermogenes effectively nameless. Yet, when Cratylus finally enters the conversation, he immediately addresses Hermogenes by name (427e5), an act that on Cratylus's own reckoning is pointless noise akin to "banging a brass pot."[57] On Hermogenes's conventionalism, since Cratylus nonetheless continues to *use* Hermogenes's name, he remains named as he is.[58] Neither can admit the falsity of Hermogenes's name, and both thereby contradict their own linguistic positions through their actions in the dialogue.

Socrates claims an unknown inspiration for the "superhuman wisdom" (396d7–8) behind his etymologies, and then identifies this source as Euthyphro of Prospalta, likely to be the same Euthyphro who appears in the eponymous dialogue.[59] Euthyphro exhibits this incongruity between speech and deed as well, and cuts a comical figure because of it. It is significant that his conversation with Socrates on piety occurs on the day that Socrates is charged with impiety, and that Euthyphro himself begins his arguably impious prosecution against his own father. That this seems to be the very same day on which Socrates's conversation with Hermogenes and Cratylus occurs is no coincidence. At issue is the congruity, or lack thereof, between one's speech and actions. Euthyphro's *hubris* is evident in both. He claims to know what pleases the gods which, unless genuinely inspired is already a hubristic claim, while unable to offer a logos for this and while doing something that few Greeks would consider pious, namely prosecuting his father.

Referring to Hermogenes's faith in Euthyphro's inspiration, Socrates, in the *Cratylus*, says, ". . . I seem to have had such a clever insight just now, that, if I'm not careful, I'll be in danger of becoming altogether *too* wise [*sophōteros tou deontos genesthai*] before the day is out." *Sophōteros tou deontos* literally means "wiser than what is binding or proper." In the *Apology*, Socrates distinguishes between the kind of wisdom he claims for himself—human wisdom, and that of sophists such as Prodicus, Hippias, and Callias, which is "a wisdom more than human" (*Apology* 20e2). Human wisdom involves awareness of one's own ignorance, whereas superhuman wisdom is ignorant of its own ignorance. Euthyphro's wisdom, given his inability to provide a suitable logos for *to hosion*, or the pious, appears to be of the latter kind, and for this, he presents a comic figure. On knowledge of the divine, piety, and impiety, Euthyphro says, "I should be of no use, Socrates, and Euthyphro would not be *superior to the majority of men*, if I did not have accurate knowledge of all such things" (*Euthyphro* 5a1–3, my emphasis). This is precisely the sort of hubristic overestimation of oneself that Socrates describes as comic fodder in the *Philebus*.[60] Euthyphro is sensitive to how his prophesying is received, repeatedly describing being laughed at (*katagelōsin*) by the assembly, to which Socrates responds by suggesting that being laughed at is not such a bad thing (*katagelasthēnai isōs ouden pragma*) (*Euthyphro* 3c, 3e). Herein lies a significant revision in the role, reception, and evaluation of laughter. Laughter, as the previous chapter suggested, is not what we ought to fear. We ought to fear instead the self-deception and ignorance that laughter can make evident.

Indeed, Socrates seems to *invite* laughter directed at the etymologies and the dubious wisdom inspiring them in the *Cratylus*. Sedley's article is not the only one to entirely ignore any "exploitable gap," as he puts it, but missing the frequency with which Socrates undermines the solemnity of his etymologies remains surprising nonetheless. Referring to this inspired wisdom, Socrates says that "It sounds completely absurd [*geloion men panu eipein*] (401e7). He claims that his etymologies of the Olympian gods are playful, as opposed to serious, saying to Hermogenes, ". . . there is not only a serious [*spoudaiōs*] way of explaining the names of these divinities but a playful [*paidikōs*] one as well. You'll have to ask others for the serious [*spoudion*] one, but there's nothing to prevent us from going through the playful [*paidikon*] one—even the gods love play [*philopaismones*]" (406b9-c3). Socrates's account is playful. He repeatedly undermines faith in his allegedly inspired etymologies, saying, "I think I'm driving my apparent wisdom pretty hard at present [*phainomai sophias elauein*] (410e2), acknowledging that those hearing his etymologies might see them as ridiculous (*pantōn katagelan*) (413c3-4), and imputing to Hermogenes a similar doubt, saying, ". . . now maybe you'll say that I'm inventing things again . . ." (415d4-5). At 426b5-6, Socrates declares, "Well, my impressions about primary names seem to me to be entirely outrageous [*hubristika*] and absurd [*geloia*]."

Taking such suggestions by Socrates, and there are many of them in the *Cratylus*, at face value might lead one to ignore the otherwise dense and difficult etymologies. Taylor writes of the etymologies that "there is no need to follow this part of the conversation in any detail, all the more since Socrates professes to be surprised by his own readiness and suggests that he must have been infected by an abnormal 'possession' from having just left the company of the 'inspired' Euthyphro."[61] I believe just the reverse to be true: given Socrates's repeated hints as to his suspicious inspiration and the dubious quality of his etymologies, the question becomes all the more important as to why approximately half of the dialogue is devoted to these. Although it is not my purpose to evaluate the etymologies in great detail, it will suffice to address them here with regard to one particular aspect of the argument already underway: the etymologies' connection to excessiveness and comedy.[62]

Socrates employs elaborate and excessive etymologies for simultaneously philosophical and comical purposes. For instance, he uses creative etymology to take a light-hearted dig at Anaxagoras. His etymology for the moon, *selēnē*, turns it into a philosophical claim that displaces Anaxagoras's originality. Anaxagoras was the first to recognize that the moon derives its light from the sun, and here Socrates has him claim that the light we see on the moon is both new and remaining light from the sun (409b).[63] Because the moon's light is therefore always new (*neon*) and old (*henon*), Socrates suggests the moon's correct name, from "the bright light whose light is always both old and new" (*selas neon kai henon echei aei*), is *Selaenoneoaeia*, which has been compressed for obvious reasons. Socrates's etymology is as thin as its gibe at Anaxagoras is insubstantial. Hermogenes remarks at what a "dithyrambic [*dithurambōdes*] name [*touto tounoma*] it is!" (409c).[64] Even Hermogenes, whose claim has been that however one uses a name is correct, remarks on the excessiveness on display here.

Hermogenes's comparison to dithyrambs makes a clear connection between the etymologies and comedy. Dithyrambs are choral songs and dances in honor of Dionysus, written in lyric meter. They are described by a number of sources as having been acutely emotive and enthusiastic praises honoring the god of comedy and drama, and connected historically with the comic revel.[65] Plutarch quotes Aeschylus, and then contrasts Apollo's paean with Dionysus's dithyramb.

> 'In mingled cries the dithyramb should ring, with Dionysus reveling [*sunkōmon*], its king.' But Apollo has the Pæan, a set and sober [*sōphrona*] music. Apollo is ever ageless [*agērōn*] and young [*aei neon*]; Dionysus has many forms and many shapes as represented in paintings and sculpture, which attribute to Apollo smoothness and order and a gravity with no admixture [*spoudē akraton*], to Dionysus a blend of sport [*tina paidia*] and sauciness [*hubrei*] with seriousness [*spoudē*] and frenzy [*mania*].[66]

The ageless, consistent, and orderly Apollo is in direct contrast to the aged, incongruous, and playful Socrates. Hermogenes's characterization of the putative original *onoma* from which *selēnē* is derived suggests his recognition of Socrates's etymological excessiveness and the comical spirit in which the etymologies are delivered. It also underscores the tone in which Socrates's etymologies are being received.

What Socrates demonstrates in his use of language in the etymologies is the *hubris* toward which humans are prone. Humans cannot be the *metron*, the measure for all things, precisely because we ourselves are prone to excessiveness. Socrates pulls back the curtain on his own performance at several points, indicating the various devices (*mēchanē*, 409d) he uses for the desired effect. It is the comic logos that Socrates employs, and of which, at various points, Hermogenes and Cratylus approve, that allows such excessiveness to be enacted. There are further warnings not to take what has been said and done at face value, including the sudden discussion of self-deception. It would be an odd topic to raise here if not for the connection established in the previous chapter between laughter and self-deception. But in a dialogue making what may be excessive use of laughter and the comical to expose sophistic pretenses, it is not all that odd.

The discussion of self-deception in the *Cratylus* is Socrates's warning to his interlocutors not to take his seemingly inspired etymological proficiency too seriously, to allow themselves be laughable, but not ridiculous. After Cratylus agrees with these, Socrates says, "But, Cratylus, *I* have long been surprised at my own wisdom—and doubtful of it too" (428d1-5). He then warns against self-deception as the "worst thing of all" (428d3), and suggests testing and retesting what he has said before assuming its veracity. This comment seems out of place if not to warn the compliant Cratylus not to concede too easily, and indeed, Socrates returns to the theme of deception, tying it together explicitly with the etymological investigation: "But don't you see, Cratylus, that anyone who investigates things by taking names as his guides and looking into their meanings runs no small risk of being deceived?" (436b1-3). Socrates concludes by making the warning more dire: ". . . surely no one with any understanding will commit himself or the cultivation of his soul to names, or trust them and their givers to the point of firmly stating that he knows something . . ." (440c2-4). Etymology alone cannot yield knowledge, a point which is underscored in Plato's *Seventh Letter*, where names are listed as a necessary component of coming to knowledge (342a-b, 342e, 343e1-6), but not alone a sufficient one (343d9, 343b1-3).

Central to the discussion in the *Cratylus* is the order of inquiry between *onomata* and *ta onta*, which is why Heraclitus and Parmenides are contrasted, with the seemingly disparate positions of Hermogenes and Cratylus. Focusing on Cratylus's naturalistic position and on Hermogenes's conventional position is somewhat misplaced, and their ultimate identification supports this. Both positions are hubristic and without measure, or *metron*. It is not Cratylus's claim that names must accord with a thing's natural essence that lands him in trouble; it is the claim that names must reflect a Heraclitean flux and that names themselves can teach us that such a flux is natural. The position itself, however, may not be so important. Socrates' response is to show with his extensive and preposterous word derivations that, according to Sprague: "it is possible to construct etymologies of rest which are just as convincing as the etymologies of motion . . ." and therefore, the etymological method of studying reality is unreliable.[67] Etymologies cannot teach us how things really are: names cannot guarantee their own truth, but must remain somewhat arbitrary and limited. Inquiry, in this sense and in line with both Heraclitus and Parmenides, cannot begin with *onomata*; it must begin with *ta onta*.

What happens when we do begin with *onomata* is dramatically and comically enacted by Socrates in the etymologies. If indeed humans are the measure (*metron*) of all things, the senseless etymologies are what result. As soon as the audience declares these to be in some capacity "false," we take a stand in the question as to the possibility of false speech, a stand in opposition to the ones explicitly adopted by Hermogenes and Cratylus. If we do not, we either accept them without a measure of their truth, or find the measure of their truth in an appeal beyond the human to the divine, or at least to the self-proclaimed authority of a divinely inspired mortal who offers access to divine or primary names. Hermogenes, repeatedly marveling at Socrates's etymological dexterity, concurs that this must be a divine inspiration, but does not flinch when Socrates proclaims his Muse to be the laughable Euthyphro, who can neither explain his alleged afflatus, nor reveal anything particularly inspiring through it, aside from his own hubris.

Cratylus's joke reveals a "peculiar seriousness" to comedy indeed. Both Cratylus's and Hermogenes's positions are identical in the sense that they lack a measure (*metron*) by which one might distinguish true from false names and, as such, their positions are contradicted by their actions in the dialogue. Further, Cratylus's position lacks measure in its need to appeal to either primary or divine names, access to which cannot be gained through logos, but could only be provided by divine inspiration. That the inspiration Socrates claims is, instead, a Euthyphronic inspiration suggests that the desire to justify logos by means of appeal beyond logos is already unmeasured, or hubristic, much like what Socrates calls more-than-human-wisdom in the *Apology*. We remain comically situated in logos despite our appeals beyond it.

What then does this illuminate about self-knowledge? If comedy is a self-forgetting, then the route to self-knowledge lies in logos, and potentially comic logos at that. Self-identity, like the referents of names, involves a papering over of incongruities in which case, we are never *fully* present or knowable to ourselves. But there is still a form of self-knowledge available to us, one that recognizes this ignorance, and that seeks, to the extent this is possible, to harmonize our words and deeds. The possibility of posing a ridiculous spectacle, when acknowledged, reminds us of the limitations inherent to the self we are attempting to understand. Reading the *Cratylus* as a comedy, and comedy within it as self-forgetting thus reveal the very obstacles lying in our way: hubris, self-deception, and the incongruity among facets of ourselves.

This chapter thus suggests laughter in the *Cratylus* to be tied up with a larger semantic issue, namely the conditions necessary for sensible logos to occur. Ignoring the laughter in Platonic dialogues is not simply ignoring their frivolity. Laughter in the *Cratylus* reveals the exceeding of limitations between humans and logos: persons defend claims that exceed the human limitation to logos, and logos itself is shown to have limitations that must be heeded in philosophical inquiry. If forgetting ourselves and our limits render us laughable, then laughter itself has the potential to point us toward greater self-knowledge. Platonic laughter, as we will continue to see in the next chapter, has philosophical significance.

The exchange between Socrates and Hermogenes concerning the etymology of Hermes's name is lengthy, but worthwhile to address in concluding. Hermes, Socrates says, is a "*hermeneus*, a messenger, a thief and a deceiver in words [*apatēlon en logois*] . . ." (*Cratylus* 408a). Responding to Cratylus's earlier pun on Hermogenes's name, Hermogenes does not see himself in Hermes, skilled as he is in the use of logos. Socrates responds:

> But it *is* reasonable for Pan to be Hermes' double-natured son. Hermogenes: How so? Socrates: You know speech signifies all things [*to pan*] and keeps them circulating and always going about, and that it has two forms—true and false? Hermogenes: Certainly. Socrates: Well, the true part is smooth and divine and dwells among the gods above, while the false part dwells below among the human masses, and is rough and goatish [*tragikon*]; for it is here, in the tragic [*tragikon*] life, that one finds the vast majority of myths and falsehoods. Hermogenes: Certainly. Socrates: Therefore the one who expresses all things [*pan*] and keeps them always in circulation [*aei polōn*] is correctly called 'Pan-the-goat-herd' ['*Pan aipolos*']

> The double-natured son of Hermes, he is smooth in his upper parts, and rough and goatish in the ones below. He is either speech itself or the brother of speech, since he is the son of Hermes . . . (*Cratylus* 408b–d)

Hermes is, after all, a trickster god. As his cunning theft of Apollo's cattle shortly after his own birth and his brazen denial of this imply, Hermes is comical. Pan, says Socrates, is Hermes's double-natured son, who has a form reflecting such duality and is either logos itself or the brother of logos, given that Hermes begot both. Laughter thus reveals fundamental ambiguities not only in the names and words that we use, but between our words and actions, and in ourselves. Such duality and the ability to express all things (and all positions) are embodied not only in logos and in Pan, as we have seen in this chapter, but also in Socrates himself, as we will see in the next chapter.

As comical, Socrates is an image of the dual nature of logos. Socrates thus warns us with laughter in the *Cratylus* and *Euthydemus* not to become a sucker as he has played at being, one who takes the complex as one-dimensional, or one who takes himself to be more than a fundamentally imperfect being, a mixture of the beastly and the divine, of the mischievous and the wise. Like the logos to which we are inextricably bound, we cannot be the *metron*, or measure, of ourselves. As Ewegen suggests, humans cannot be measure of things without making naming and logos itself impossible.[68] Humans are instead laughably limited. Chance writes that, "By investing [the *Euthydemus*'s] form with a content, now-playful, now-serious, with the comic antics of the brother-pair predominating, Plato gives clear evidence of loosely modeling his dialogues after that easily recognizable but little appreciated genre known as the satyr play or tragicomedy."[69] This is the figure staring back at us in the mirror. Logos, like Socrates and the beings limited to logos, is a satyr. This, as we will see in the next chapter, has significant implications for the possibility of self-knowledge.

5

Bawdy Politics: Satyrical Laughter and Self-Knowledge in the *Symposium*

The first chapter asks what sort of hero Socrates is, and the answer, as the next two chapters suggest, is a comical one. The fifth chapter returns to this question to further develop and specify this notion, drawing from the third and fourth chapters to do so. Through this, it becomes possible to understand Alcibiades's claim in the *Symposium* that Socrates cannot be compared to anyone except, perhaps, a satyr. For like the comical satyr, Socrates is a composite of beast, human, and divine. Here it also becomes possible to see how far Socrates the comical hero alters the given paradigms for comical heroes, for Socrates is a self-conscious and virtuous hero, one who uses comedy at others' and his own expense for purposes such as turning people toward doing philosophy and away from what undermines such efforts. He has—at least in part—removed shame from being laughable. Virtue for Socrates, as supported by the third chapter, is not incompatible with self-knowledge, for the self-consciously comical figure of Socrates embodies both. If humans in general are, like Socrates, inherently laughable, this casts light on the possibility of self-knowledge. On the one hand, complete self-knowledge becomes impossible. On the other hand, the very basis of this impossibility—the ultimately incommensurable and mutable self, also presents the possibility of a sort of personal transcendence. Recognizing the dialogues' comedy thus liberates us from a tragic pessimism to a comical, Platonic optimism.

The only dialogue named after an occasion, the *Symposium* presents one at which it is not at all surprising to find comedy and laughter. The drinking party's laughter exposes pretensions toward a conception of eros that forgets the self, here particularly in the form of the body. While Aristophanes's hiccups and speech emphasize the body's significance for eros, Alcibiades's praise of Socrates, whom he describes as the very embodiment of eros, takes this further to build to a comical punch line that exposes how much the earlier speeches overlook the role of the body. If the body's role in eros is significant, the physical aspect of Alcibiades's comparison of Socrates to a satyr must be too. Alcibiades also offers an image that answers the question posed at the beginning of the book as to what sort of hero Socrates is. Socrates is a satyr—a comical, incommensurable, epitome of the erotic and Dionysian spirit. The embodiment of the beast-human-divine complex, Socrates is a comical hero. The laughter of the dialogue thus brings to light two things that otherwise go unnoticed: the question of the importance of the body in eros, and an optimistic spirit at play in the dialogues.

While an optimistic spirit is acknowledged by Nietzsche, it is seen as an expression of the arrogance of a superficial rationality regarding itself as omnipotent. What we have seen from Critias in the *Charmides*, is that a rationality mistaking itself as omnipotent is something deficient to be laughed at. If we instead acknowledge the comical spirit at work in Platonic dialogues, just the opposite comes to light. Rather than regarding rationality, humans, or any individual as omnipotent, recognizing the comical spirit in the dialogues demands the simultaneous recognition of limits and an attending attitude of humility. The optimism stems from possibilities existing within such limits, for what the comical reading of Plato presents is a view of the self as a beast-human-god composite, a limited being—one bound to logos for whom eros is a permanent state, but one having the possibility of a finite transcendence of these parts of the self depending on how we comport ourselves. For the self described by Alcibiades and enacted by Socrates in the *Symposium* is a comical and fragile composite vulnerable to shifts in either direction.

It is possible to see in the chapters preceding, the beginnings of a response to Nietzsche's claims about Socrates and Plato in the *Birth of Tragedy*. In it, Nietzsche writes that Plato's "creative gifts forced him to develop an art form deeply akin to the existing forms which he had repudiated."[1] While

I have explicitly argued against the notion that Plato repudiates poetry elsewhere, the preceding chapters should already begin to form a case against Plato's alleged hostility toward specific forms of poetry, namely comedy and tragedy.[2] Can we not reverse this to see in the likeness evidence against such repudiation? Nietzsche describes Plato's seemingly favorable comments about poetry as being "ironic."[3] While irony admits a modicum of humor in Nietzsche's assessment of Plato, it does not go far enough, for irony is largely divorced from the Dionysian, since it can be seen to subject its humor to the rationalist project that Nietzsche attributes to Socrates. As this book has thus far suggested, Socrates cuts a comical (and not merely ironic) figure, one embodying both Apollonian and Dionysian forces. In this chapter, we see this most directly in Alcibiades's description of Socrates as a satyr.

More specifically, in the *Birth of Tragedy*, Nietzsche attacks Socrates as Dionysius's "chief opponent" who has a "corrosive influence upon instinctual life."[4] In this early work, Nietzsche presents Socrates as curbing the Dionysian and replacing it with a rationality that leads to the demise of the Aeschylean tradition. Further, Nietzsche understands Socrates's physical ugliness as grounds for his resentment and envy of established society, and the turn towards philosophy. Does this not overemphasize the body and its beauty? Cannot Socrates's ugliness, and Plato's regular emphasis of this, instead suggest his affinity with the very exemplar of contradictory qualities and of instinctive, Dionysian impulses, namely, the ugly satyr? Does Plato's closer and more symbiotic relationship with comedy and tragedy suggested here not instead further the Aeschlean and Aristophanean traditions? I hope to present an alterative understanding of Socrates here, a figure compared to both beasts and the divine, and for whom Alcibiades's comparison to a satyr may best balance these polarities.

While regularly compared to animals in the dialogues, according to Alcibiades in the *Symposium*, Socrates might most fittingly be likened to a mythical beast, akin to Typhon, Marsyas, or Silenus. The question becomes one as to the significance of Socrates's comical depiction as a satyr, and it is a question to which Socrates himself provides a possible answer elsewhere. Concerning the being of mythical creatures, Socrates explains his approach to Phaedrus, saying, "I'm not yet able, in accordance with the Delphic inscription, to know myself, and it seems ridiculous [*geloion*] to me to investigate things that don't concern me while still lacking that knowledge" (*Phaedrus* 229e). Lacking self-knowledge, Socrates pursues it by way of comparisons of himself to mythical figures. Instead of inquiring into traditional, mythical representations, Socrates says, "I investigate (as I was saying just now) not those things but myself, as to whether I happen to be a beast more complex and agitated than Typhon, or a gentler and simpler animal, possessing by nature a divine and un-Typhonic lot" (*Phaedrus* 229e–30a). Socrates himself is likened to such mythical creatures. I propose that an answer to Socrates's musings is suggested by Alcibiades's encomium of Socrates in the *Symposium*. What can we learn about ourselves from Socrates, as presented in the *Symposium*? And what does the way in which Socrates is presented reveal about self-knowledge? My proposal is to take the satyr much as Socrates himself suggests we do with other mythical figures, such as Typhon, and to use it for the purposes of acquiring self-knowledge. Doing so will reveal at least as much about Socrates. In the *Symposium*, I will argue, Socrates is presented as a mythical and comical beast to whom we can compare ourselves, asking whether we are as courageous, as *sōphrōn*, as complex, or perhaps even as mischievous, as he is. We are invited, in other words, to discover ourselves in and through Socrates—as he suggests in the *Phaedrus* one might do with figures such as Typhon, to understand ourselves better through a figure who simultaneously enables and renders impossible the quest for self-knowledge.

In this picture, humans appear precariously poised between beasts and the divine, and potentially drawing from both. This tension between human deficiency and excess, and the endeavor to exceed our limitations are at the fore of Alcibiades's depiction of Socrates in the *Symposium* and most clearly in his comparison of Socrates to a satyr. As Alcibiades portrays him, Socrates is incomparable to humans and most closely akin to satyrs like Silenus or Marsyas. He and his *logoi* are depicted as divided much like a satyr, having a crude, comical, and ugly exterior, but possessing an interior of divine, virtuous beauty. This veneer, however, is not expendable: the satyr and his characteristics permeate the entirety of Alcibiades's speech and, inasmuch as his speech is true, the satyrical tension between the beastly and the divine, the mischievous and the wise, and the comical and the serious best illustrates Socrates's very nature. The case can be made, then, that Socrates is, at least in part, a comical figure. Far from enabling us to dismiss this aspect of Socrates and his *logoi*, however, I will suggest that recognizing it can instead shed light on philosophical consequences concerning what has been neglected, not only in interpretations of the dialogue, but in the preceding encomia of Eros: the body, the Dionysian, and laughter.

The laughter of the *Symposium* is satyrical and comic, both forms of which could be, and have often been, easily ignored. The comic laughter that this chapter will address occurs in three parts: the curious form of Aristophanes's case of hiccups; in Aristophanes's myth; and in Alcibiades's encomium of Socrates. Its satyric laughter derives from taking Alcibiades's speech and its central simile "seriously," as though it might be describing Socrates truthfully. This chapter will first turn to Aristophanes's hiccups, arguing that the hiccups remind us of what has been forgotten in the dialogue, and then examine the satyrical rendering of Socrates for what it might tell us both about Socrates's nature and our own. The *Symposium*'s laughter hinges on self-forgetting in the form of forgetting the body, a facet of eros that a number of encomia leave out or vulgarize. In this sense, Alcibiades's accusation of hubris against Socrates is a joke revealing the culmination of such a self-forgetting, and the laughter it generates exposes the pretension of those who venerate an incorporeal eros. That laughter betrays those laughing, for if they believed what they claimed, Alcibiades's pursuit of the ugly Socrates without physical consummation would be an ideal, rather than a punch line.

While I am not making the claim that the *Symposium* itself constitutes a satyr play, I will argue that the dialogue's laughter is a satyrical laughter, one that combines the serious with slapstick comedy. Sutton insists that satyrical laughter is that resulting from incongruities: the serious with the ludicrous, high-brow drama with low-brow buffoonery, the divine and the crude, and the heroic with the comic. He writes: "the satyr play is not a wholly farcical genre, but a serio-comic form insofar as its characteristic humor comes from the collision of the serious and the comic and requires the presence of both."[5] Satyric humor, according to Sutton, is largely "the wildly ludicrous juxtaposition of the heroic and the comic."[6] It is such incongruity, ". . . together with the slapstick buffoonery of low-brow Greek stage-comedy, [that] is the principle source of satyric humor."[7] We find such humor throughout the *Symposium*, but most particularly embodied in the figure of Socrates and in incidents such as Aristophanes's hiccups. It is to these hiccups that the chapter turns first.

Aristophanes's Hiccups

From a philosopher who was reputed never to have laughed out loud, the *Symposium* lands us in a rather funny interpretive predicament: how should we make sense of its moments of hilarity? Why, for instance, does Aristophanes contract a case of the hiccups? And what, if anything, are we to make of the buffoonery subsequently taking place "off-stage,"[8] namely the assorted cures Eryximachus prescribes him? As Eryximachus stands in for Aristophanes to deliver his own speech on love, Aristophanes proceeds to hold his breath, only to hiccup again, then gargle water, only to break into more hiccups, and then he tickles his own nose with a feather until he finally sneezes the hiccups away. Read in line with the notion of comedy discussed in the *Philebus*, this incident might be taken as derisive toward another of the speakers. Are we to interpret this as making a mockery of Aristophanes—in retaliation, perhaps, for his jests about Socrates in the *Clouds*—or should we read this as a comedic undermining of the pompous speech Eryximachus is simultaneously delivering?

The hiccups need not be read as simple mockery of any of these figures, but neither are these possibilities entirely left behind. The hiccups do indeed deliver a certain amount of comic justice to Aristophanes, deny Eryximachus's speech the gravitas he clearly intends, and alter the speaking order. But the hiccups and their ensuing remedies, seem more than simply satire; indeed, this episode can alternately and easily be read as slapstick. Nor can the significance of the hiccups be relegated to their consequences on the speaking order. This section asks whether listening a bit more closely to Aristophanes's hiccups might not uncover overlooked meanings in Plato's comic moments. This curious little incident instead casts light on Plato as a writer of what is comical in addition to the humorless philosophy that tends to be attributed to him.

At the outset, it might be held that this could be all there is to this little incident: a simple, innocuous moment of play for comic relief, to be left aside for more serious matters. This assumes that serious matters are decidedly not comic, and that an incident with significant consequences for the dialogue remains, nonetheless, itself insignificant. As Taylor sums up the significance of the hiccups: "There is nothing here which calls for a 'serious' explanation."[9] The comment is important in how dismissive it is of Aristophanes's malady as being any more than a "small joke" filling a gap between speeches. The "small joke" is opposed to any "serious" explanation. Logos belongs on the side of the serious (unlike what the *Cratylus* has been shown to indicate). If such a perspective were limited to Taylor, it would hardly be worth mentioning, but it is not. Why do we commonly assume the comedic to be superficial or to lack meaning? And what if, in this instance, we are wrong?

Recognizing literary and dramatic dimensions of the dialogues as, at least potentially, philosophically meaningful offers a starting point from which to begin to answer this second question. Bury points out that Apollodorus had only been asked for the *logoi* spoken at the banquet (172b, 173e), but offers instead a full account of the evening's dramatic incidents, an indication that we are meant to pay attention to both.[10] Laughter is interlaced throughout.[11] Socrates readily displays a sense of humor appropriate to the occasion, jokingly referring to Homer (174a, 174b), and punning on the names of Agathon (175c–e) and Gorgias (198c).[12] Apollodorus points out his own pun on Pausanias's name (185c). Alcibiades's arrival is in keeping with this tone, as already discussed. Alcibiades uses comic imagery to portray Socrates and builds to a comical accusation of hubris, both of which operate on the simultaneous distinction and confusion of body and soul. The laughter of Aristophanes's hiccups, I contend, operates consistently with this, and this consistency supports rereading the role of the body and the Dionysian in the dialogue. Taking the *Symposium*'s laughter—both actual outbursts of laughing and humor, more broadly, within it—"seriously" prompts a reevaluation of the significance of the body and the Dionysian in philosophical eros.

Arieti deems them "the world's most annotated case of hiccups."[13] Their frequent mention in secondary literature tends toward understanding the significance of the hiccups in terms of their effects on the speaking order. Friedländer claims that the order's interruption underscores the significance of the speaking order and points to its culmination in Socrates.[14] Howland stresses the alteration of the speaking order, and how this anticipates similar interruptive exchanges of dramatic voices, just as the entrance of Alcibiades interrupts Aristophanes's objection to Socrates's speech.[15] Clay underscores the hiccups' interruption of civil discourse, and particularly their effect on the speaking order, bringing the speeches of the comic and tragic poet into greater juxtaposition.[16] For Rosen, the hiccups represent the triumph of technicism over poetry despite their moving Aristophanes's speech one step further in the dialectical progression.[17] Quite to the contrary, Guthrie suggests the hiccups may "warn the reader that the order of speeches is not significant but accidental."[18] While recognizing the possibility that there may be no qualitative progression in the order of speeches, Lowenstam casts doubt on Guthrie's claim that it is the role of the hiccups to indicate this. Indeed, the hiccups would seem to be a remarkably inefficient device with which to signal merely that something is insignificant.[19]

While a comprehensive understanding may very well need to account for the hiccups' effects on the speaking order, their significance need not be relegated to such effects.[20] Nor must an assessment of the hiccups' significance begin with their effects on the order. Doing so implies that it could have been anything else that had these effects on the speaking order, and the question remains largely unanswered as to why it is the hiccups that are given this power. I propose instead to begin with a focus on what specifically is given the power to alter the order: the benign, corporeal malady of hiccups, and I will suggest that the hiccups comically illustrate the power of something that has been neglected and underappreciated throughout the discussion of eros—the body. It is the body that interrupts the order and moves Aristophanes's speech forward, a speech that proceeds to ground eros in the body. If there is a qualitative progression of speeches, then it is even more important to recognize that it is Aristophanes's body that—however inadvertently—propels his speech up the order, and it is Aristophanes' speech that attributes positive worth to the body in eros.

The body, although maligned or even left out of some accounts of eros, has a curious and dramatic way of reinserting itself back into the discussion by way of Aristophanes's hiccups. In doing so, it simultaneously alters the order of speeches and moves Aristophanes's speech one position closer to the last or uppermost (*eschatos*). Paralleled by the play for position on the couches, these transpositions are significant in what they suggest regarding the physical dimensions of eros and how we are to value these. Read together with the content of Aristophanes's encomium and the transpositions they induce, these hiccups are a playful foregrounding not only of the body, but also of the dramatic action that underpins the dialogue itself. Aristophanes's definition of eros as a "desire for wholeness" (192e) refers to physical wholeness, though not a "mere union of sexual passion," because the souls of each also desire one another (192c). In his positive valuation of the body, Aristophanes diverges considerably from the speeches preceding his.

The role of the body is at issue in the content of the preceding speeches as well. While Phaedrus praises eros for its instrumental value in cultivating virtue in lovers and beloveds (180a), Pausanias splits eros into heavenly and common forms, the latter of which he associates with the body and women (180d–81d). He states that it is most noble "when one loves the noblest and best youths, even if they are uglier [*aischious*] than the others" (182d). Pausanias esteems the person pursuing a common love as "worthless, because he loves the body [*tou sōmatos*] instead of the soul [*tēs psuchēs*]" (183e). When Alcibiades exhibits precisely such love for one who, according to his own description, is uniquely virtuous even if "uglier than the others," he is met with laughter (222c). This laughter—one of two explicit episodes in the dialogue—exposes the earlier speakers' pretensions to the noble forms of love by showing how ridiculous such attraction would appear, as it does in Alcibiades's speech. As it was shown to do in the *Cratylus*, laughing exposes pretension, and in this case, it is self-reflective laughter.

Several interpretations attempt to make sense of why it is hiccups that interrupt the speaking order. Arieti points out that the hiccups allow Eryximachus to display his power as a physician, a power diminished comically, perhaps, by comparison to that of Diotima, who postponed plague in Athens for a decade (201d).[21] Halper reads the hiccups and their cure as refuting Eryximachus's (and other prior speakers') debauched understanding of the physicality of love by attributing to the bodily a positive value.[22] Halper sees the hiccups as ridiculing these earlier encomiasts, pointing out the speakers' foolishness in dismissing the corporeal. In conjunction with Halper's reading, I will attempt to show that the hiccups expose the pretensions of the earlier encomiasts to a nobler, more disembodied sort of eros than they truly believe in, but the hiccups' significance need not be relegated to a negative, mocking function. Their power on the speaking order accords the body a potentially positive role in philosophical eros, a role that is reinforced by the content of Aristophanes's transposed encomium.

The hiccups might be read as a dramatic device, inserted so as to affect this order of speeches, which they do in fact alter. But if affecting the order of speeches were the main purpose of introducing the hiccups, one could not help but wonder again at such a thorough lack of authorial economy.[23] Plato could easily have swapped Aristophanes's and Eryximachus's positions on the couches at the outset, thereby beginning with the revised order of speeches, and so maintained a more solemn orderliness within the dialogue, assuming that such solemnity and order were indeed what he was after. This is not to say that the transposition of speeches is insignificant, but rather that this effect cannot be the *only* reason why the hiccups occur.

Indeed, inasmuch as the ordering of speeches is taken to be significant, the hiccups have two important consequences: they move Aristophanes's speech to a central position, and so also, one position closer to the uppermost. What affects this transposition of speeches in the dialogue is not any orderly, metaphysical necessity; it is physical, disorderly chance. Support for the significance of this order might be gleaned from the explicit discussion of it at the beginning and end of the dialogue. Toward the end, a playful quarrel breaks out among Alcibiades, Agathon, and Socrates over the seating arrangement, namely, over who gets to sit by Agathon. The order of speeches proceeds from left to right, beginning with Phaedrus. This is the same order that the remaining imbibers—Agathon, Aristophanes, and Socrates—drink from (that is, left to right) at the dialogue's end, after revelers burst in on the party. If eros is ultimately not at all corporeal, then why should whom anyone sits next to matter? Taking the *Symposium*'s laughter "seriously" brings into relief a greater role played by the body and Dionysian elements, as we will see.

To understand the hiccups, one might ask whether this is an instance of derisive laughter, in which a target is ridiculed. Aristophanes himself, Eryximachus, and Pausanias each present such a possibility. We will discuss each briefly, in turn. If Aristophanes is the butt of the joke, as has been suggested by a number of commentators,[24] the hiccups can be read as no more than what Aristotle deems "ridiculous [*to geloion*]" namely "a mistake or deformity not productive of pain or harm to others."[25] The hiccups may simply be a harmless source of fun at Aristophanes's expense, comparable to the case of cramps Aristophanes assigns to one of his own characters while his wife is assembling Athenian women to overthrow male rule in *Ecclesiazusae*.[26] After all, it is Aristophanes's scathing satire of Socrates that presents philosophers, and for that matter, philosophy, as proper subjects of ridicule. What delicious irony, then, to subject Aristophanes to such a corporeal malady as he subjects his own characters.

Aristophanes plays the joke off, however, as though it were on Eryximachus, which Eryximachus recognizes, in saying: "Do you think you can make me a target and get away with it, Aristophanes?" (189b6–7). Eryximachus and his medical account of love have been read, notably by Schleiermacher, as the joke's target.[27] The hiccups undermine the haughty speech that Eryximachus delivers while Aristophanes attempts a variety of cures. The hiccups may be a pun on Eryximachus's very name, which means "belch battler."[28] Although not described any further, the cures could hardly have been ignored by those present, particularly when delivered by so ostentatious a character. If the *Symposium* were staged, this scene would constitute a comedic interlude.

If love is that of repletion and evacuation, as Eryximachus posited, then a sneeze might well offer a base illustration of Eryximachus's speech. The tone here need not be one of mockery. Indeed the word used for repletion also connotes the process of childbirth.[29] Eryximachus's claims about eros anticipate those of Diotima. To take Diotima's claims as a culmination in the quality of speeches means to take earlier speeches as, perhaps less developed, but nonetheless significant contributions. Eryximachus is undoubtedly pompous—as evidenced by his evaluation of his own speech as conclusive, leaving only a few gaps for Aristophanes and later speakers to fill, but his speech need not simply be dismissed.

Pausanias represents another possible satirical target.[30] The party has decided to substitute indulgence in speeches for that in wine at this symposium.[31] Aristophanes, who has not imbibed, cannot have contracted hiccups from excessive drink, but due to, as is described, "overeating or something else" (185c7-8). Overindulgence in speeches is the implied cause. The speech immediately prior to the hiccupping would be that of Pausanias, whose verbose encomium on Athenian customs may be the culprit. What was it in his speech that Aristophanes might have overindulged in?

Pausanias's speech presents eros of bodies as being for the sake of, and thus secondary to, moral education.[32] Diotima will take this devaluation of the body yet further in suggesting the highest step on the ladder to involve the contemplation of beauty entirely disembodied, or "not contaminated with human flesh" (211e). So why the hiccups? After Pausanias speaks, Aristophanes's body manages to remind us of what is being neglected and denigrated. The body has a dramatic way of reasserting its importance in the discussion by forestalling Aristophanes's speech and suggesting the kind of disembodied philosophical dialogues discussed in the *Phaedo* to be impossible. To the extent that we, the interpreters, then ignore what is happening "off-stage," we too neglect consideration of the body. But if Pausanias is the target, Aristophanes's hiccups would seem to be an affectation, feigned for the sake of showing disapproval of Pausanias's speech, a reading that appears, as Bury puts it, "far-fetched and improbable."[33]

The notion of comedy attributed to the *Philebus*, as based on feelings of superiority and malice, however slight here, might be brought to bear on this reading. To read the comedy involved in Aristophanes's case of hiccups as malicious, as Socrates's statements in the *Philebus* would have us do, may square with any of these targets. But to do so seems to ignore the tone of this drinking party: a jovial, friendly and playful symposium. This is not the setting of the early *Republic*, the *Protagoras*, or the *Ion* in which Socrates's opponent is identified expressly and the antagonism made clear in the form of rhetorical jousts. There may be *agon* here, but antagonism is harder to locate. Socrates does not expose possible contradictions within, and absurd consequences to, Phaedrus's naïve opening speech (nor does the format enable him to do so). The purpose of the hiccups cannot be exclusively to mock one of these speakers for, as Rüchert and Bury argue, "such rude antics seem out of place of so convivial a setting."[34] Such an interpretation, frequent though it may be today, is at odds with how the hiccups were read in antiquity.

Ancient interpreters consistently read the hiccups as playful and comical, rather than in any sense malicious.[35] Plutarch reads the entirety of Aristophanes's speech as a form of comic entertainment devised by Plato, who ". . . brought in Aristophanes's discourse of love, as a comedy, into his entertainment; and at the last, as it were drawing all the curtains, he shows a scene of the greatest variety imaginable—Alcibiades drunk, frolicking, and crowned."[36] What follows is "pleasant raillery" among Aristophanes and Socrates, and "facetious raillery" amongst the interlocutors generally.[37] The tone of the symposium itself is one of "extreme pleasantness" of discourse.[38]

Ancient readings of the *Symposium* underscore its Dionysian elements. Athenaeus describes several points in various symposia deserving of censure. Plato's *Symposium*, he describes, ". . . is full of sneerers [*muktēristōn*] mocking [*tōthazontōn*] each other . . ."[39] He claims Plato is inconsistent for putatively banishing the poets and oratory from "Plato's" ideal city in the *Republic* and yet using poetic flourishes and devices in his own dialogues. His example is Aristophanes's comical hiccups and cures effected in the *Symposium*: "As for Plato—I ignore the man who was troubled by hiccoughs and cured by gargling water, as well as by tickling his nose with a piece of straw to make him sneeze" (*Sym.* 185d–e), and claims that Plato "wanted to mock and ridicule [*kōmōdein gar ēthele kai diasturein*]—he makes fun of [*chleuazei*] Agathon's balanced clauses and antitheses" (*Sym.* 194e–7e).[40] He is puzzled as to why this is coming from the same author who is alleged to expel poetry. Athenaeus uses the word *kōmōdein* to describe Aristophanes's hiccups and cures. Although he notes the symposiasts' "mocking" and "making fun" of each other (without specifying targets), neither of the terms used imply maliciousness.

Olympiodorus understands the tone of Aristophanes's hiccups as playful, good-natured comedy with no hint of spite or malice. Plato, Olympiodorus tells us, took "great delight in Aristophanes, the comic writer, and in Sophron."[41] Olympiodorus reports on the comic treatment of Aristophanes in the *Symposium*, writing that Plato "made fun of [*ekōmōdēse*] Aristophanes in his dialogue [called] the *Banquet*, as having derived some benefit in the style of comedy. For after making him hymn the god of Love, he introduces him as seized during [the conversation] with hiccups, and unable to finish the hymn."[42] But Olympiodorus's interpretation of Plato also offers an oblique possibility as to how the body, comically excluded in the *Symposium*, can bear significance.

Several points concerning the significance of the body can be culled from Olympiodorus's interpretation. Taking Alcibiades's image of Socrates as a Silenus "seriously," as will be done in the second half of this chapter, presents the temptation of discarding the ugly, embodied shell to leave us with the divine, golden treasures on the inside. Like the discussion concerning the morality of suicide in the *Phaedo*, one's body might be likened to "a kind of prison," as Socrates suggests, in which one's soul dwells under the guardianship of the gods, a comparison suggesting a divisible and hierarchical relation of soul to body (*Phaedo* 62). But Socrates introduces this argument as one originating in the mysteries, and the prison analogy is hardly the stuff of religious secret. Olympiodorus takes this cue to suggest an alternate, mythologically grounded reading in which human bodies do not so much comprise a prison for our souls, but rather, belong to Dionysus, and because of this, suicide is unacceptable. As Olympiodorus suggests, Dionysus, a successor to Zeus, was dismembered and consumed by the Titans. When Zeus struck the Titans down with thunderbolts, he used the vapors and soot arising from the corporeal conflagration to make the matter from which humans are formed.

Our bodies, for Olympiodorus, are thus comprised of Dionysus's flesh, and sacred because of this.[43]

On Olympiodorus's reading, Socrates is not denigrating the body so much as alluding to its religious and, specifically, Dionysian significance. If he is right, and as will be argued in regards to the image of Socrates-as-Silenus, the body cannot and ought not to be discarded in favor of the soul. Moreover, if he is right, the body retains a distinctly Dionysian element linking it at a compositional level to the god of comedy, tragedy, and regenerative growth. It is this element and any significance it may hold that are ignored when we read the dialogue solemnly. It is the possibility of such a reading that is interrupted by the bodily disruptions of a comic poet's hiccups and their outlandish series of cures.

Aristophanes's hiccups are an eruption of the physical into the metaphysical, and increasingly bodiless, discussion. As interruptions of the flow of breathing, they are simultaneously interruptions of the flow of logos, or dialogue. Speeches cannot continue without physical cooperation. Aristophanes's hiccups, as Plochmann reads them, "betoken a temporary overturn of the order established."[44] If we assume that there is a qualitative progression in the speaking order, then we must credit the body—namely, Aristophanes's—with forcing the rearrangement. If we assume no such progression, then the question becomes one as to why this order is mentioned at all, let alone repeatedly. Bodily positions create this order: ". . . each of us, starting on the left, should recite the fairest praise of Eros that he can, and Phaedrus should be the first to begin, inasmuch as he is lying on the head couch and is also the father of the argument (177d2-5). This amounts to a humorous refutation of Eryximachus because it suggests a positive value for the debauched physical love that Eryximachus aims to dismiss; for an itch provokes not only a sneeze, but also, as Socrates regularly claims, sex."[45] Eryximachus's speech need not be the only focus here. The broader suggestion is that seemingly disorderly, inadvertent, and comical functions of the body—itches, sneezes, and, I submit, hiccups—establish order. Similarly in Aristophanes's myth, Apollo is said to turn around each human's head "so that when it looked at its own scar the person might be more orderly" (190e). The body thus serves as a reminder of human nature and our tendency to excessiveness, and in this way, the body serves to maintain order.

The encomium Aristophanes delivers, once he is able to, further shades this. While Aristophanes expressly denies that pleasure alone is at the heart of eros (192c4–d2), he presents eros as love of the whole, and more specifically, a physical whole. His mutated, bifurcated bodies desire completion though union with their other halves. But where Diotima's love of the whole will be disembodied, Aristophanes's is very much corporeal. Eros, for Aristophanes, "collects the halves of our original nature" (191d), bodily wholes to which we can only temporarily return. Read as a comedic interlude as well, the fifth Book of the *Republic* parallels this in that the comedy seems based on Socrates's ignoring of the body. The Guardians' bodily skills, gymnastics for the sake of the soul rather than the body, strict communism (in which the body alone cannot be shared) and the differences in body among genders exercising naked together are all left out of the account of the city.[46] Comedy is triggered not only by the body, as is evidenced by several millennia of jokes on inadvertent bodily functions—including hiccups, but also by the neglect of the body. Thales's falling into a well as he is gazing heavenward is such an instance. Forgetfulness of the body is also self-forgetfulness.

Several points emerge from this case of the hiccups that will be brought to bear on what follows. First, the significance of the body is, at the very least, brought into question through the hiccups, which underscore what has been left out of the discussion of eros and how the symposiasts have forgotten themselves. This potential valuation of the physical will come into play both in how Socrates is described—an amalgam of ugly body and beautiful soul—and in Alcibiades's dramatic confession of the sort of psychic love earlier speakers held up as an ideal, at which they now laugh in practice. Second, the hiccups scene presents the sort of lowbrow laughter typical of both Attic Old Comedies and of satyr plays. Such laughter sets the tone for what is to come. Both points belie the *Symposium*'s infusion with a Dionysian spirit.

Socrates as Satyr

Aristophanes's hiccups and Alcibiades's arrival are linked by both of the dialogue's explicit mentions of laughter and several similarities. Both constitute interruptions and entail modifications of the speaking order, if we count Alcibiades's as an encomium. It is precisely when Aristophanes is about to respond to the anachronism in Socrates's speech (214c) that he is once more interrupted, this time not by his body but by the entrance of Alcibiades.[47] The scenes are comically linked. For Bury, "The comic relief which, in the earlier scenes, had been supplied by Aristophanes, as *gelōtopoios*, is now supplied by Alcibiades."[48] Aristophanes offers such relief in comic language and outlandish themes (such as playing hopscotch and slicing eggs) within his speech, as well as the comic circumstances surrounding his speech, most notably, his case of the hiccups (*lugx*, a phonetic rendering of the occurrence). Alcibiades offers comic relief by way of a comical accusation of *hubris* and satyric imagery. The comparison to a satyr reveals in Socrates and his *logoi* an inherent bifurcation as well as an ineliminable link to comedy. Inasmuch as they constitute wholes, Socrates and his *logoi* cannot undergo bisection, as do Aristophanes's original humans. Although Socrates, like these mythical prototypes and like many satyrs, stands accused of hubris,[49] the very accusation reveals a comical confusion of soul and body, and an exposure of the hypocrisy of earlier encomiasts. Despite the reminder from Aristophanes's hiccups and his corporeal encomium of eros, the body is nonetheless forgotten.

Alcibiades's entrance returns to the symposium what has been uncharacteristically kept out of it: music, flute girls, heavy drinking, and an acute Dionysian presence. Alcibiades shows up uninvited and drunk, purportedly there to crown Agathon for his dramatic victory the night before. He appears in the guise of Dionysus, with garlands of ivy and violets in his hair, flute girls in tow, and revelers all about him.[50] Seating himself next to Agathon, he recoils in surprise to find Socrates on the same couch, rebuking Socrates for this and asking why Socrates is seated next to the beautiful Agathon, rather than next to another "intentional jokester" (213c) such as Aristophanes. Socrates is a comic figure for Alcibiades, but one who nonetheless prompts Alcibiades immediately to crown Socrates for his constant triumph over all others in *logoi* (213e). In lieu of an encomium in honor of Eros, Alcibiades's impromptu speech, at the suggestion of Eryximachus (214d), will concern what Alcibiades appears most erotically preoccupied with—the figure of Socrates. His speech is neither unmitigated praise nor does it render Socrates a "laughingstock" as Socrates fears (214e).[51] It presents him instead as a serio-comic figure, simultaneously ugly and beautiful, heroic and comic, virtuous and hubristic, and it does so by comparing Socrates's incongruous nature to that of a satyr.

Alcibiades begins with the claim that Socrates's physical resemblance to satyrs is indisputable. Alcibiades begins, "Now, this is the way I will attempt to praise Socrates, gentlemen, by means of images [*di' eikonōn*].

He'll probably think that it's to make him a laughingstock [*geloiotera*], but the image aims at truth. It's not a joke [*ou tou geloiou*]" (215a). Alcibiades begins with an image and declares it not to be a joke, much akin to how Socrates begins his defense in the *Apology*. The image Alcibiades uses is a Silenus statue: "what he's most similar to are the Sileni that sit in the statue-makers' shops, the ones artisans make that hold shepherd's pipes or flutes, which when pulled apart are found to have statues of gods inside . . . especially like the Satyr Marsyas. That your form is similar to theirs, Socrates, you yourself can't deny" (215a–b). But not only does Socrates resemble the satyrs in form and body, he resembles them in behavior. Alcibiades tells Socrates, "You behave outrageously [*hubristēs*], don't you? . . . And you're a flute-player, aren't you? In fact, you're a more amazing one than Marsyas. He used instruments to bewitch human beings with the power that emanated from his mouth, as do those who play his tunes today . . . The only way you differ from him is that, while you do the same thing he does, you do it using plain words [*philois logois*] without instruments [*aneu organōn*] (*Symposium* 215c–d). Socrates can only be compared to a satyr, a mythical creature that is half goat, half human, and semidivine.

Alcibiades's warning aside, we are in well-trodden, comical territory and it is territory that Plato's dialogues regularly venture into. Usher notes the comical precedent of Alcibiades's comparison: "to compare a man to an animal *di' eikonōn*, as Alcibiades does in his speech, is a familiar trope of Old Comedy."[52] Socrates's physical resemblance to satyrs is referred to by various sources, including Socrates himself. Although there are some geographical and historical variations regarding their appearance, satyrs are routinely described as snub-nosed with protruding eyes and receding hairlines. In the *Theaetetus*, Theodorus describes the title character to Socrates as "not beautiful at all, but is rather like you, snub-nosed, with eyes that stick out; though these features are not quite so pronounced in him" (*Theaetetus* 143e). Socrates's snub-nose is described at length in the beauty contest in Xenophon, where he is also said to have a big mouth and thick lips.[53] These features are said to be like those of a satyr, a visual similarity to which both Critobulus and Socrates will themselves refer. When Socrates questions whether Critobulus thinks himself more beautiful than Socrates, Socrates says, "Of course . . . otherwise I should be uglier than any Silenus in the satyr-plays."[54] Socrates himself later recognizes that "the Naiads, who are goddesses, are mothers of the Sileni, who resemble me more than you."[55]

Socrates is portrayed regularly as having a comic exterior, whether due to his unattractiveness or his resemblance to comic masks and satyrs. Artistic renderings of Socrates visually make the connection between Socrates and satyrs. Arguably, such renderings themselves may be based on these physical descriptions of Socrates in Plato and Xenophon, making any "evidence" they provide potentially circular. Regardless, the depictions visually underscore the similarities between Socrates and satyrs. Details other than those suggested in Platonic and Xenophonic works also support the comic depiction of Socrates. Typically, Socrates is shown already at an advanced age. In a relief from Pompeii discussed by Amelung, Socrates is shown leaning on a stick.[56] The bronze shows an elderly, satyr-like Socrates listening intently to a seated female figure (presumed to be Diotima). Beyond suggesting senescence, the motif of using a cane also implies the onset of physical infirmity, dependency, and feebleness. Socrates is said to have stood up in the audience attending a performance of *The Clouds* once the character wearing his comical face mask came onstage, which has been read as his illustrating the likeness the mask bears to his own face. For Usher, this opening by Aristophanes is a contemptuous rebuke of Strepsiades, one in which Aelian has found parallels to Silenus's haughty disdain for Midas, a parody that would seem to emphasize Socrates's satyr-like visage.[57] All of these would have been considered comical in antiquity.

Beneath Socrates's comical exterior lies a "serious" interior, but this claim, seeming to imply a spatial distinction, must be heavily qualified. Alcibiades's speech about Socrates in Plato's *Symposium* is a lengthier and explicit account of Socrates as a satyr or Silenus. After pointing out that Socrates *looks* undeniably like a satyr, Alcibiades says the resemblance goes well beyond the physical. Alcibiades extends the comparison to Socrates's *logoi*:

> his arguments [*logoi*] are most like those Sileni that can be opened up. If anyone is willing to listen to Socrates' arguments, they at first appear to be quite ridiculous [*panu geloioi*]. They're covered over on the outside with words [*onomata*] and phrases [*rhēmata*] that are like the hide of an outrageous Satyr [*saturou . . . hubristou*], for he talks about donkeys and pack-asses, about blacksmiths, cobblers, and tanners, and throughout it all he appears always to be saying the same things, so that an inexperienced and ignorant

> person would take everything he says as a joke [*logōn katagelaseien*]. However, anyone who sees his arguments opened up and gets inside them will find in the first place that they are the only arguments that make sense and that they are the most divine, that they contain within themselves many marvelous images of virtue, and that when they are fully expanded they deal with everything that a person who wants to be good and beautiful [*kalō kagathō*] needs to consider. (221d–22a)

Socrates's *logoi*, just like he himself, exhibit this comical beast-human-god structure. As Alcibiades suggests, these *logoi* are themselves satyr-like. Given the turn to *logoi* and the application of the incongruities to the *logoi* themselves, spatial distinctions such as between one's internal and external self become inapplicable. Socrates's *logoi* themselves exhibit this sort of incongruity. They are simultaneously comical and of profound substance, with the capacity to elevate to divinity.

Socrates's use of lowbrow examples from common trades and the animal world is already familiar to us from several dialogues. In the *Apology*, Socrates prefaces an argument concerning mules with an appeal to the jury not to "create a disturbance, if I proceed in my usual manner" (*Apology* 27b), suggesting that he is entirely aware of the agitation caused by his provocatively comic *logoi*. The argument, comparing mules to daimones, horses to gods, and pack-asses to humans, has been considered so outlandishly comical by some translators, as to have been left out entirely.[58] But such comic *logoi*, as Alcibiades claims, are entirely consistent and even typical for Socrates who, in the same dialogue, swears "by the dog" (*Apology* 22a) and compares himself to a gadfly stinging the rump of a lazy horse—Athens, including the jurors determining Socrates's fate (*Apology* 30e–31b). The comical veneer of Socratic *logoi* is itself intended to do some of the stinging. Crude, base, and surprising as it is, the veneer can provoke Socrates's audience into a response. As discussed in chapter 2, Socrates asks whether doing something scientifically is like cutting leather, and associates the science of happiness with the art of playing checkers, to an outraged, offended, and thoroughly aristocratic Critias (*Charmides* 173e–74b). The "usual manner" of Socrates is often one that gets a rise out of his audience, like the stinging of the horse fly. Socratic *logoi* are beautiful images of virtue covered over in the shaggy, base hides of satyrs. As such they, and he, are comical.

Although Alcibiades's comparison of Socrates to a satyr has been commented on in the literature, what seems to have been neglected is how deeply the comparison pervades the entirety of his speech.[59] That Alcibides begins and ends with the analogy is explicit, but the characteristics Alcibiades chooses to praise Socrates with are direct, albeit inverse, comparisons with satyrs. Socrates is said to be incomparable to other humans; the only valid comparison that Alcibiades says one can make is to the Sileni and satyrs (221d). Whereas satyrs are salacious pursuers of beautiful youths, Socrates is said to appear "fixated on beautiful young men" (216d) and yet he resists physical consummation (219d).[60] Satyrs are wine-loving and easily intoxicated. Socrates, we are told, does not desire wine, can outdrink anyone else when compelled to do so, and yet has never been seen to be drunk (220a). While satyrs are characteristically skittish, Alcibiades depicts Socrates as having superhuman endurance, being steadfast (220a–d), and particularly brave (220d–e).[61] Alcibiades's description of Socrates thus also diverges sharply from characteristics typical of satyrs and, in this way, forms an inverse image of satyrs. If these virtues and characteristics may be what Alcibiades reveals as the divine treasures inside Socrates, then the satyr image pervades Alcibiades's encomium. The question then becomes why Alcibiades stresses the comparison of Socrates and Sileni or satyrs, given the inverse portion of his comparison.

Satyrs themselves enact such reversals. Traditionally, a satyr "plays in a different key, with the displacement, distortion, and reversal of what constitutes the world and culture of men . . ."[62] Lissarrague calls them "antitypes of the Athenian male citizenry," stresses the "inverted anthropology" they represent, and deems this an "anthropology of laughter."[63] In modern psychological terms, satyrs are manifestations of the Id and thoroughly lacking in Superego, a reversal of the priorities expected of an Athenian citizen. Socrates is the virtuous satyr, one who distorts and reverses the world of Athenian men as well as their mythology.

Satyrs are complex figures: crude yet wise, beastly yet divine. The reversals satyrs bring about are a part of their mischievousness, and we see both in the figure of Socrates, as presented in the *Symposium*. Socrates's association with satyrs raises several points of comparison to be examined. Satyrs are tricksters who create a benign sort of mischief, often in the form of reversals, and yet are credited with a superhuman wisdom. The plays in which they are depicted make heavy use of myth, particularly by parodying it. The tone of satyr play thus combines heroism and comedy, seriousness and play, and the vulgar and the sacred.

There are two types of satyrs and, more strictly, *silenoi*, both of which I refer to as satyrs: those associated with Pan, including Marsyas, depicted as having a horned head, the torso of a human, and the bottom half of a goat; and those said to have descended from Silenus, depicted with snub-noses, and oftentimes, pointy ears, and equine tails. Satyrs are seen as *daimones*, vulgar hedonists, seemingly immortal, generally close companions of a god, and yet unconcerned with the status of the gods.[64] Seaford describes the satyr as "an ambiguous creature, cruder than a man and yet somehow wiser, combining mischief with wisdom and animality with divinity."[65] As such, satyrs are in an odd position in relation to mortals. King Midas seeks wisdom otherwise inaccessible to him by catching Silenus in his garden.[66] At the same time, as creatures of nature, they belong fully neither to the realms of gods, nor to that of mortals. They stand instead at the very beginnings of civilization as *prōtoi euretai*, or inventors of culture.[67] In a categorization of styles of dancing as either peaceful or bellicose, the Athenian in Plato's *Laws* describes the dancing of satyric drama, here linked expressly with a ritual context, as *ou politikon*, or not of the polis[68] (815c). Nietzsche expands on this, seeing satyrs as having "expressed nature in a rude, uncultivated state," and so constituted "man's true prototype, an expression of his highest and strongest aspirations," in which "archetypal man was cleansed of the illusion of culture, and what revealed itself was authentic man, the bearded satyr jubilantly greeting his god."[69]

Satyr plays, like comedies, seem to have broken the fourth wall, incorporating or addressing their audiences in the performances. Nietzsche dissolves any opposition of audience and chorus in satyr plays. Citing ancient Greek theater's architectural structures of rising, concentric arcs about the stage, Nietzsche writes, "Audience and chorus were never set over against each other: all was one grand chorus of dancing, singing satyrs, and of those who let themselves be represented by them."[70] Horace's claim that spectators, in a drunken and lawless mood, had just come observing the rites, supports Nietzsche's suggestion that the audience sees themselves in the satyr chorus, a vision so powerful as to "blur the actors' sense of the 'reality' of cultured spectators ranged row on row about him."[71] Such Dionysiac *ekstasis*, literally in the Greek "standing outside of oneself," or "projecting oneself outside oneself and then acting as though one had really entered another body, another character," is the basic dramatic phenomenon for Nietzsche.[72] The audience may thus be part of the performance. It will become apparent how this is the case for the *Symposium*'s audience.

How Alcibiades's portrayal of Socrates distorts the values of Athenian citizenry can be seen in how Socrates differs from Alcibiades himself. Whereas Alcibiades represents traditional, typical, Athenian virtues such as physical beauty and charisma, Socrates challenges these with his own ugliness and offensiveness. Ugly on the outside, Socrates, per Alcibiades's description, is extraordinarily beautiful on the inside; Alcibiades, a physically beautiful youth, is of highly dubious moral integrity, at best, and this event, occasioning the eve of his alleged desecration of the Herms, underscores this. Socrates recognizes this inequality when he describes Alcibiades's attempt to engage in an erotic relationship with Socrates as an exchange of "gold for bronze" (218e). The impassivity of Socrates contrasts sharply with the emotional volatility of Alcibiades. Socrates's interior exceeds his exterior, and in this way the image of Socrates as a satyr is a reversal of Alcibiades, whose exterior greatly exceeds his interior.

Satyrs are ambiguous figures, mediating between several pairs of opposites. Seaford describes the satyr as "an ambiguous creature, cruder than a man and yet somehow wiser, combining mischief with wisdom and animality with divinity."[73] On this ambiguity, Seaford writes, "On the one hand they are men and boys, dressed up for frolics at the festival; and on the other hand they are, within the *thiasos*, the attendants of the god and the initiated custodians of a solemn and secret tradition."[74] Socrates is just such a figure in the *Symposium*: washed and dressed for the occasion, and recounting his own initiation into the wisdom revealed by Diotima. Alcibiades suggests such religious initiation as well, indicating that all of those present have "taken part in the madness [*manias*] and Bacchanalian frenzy [*bakcheias*] of philosophy" but that the slaves ought to cover their ears before he reveals Socrates's deed (218b). If the satyr image is taken "seriously," as I am suggesting it ought to be, then the nature of Socrates cannot be allocated to either of his halves. His function as mediator between opposites must be taken into account as a key insight into who Socrates is, and thus also into the question of what philosophy is.[75]

For Nussbaum, Socrates is the embodiment of an ideal expressed by Diotima, representing the life, values, and knowledge of philosophical eros, a life removed from the turbulence of emotions, personal desire, and the volatility of the body.[76] Alcibiades, on the other hand, represents the life of humanity—tempestuous and corporeal. Socrates and philosophy are, in this way, "not fully human," but humanity and what it leads to are also terrifying.[77] Indeed, the Socrates described by Alcibiades,[78] unaffected by hunger, cold, bodily desire, wine, sleeplessness, and fear, is not fully human, but rather something above and below us at the same time. He is self-sufficient and utterly invulnerable, a "whole" who does not seem to desire his other half, pace Aristophanes (193a). And yet, as simultaneously heroic and comic, ugly and beautiful, superhuman and subhuman, neither is he a uniform whole. Satyr-like Socrates is two, almost irreconcilable halves at odds with one another and, in this way, a comic figure.[79] But the seemingly akrastic Alcibiades, torn between what he has learned from Socrates about pursuing a virtuous life, and the honor offered by the masses, is clearly bifurcated, limited, and deficient. The question then is one as to whom the comic figure really is—the satyr-like and self-sufficient Socrates, or Alcibiades and the rest of those representing "humanity," who are limited and deficient in what are, perhaps, less obvious ways.

Satyrs and satyr-plays are replete with trickery, scheming, and mischief.[80] It is thus not surprising to find that tricksters such as Odysseus, Hermes, and Sisyphus are recurrent characters in satyr plays. Such mischief and trickery need not indicate any perceived moral lapses. Sutton argues that "the morality of satyr plays is more relaxed than that of tragedy regarding trickery, which plays an important role in many satyr plays . . ."[81] Sutton claims that classical audiences would not have taken moral offense at the sort of mischief and trickery of, say, Odysseus's brutal revenge on Polyphemus in Euripides's *Cyclops*, as would be more typical of contemporary moral sensibilities. There is no textual censure of Odysseus's treatment of Polyphemus or of Silenus's trickery in the *Cyclops*, nor is Hermes in any way punished for stealing Apollo's cattle in Sophocles's *Ichneutae*.[82] Indeed, the *Ichneutae* ends happily, as is typical of satyr plays and of comedies, with the budding friendship between Hermes and Apollo.

Socrates plays the trickster role with some regularity. In the *Symposium*, he is accused by Alcibiades of having schemed (*diemēchanēsō*) to sit next to the most beautiful one in the room (213c).[83] Socrates creates further mischief regarding the seating order by suggesting that he will praise the person on his right, thus scheming his way to a seat between Alcibiades and Agathon (222e–23a). But the more substantive trick Socrates plays in the *Symposium* is what Alcibiades implies: Socrates reverses the roles of beloved (*erōmenos*) and lover (*erastēs*), and the mischief that this generates underlies the entirety of Alcibiades's speech. Alcibiades's self-professed purpose in offering this mitigated praise of Socrates is to warn Agathon and others of Socrates's deception at acting more like a beloved than a lover, something Alcibiades himself has apparently failed to recognize (222b). As we will see, Socrates is not guilty of hubris, understood as a classical Athenian audience in this context would have understood it; rather, he is guilty, as a satyr would be, of philosophical mischief.

Echoing what is appropriate to its content, Alcibiades's speech is, like a satyr play, serio-comic in tone and function. Socrates himself, in referring to Alcibiades's speech, deems it a "satyrical drama" (*drama . . . silēnikon*) (*Symposium* 222d).[84] Although Alcibiades expresses concern that his speech will be taken as a joke (215a) and insists that the image aims at the truth, Alcibiades's description of Socrates borrows directly from comedy, and shows Socrates to cut a comical figure. He quotes Aristophanes's *Clouds* to describe how, in the retreat from Delium, Socrates is said to have been " 'holding his head high and glancing from side to side' to use your phrase, Aristophanes" (*Symposium* 221b).[85] His portrayal of Socrates and the punch line his speech leads up to elicit laughter, and simultaneously contain moments of seriousness and tragedy, but the latter two have been addressed with some regularity by commentators, and require less further substantiation than my claim that there is substantial comedy in this as well.[86]

Alcibiades builds up expectations to his punch line in dramatic fashion. Alcibiades describes himself as "a drunken man" (214c) and "totally drunk" (215d) and couches his great revelation about Socrates with the saying that, "wine makes for truth when the servants are absent" (217e). With this, Alcibiades promises to reveal Socrates's "contemptuous deed" (*ergon huperēphanon*, 217e). *Huperēphanon* can mean contemptuous, arrogant, or haughty, but it also has a positive sense in which it means magnificent or splendid. Alcibiades expresses anger toward, as well as admiration for, Socrates, and such duplicity in the characterization of Socrates's deed may be intentional. Alcibiades is not done building up to his revelation. Describing philosophy as Dionysian, he warns that while all present have taken part "in the madness and Bacchanalian frenzy of philosophy . . . But you slaves and anyone else who is uninitiated and uncivilized, cover your ears very tightly" (218b). While the servants remain, they must brace themselves, like Odysseus's crew against the sirens, for what he is about to reveal about Socrates.

Like Midas attempting to ensnare Silenus for the sake of his special wisdom, Alcibiades tries to seduce Socrates for the sake of his wisdom. Having set himself on the task of "gratifying Socrates," so that "I would provide myself with the opportunity to hear everything he knew" (217a), Alcibiades repeatedly, and frustratingly fails to seduce his lover, who increasingly turns out to be more of a beloved. Alcibiades says that he thought that he had ". . . let loose my arrows, I thought I had smitten him. So, I stood up, and not letting him say anything further, I put my own cloak over him, since it was winter. Then I lay down, getting under his own worn garment, threw my arms around this truly daimonic [*daimoniō*] and amazing [*thaumastō*] man, and lay there the entire night. (And you can't say that I am lying about this, Socrates!)" (219b–c). But the night does not proceed according to Alcibiades's wishes.

Alcibiades clarifies just what impact the night has on him, and then puts the audience in a peculiar position. After "having slept with Socrates in a way that had no more significance than sleeping with a father or an older brother" (219d), Alcibiades claims that Socrates "disdainfully laughed [*katephronēsin kai kategelasen*] at my youthful good looks, in a quite outrageous manner [*hubrisen*]—and this was about something I thought was of real importance, gentlemen of the jury (for you are a jury, judging Socrates' arrogance [*huperēphanias*], and you know it!)" (219c). Alcibiades interrupts his own account to deem the audience a jury who judges Socrates's deed. We will see exactly what he has in mind by this later.

Between Socrates's laughter and his resistance to Alcibiades's charms, it is not surprising to find Alcibiades distraught: "I believed I had been dishonored [*ētimasthai*] but I also admired his nature [*phusin*]—his judiciousness and his courage [*sōphrosunēn kai andreian*] . . ." (219d). Alcibiades's response to Socrates is confused. Is Socrates "arrogant" or "marvelous" in having resisted Alcibiades? This, Alcibiades recounts, was one of the "times he treated me outrageously [*hubrisen*]" (222a). Alcibiades's revelation is met with laughter: "Some of the group laughed at [*gelōta*] Alcibiades's frankness [*parrēsia*] in saying this, because he seemed still to be in love [*erōtikōs echein*] with Socrates . . ." (222c). What exactly is so funny here?

Alcibiades's image of Socrates as a satyr further supports his accusation, and the call to judgment, of Socrates's hubris, an accusation that turns out to be effectively a joke.[87] According to Lissarrague, satyrical behavior "is almost always an excess or a transgression . . ."[88] Socrates's behavior and his endurance are indeed excessive, but Alcibiades also suggests him to be the model of *sōphrosynē*, the very opposite of hubris.[89] The contradiction is more apparent than real. It is tempting to read Alcibiades's accusation of hubris against Socrates as an accusation of moral viciousness but doing so may be misdirected. According to Dover, an accusation of hubris by a potential *erōmenos* against an *erastēs* would have implied rape, particularly in a context as erotically charged as this symposium.[90] Alcibiades accuses Socrates of hubris (219c), suggesting that the contemptuous (*huperēphanon*) deed (217e) he is building up to exposing will be some sort of transgressive erotic assault, and then finally reveals the source of his own dishonor: Socrates *in no way* took advantage of him (219c–d).[91] Alcibiades feels dishonored and violated by *not* having been violated. This revelation is met with laughter (*gelōta*) at Alcibiades for having said this in the way he did, and "because he still seemed to be in love with Socrates" (222c). Euripides's satyr play, *Cyclops*, pokes fun at Greek pederasty and the norms of Athenian beauty in pairing together a cyclops and a satyr.[92] The *Symposium* does something similar to this by pairing together a beautiful, younger, would-be-beloved with an elderly and ugly satyr—a would-be-lover. The salacious satyr, the active lover, in this case turns out to be a coy and reluctant *erōmenos*.

What would it have meant to be hubristic? Bury describes the *hubristēs*: "A man of strong sexual appetites, more shameless, importunate and headstrong in pursuit of their satisfaction than society regarded as acceptable, was *hubristēs*, and the man of opposite character, inclined to stop and think before acting in furtherance of his own short-term interests or appetites was *sōphrōn*, an invariably complimentary word which can be translated, according to context, as 'sensible,' 'careful,' 'disciplined,' 'law-abiding,' 'moral,' 'chaste,' 'frugal,' etc."[93] Socrates has shown which category he falls into in the *Charmides*, where his glance under Charmides's cloak leads to a long consideration of *sōphrosynē*. Bury notes that ". . . anyone who attached the highest importance to the satisfaction of his own bodily desires could reasonably be called *hubristēs*."[94] The emphasis on the importance of the body to eros is not without limits, and Alcibiades, who pursues physical consummation of psychic admiration, exceeds these limits. In this case, another reversal occurs: it is Alcibiades who is *hubristēs*, not Socrates.

The interlocutors laugh at Alcibiades's *parrēsia* (his frankness or openness) for more than just its excessive disclosure. Contrary to his warning, Alcibiades's revelation turns out to be a joke after all. He builds up his listeners' expectations, promising to reveal the most sordid details of Socrates's egregious act (Alcibiades's drunkenness only enhances these expectations), only to substitute a thoroughly unexpected revelation. He has, indeed, built up expectations, referring to Socrates's contemptuous deed (217e). Such buildup is a standard comical trick, called *para prosdokian*, or "contrary to expectation." It was used regularly by comedians, including Aristophanes, as a comic trick employing and then dashing the audience's expectation of what was about to be said.[95] Halper notes this parallel between Alcibiades's and Aristophanes's speeches: "Aristophanes is doing exactly the opposite of Alcibiades: whereas the latter led us to expect a sex scene in order to show us Socrates' virtue and, consequently, his own foolishness, Aristophanes draws on the expectations of noble love generated by previous speakers to show us the physical motivation and, consequently, the previous speaker's foolishness."[96] But there may be personal tragedy in the reversal for which Socrates is responsible.

A reversal of expectations is at the heart of why Alcibiades feels himself to have been dishonored. As has been argued by some, there is personal tragedy in this, but in keeping with the satyrical imagery and tone, it is also comical. The "contemptuous deed" Alcibiades has built up to is just the opposite of what was expected, and this is met with jovial (and not malicious) laughter (*gelōta*), at the punch line, as Edmonds calls it, of Alcibiades's speech.[97] Alcibiades has been led on, perhaps less so by Socrates himself, than by Alcibiades's own traditional expectations of a very *atopos* (215a, 221d) and untraditional man. The reversal goes further than this. Alcibiades says of Socrates's relationships with a number of young men, including himself: "this man deceived by acting more like a darling than a lover so that they adopted for themselves the role of lover" (222b). Alcibiades may feel genuinely humiliated by Socrates, but his suggestion here is that he himself is at least partly responsible, having let himself be deceived by the satyrical Socrates. But if Alcibiades is right, and Socrates's internal treasures are as beautiful as he claims, then Socrates seems an appropriate *erōmenos*. It is Socrates's aged, ugly, shaggy hide—his body, that prevents him from this role. Once again, the old man is playing the role of a youth to comic and mischievous effect. Socrates has tricked Alcibiades into acting the part of an *erastēs* to his own *erōmenos* and entirely blurred these roles in the process.[98]

The effect of, and perhaps the reason why, Socrates performs such reversals is implied in what Alcibiades claims: Socrates is prompting passive admirers to become active participants instead, even if his efforts frequently fail. But rather than becoming lovers of Socrates, Socrates is attempting to entice them into becoming lovers of wisdom. A defense against his failure to do so may lie in Alcibiades's claim that, in his heart, he knows Socrates is right about becoming a better person, "but then I go away, a slave to the honor given by the masses" (216b). Edmonds claims that this trick also applies to Socrates's relationships with Agathon and Aristodemus, as presented in the *Symposium*, and that the reversal breaks down these traditionally hierarchical relations to replace them with a philosophical reciprocity. Inasmuch as the beauty by which Socrates transforms himself into a beloved is a philosophical beauty, the activity such a reversal invites is philosophical activity. Alcibiades is exposed to this sort of mischief elsewhere. In the *Alcibiades Major*, Alcibiades predicts that he and Socrates are "going to change roles" in such a way that Alcibiades becomes the pedagogue and, Socrates, the pupil (135d–e).[99] He declares that because of the reversal, he will "start to cultivate justice in [him]self right now" (135e). The philosophical, and characteristically satyrical, reversal thus invites us into the doing of philosophy.

In addition to displaying mischief, satyr plays make significant use of mythology, often by parodying it. In *De Elocutione*, Demetrius describes satyr play as "playful tragedy."[100] What is funny about satyr play, according to Lissarrague, follows from its "recipe": ". . . take one myth, add satyrs, observe the result . . . The joke is one of incongruity."[101] Sutton describes the satyr play as "a genre devoted to farcical mythological travesty."[102] We see just such farcical spins on mythology in the *Symposium*. Silenus is said to have played a pedagogical role vis-à-vis Dionysus, and satyrs are frequently represented as educators.[103] Alcibiades, garlanded in the *Symposium* with ivy and violets, and followed by a trail of revelers, much like Dionysus, is either unable to learn or then the Socratic Silenus is unable to teach him anything enduring (216a).

Alcibiades's satyrical speech can be seen to parody Socrates's myth of the generation of Eros, from Penia and Poros.[104] The Sileni statues to which Alcibiades compares Socrates are empty and full simultaneously.

Like Eros, Socrates is such an amalgamation of resource (*poros*) and deficiency or need (*penia*), but in such a parody, Socrates would seem to play Poros. Alcibiades is compared with Penia, scheming to amend her deficiency by seducing Poros, or Socrates. Just as Penia lays down with the sleeping Poros, Alcibiades lays down beside the resting (but "certainly not" sleeping) Socrates to benefit from his wisdom (218b–d).[105] Agathon previously alluded to such benefits from touching one another in his demand that Socrates recline beside him, and Socrates has already lamented the thought, regretting that wisdom is not the sort of thing that, like water through a piece of yarn, flows from the fuller cup to the emptier (175c–e). Agathon responds that such claims about wisdom will be argued later, "when we'll use Dionysus as the judge" (175e).

Another candidate is the myth offered by Aristophanes. The satyr is a whole whose halves can neither be fused nor pulled apart. As such, the satyr image renders Aristophanes's myth, in which whole selves are bifurcated and, at least potentially, reconnected, impossible. Indeed, because it is the bifurcation in Aristophanes's myth that gives rise to the desire for wholeness that is eros, eros too becomes impossible. Alcibiades's satyrical speech can thus be seen as parodying and ultimately rejecting the myth Aristophanes proffers. But what we find in Alcibiades's "speech" nonetheless echoes the emphasis on bodily eros.

With Alcibiades's arrival comes the distinctly Dionysian presence who can serve as such a judge regarding these claims about wisdom.[106] Alcibiades has come to crown the head of Agathon in honor of his victory in tragic drama the previous night, and he does so, but then also crowns Socrates with a garland because he is always victorious in the realm of *logoi*. Alcibiades appears to judge in favor of Socrates, recognizing that wisdom is not transferrable as Agathon implies, but there is ambiguity in this verdict as much as there is in Alcibiades's speech. On the one hand, Alcibiades's speech assessing Socrates as a satyr shows a remarkable degree of insight into the nature of Socrates. On the other hand, Alcibiades does not seem to understand the significance of this insight. Nor does his revealed humiliation vis-à-vis Socrates suggest any recognition that his beauty is no match for that of Socrates. Perhaps more critically, Alcibiades fails to put into practice anything he may have learned from Socrates. Silenus is said to have been the *paidagōgos* to the young Dionysius, much as Socrates the satyr here appears the unsuccessful teacher of Alcibiades.[107] Socrates may continuously triumph in the realm of *logoi*, but if Alcibiades represents Athenians, Socratic claims about beauty and wisdom nonetheless fail with the masses.

Alcibiades's mistake may lie in identifying Socrates as either one of his halves. Socrates is neither the divine, golden figures inside the Silenus statue—invulnerable and impermeable, nor is he the ugly and comical veneer. Socrates's comic appearance cannot be dismissed as insignificant or merely superficial. Where Alcibiades's simile appears to break down is that, unlike the Sileni statues, Socrates's interior cannot be separated out from his exterior. Socrates's resemblance to satyrs extends through his very *logoi*, claims Alcibiades. But the key to understanding these *logoi* properly seems to be precisely that we do not dismiss them as merely a joke (*katagelaseien*) as the "inexperienced" or "ignorant" person might, but to take them in some sense "seriously." Taking them "seriously," however, should not entail ridding the *logoi* of their comic veneers, as though, like Apollo, we too are flaying Marsyas.

An important conclusion can be drawn from this immediately. If Socratic *logoi* appear *geloioi* (216b1), and this book has already shown several places where Socrates seems deliberately to employ the language, imagery, and logic of comedy, then interlocutors and readers make a significant mistake when we dismiss these. As Sheffield puts it, the "same *logoi* which cause ridicule need to be examined carefully and not dismissed as foolish nonsense."[108] Laughter can, it seems, have serious undertones and we ignore these, and the phenomenon of laughter, at our own hermeneutic peril. Similarly, it can be argued that Socrates' physical appearance may be more important than otherwise thought. At issue is the significance of the bodily and specifically, the significance of the satyr, to the *Symposium* as well as to the dialogues more broadly.

The question as to Socrates's hubris underscores the element of pretense in Socrates's character, but if Socrates's being exceeds his pretenses, how we evaluate such "dissembling" becomes more difficult. A long-standing tradition attributes the incongruity to Socratic irony, from *eirōneia*, which has itself been assessed ranging from the benign to the downright dangerous. For Aristotle, the difference between conduct in words and actions concerns truth: "With regard to truth, then, the intermediate is a truthful sort of person and the mean may be called truthfulness, while the pretence which exaggerates is boastfulness and the person characterized by it a boaster, and that which understates is mock modesty and the person characterized by it mock-modest."[109] The truthful mean is embodied in a straightforward (*authekaston*) and sincere (*haplous*) person: "The sincere and simple, or, as he is called, straightforward man, is a mean between the dissembler [*eirōn*] and the boaster [*alazōn*]. For the man who knowingly and falsely depreciates himself is a dissembler; the man who exalts himself is a boaster; the man who represents himself as he is, is sincere."[110] Socrates, as a satyr, becomes difficult to categorize, for his *logoi* do reflect the complex being that he is. The difficulty is exacerbated when we read Theophrastus's scathing assessment of the *eirōn*.

Initially echoing Aristotle, Theophrastus writes, "[Dissembling [*eirōneia*] . . . would seem to be a false denigration of one's actions and words.]"[111] Such a definition resonates well with Socrates and his *eirōneia*, but the description that follows suggests a different character and quite possibly the spuriousness of this definition.[112] The *eirōn*, in the *Characters*, is one who breaks promises (1.5), lies explicitly in his own favor (1.5), and speaks vaguely and vacuously (1.6). Of the *eirōn*, Theophrastus warns that "one must be more cautious . . . than of vipers [*echeis*]."[113] Although Alcibiades uses the same imagery and term in his comparison of the effects of Socrates's philosophical *logoi* to the venomous bites by a viper (*echeōs*, *echei*), it is difficult to assess Socrates as particularly self-serving in whatever degree of duplicitousness one can reasonably ascribe to him (*Symposium* 217e–18b). Far from breaking promises, Socrates is the character who chooses to stay in his prison cell rather than fleeing for his life. And far from lying in his own favor, Socrates's more questionable claims tend to work against his selfish interests, such as his frequent claims to be the elderly student of figures such as Euthydemus and Dionysodorus, and possibly even a more youthful student of a woman such as Diotima.

Socrates's pretense is not self-serving, flattering, or self-interested, other than the ways in which his acting this way shows that our goals of furthering specific interests, such as not looking ridiculous, are themselves silly. To the extent that Theophrastus's evaluation is indicative of cultural valuations of *eirōneia*, Socrates may be doing what Vlastos attributes to him: changing that evaluation from more strictly negative connotations to something akin to innocent pretense.[114] If Socrates is playing a partly comic role in the *Symposium*, then the emphasis on *eirōneia* and moral accusations of *hubris* may be exaggerated. There are good reasons, as have already been suggested, for considering such innocent pretense in the light of laughter and comedy, rather than the more traditional irony. As this chapter has suggested so far, if Socrates can be fairly represented by the image of a satyr, then his very nature is serio-comic and Dionysian, and we miss something important when Socrates is represented otherwise. Neither element can be subsumed in another. It is, in other words, only the writer of both comedy and tragedy who can properly depict Socrates.[115] As the *Symposium* and the comic moments and imagery within it suggest, Plato is such a writer.[116]

Such a possibility has been obscured by the conflation of potentially malicious ridicule (*katagelasta*) and playful laughter (*geloion*) in Plato. That Plato was at least aware of a significant distinction between what is *geloion* and what is *katagelasta* is proven by what Aristophanes says to Eryximachus (189b). Eryximachus has just complained that instead of a speech, Aristophanes is making jokes (*gelōtopoieis*) (189a). "Laughing [*gelasanta*], Aristophanes responded, 'You're right, Eryximachus, let what I said be unsaid? Don't be on your guard against me; what I'm afraid of is not that I may say something funny [*geloia*] (that would be a good trick and natural for my Muse), but rather that I may say something ridiculous [*katagelasta*]' " (189b). What is comical, funny or laughable is separable from what is to be laughed *at* in any pejorative sense. That Plato may have used such a distinction in the writing of the dialogues is suggested, if not proven, by the slapstick comedy of Aristophanes's case of hiccups, which seems far closer to being simply funny than to constituting a hostile or malicious kind of ridicule.

Incongruous laughter is also at the heart of Alcibiades's "joke." Alcibiades's accusation of hubris arouses in us and those present at the symposium the expectation of a physical, erotic encounter between him and Socrates. Using a standard comical trick of dashing expectations, what Alcibiades reveals instead is a "violation" only in its being an utter lack of violation. What has been forgotten is the physical. Alcibiades expects physical consummation from Socrates, who summarily rejects this with Alcibiades. Opposite of this is the case of Aristophanes's hiccups, as Halper indicates.[117] The first three speeches present noble eros as disembodied and ethereal. Even the physician praises eros as though it were a celestial and cosmological phenomenon, rather than physical attraction among bodies. Aristophanes's speech "draws on the expectations of noble love generated by previous speakers to show us the physical motivation."[118] Aristophanes's hiccups, as well as his encomium, return us to the bodily.

A further connection between Alcibiades's speech and Aristophanes's hiccups becomes evident on this interpretation. Alcibiades is attracted to Socrates because of the beauty of his soul, not that of his body, and as such, Alcibiades "displays in his behavior the conclusion that earlier speakers *should* have drawn."[119] He desires Socrates for his virtue—for his beautiful inner goods, even if he is ugly like a satyr on the outside, but when he makes this love explicit, his fellow symposiasts laugh at his doing so. Desiring physical consummation of his psychic love of Socrates, Alcibiades separates Socrates's shaggy hide from him, and the result is laughter.

If Alcibiades's love for Socrates is laughable, so too are those earlier speeches that denigrate the corporeal and esteem the erotic attraction to virtue alone. And yet, Alcibiades pursues physical, not psychic, consummation of that attraction to Socrates. So too, Alcibiades promises to reveal Socrates's hubris, conventionally implying a physical violation, when it is precisely a psychic violation that Alcibiades finds offensive (217e–18b). According to Halper, "What makes [Alcibiades's] speech funny . . . is the sudden recognition that the previous speakers' accounts of noble love were self-righteous and pompous efforts to disguise physical attraction and right physical fit as something else."[120] Eros, as they present it, strives to shed its physical limitations despite, as we are reminded by both the hiccups and the satyrical imagery, being fundamentally corporal.

Laughter exposes the pretensions of earlier speakers in this way, but its philosophical importance does not stop there. Inasmuch as the speaking order itself is important, its physical and comical interruptions underscore the significance of what has the power to interrupt it, namely, the body and laughter. Aristophanes's hiccups remind us of the body's relevance, both as a precondition for philosophical dialogue and as a vital dimension of eros. Alcibiades's joke, Aristophanes's hiccups, and Socrates's comical depiction do not so much stake a specific, positive claim for the significance of the body as they do bring such a possibility, radical as it may seem, into question. They serve to indicate what has been forgotten, or left out, of a number of accounts of eros, but not necessarily how to account for the body. As such, the comical serves to provoke us into the doing of philosophy.

Conclusion

This chapter has suggested that the laughter of the *Symposium* is satyrical laughter, and it is possible now to see more clearly what that means. The satyr is an incongruous whole, a being whose parts comically cannot be reconciled with each other. The laughter of satyr plays combines slapstick with the serious, the heroic with the comic, and highbrow drama with lowbrow buffoonery. This crystallizes in the figure of Socrates, who embodies such opposites and their incongruity. The dialogue's laughter is thus satyrical in arising from the collision and incongruity of these opposites. The *Symposium* makes pivotal use of incongruous laughter that, while predominant in this dialogue, is not the only form of laughter in Plato's comical repertoire.

The tension between comic and serious layers is at the heart of Alcibiades's portrayal of Socrates: what meets the eye about Socrates may appear ridiculous, ugly, deficient, and comic, but what is beneath that veneer is quite the opposite. If Alcibiades's image of Socrates as a satyr is, in any sense, truthful, then taking his comical veneer seriously means also accounting for the body. Socrates is the tension among incongruous aspects of himself. Socrates qua satyr cannot be categorized as simply comic (or as tragic), any more than he can be categorized simply as ugly (or as beautiful) or as superhuman (or as subhuman). Socrates is incongruous, but so too are the Athenians whose values Alcibiades can be said to typify. If this can be extended to ourselves, we too might be said to comprise incongruous wholes. Howland writes: "Socrates is not, any more than a satyr, an amalgam of tragic and comic elements. He is rather a Dionysian original, of which tragic and comic protagonists are at best one-sided, incomplete imitations."[121] This is equally true of the *Symposium*'s laughter, and may be true of the dialogues more generally. If so, the elusive writer of both comedies and tragedies may be less elusive than thought, but his comedies and tragedies may not be disambiguated from one another any more than Socrates's satyrical halves may be. Just like Socrates, comic and tragic elements of the dialogues may be amalgamated more fundamentally.

Comedy and laughter thus appear to be, as Socrates tells us in the *Philebus*, furthest from the fulfillment of the Delphic imperative. If, as Socrates suggests in the *Phaedrus*, mythical figures provide a basis on which to arrive at greater self-understanding, then the mythical figure Socrates is presented as in the *Symposium* may be instrumental for this purpose as well. The paradigm of the satyr, however, is one of thorough complexity and incongruousness. If human souls are akin to that of Socrates, and thus also to the satyrical, self-knowledge does indeed appear an impossible quest. Further, self-knowledge also appears impossible for a comical figure because of the persistent possibility of transformation.[122] It is always still possible for a philosopher to become a sophistic charlatan like Euthydemus, or for a Clinias to become wiser, a message echoed by Socrates's repeated self-description as the aged schoolboy.

Laughter and eros are intimately related in the exposure of human limitation and deficiency. Eros may expose human incompleteness, but comedy and laughter may enable recognizing and going beyond said deficiencies. The erotic structure implied by Aristophanes's myth is one, as Hyland describes it, of "incompleteness, recognition thereof, striving for wholeness . . ."[123] Socrates's attempt to separate shame and laughter, and to offer an alternative to derisive laughter—namely, self-reflective laughter—makes possible a disarming of the self that is critical to accomplishing the latter two dimensions. Socrates invites us to join him in laughter, in laughing at ourselves, or even in being laughed at by logos, the inquiry, or Courage herself without the shame or loss of face such laughter would have entailed in classical tragedy.

Eros, for Hyland, is what transforms us from animals (characterized by *epithumia*, or desire without logos, *Phaedrus* 238b) into humans. A possible difference between humans and animals may be derived from Hyland's reading of Plato as lying not in the possession of logos, but in the "possible presence of logos . . . in human beings," but this is a "precarious presence."[124] This may be further shaded from the preceding discussion of the *Charmides*, in which Socrates's erotic response to Charmides is noted, but triggers a philosophical discussion, an inquiry into the logos of *sōphrosynē* or one's internal goods, rather than any physical interaction on the basis of external goods. One suggestion emerging from the discussion of the *Cratylus* and *Euthydemus* is that a difference is made in how we use logos, the consistency with which we employ it, and that this is determined, if not by the explicit recognition of its own preconditions, at least in compliance with them. In this sense, Euthydemus and Dionysodorus's use of logos can be compared to Socrates's. By denying the preconditions of the possibility of logos, we deny ourselves higher orders of existence, including the human and the divine.

In this possibility of transcending the beastly part of ourselves, just as in the possibility of achieving divine internal treasures like Socrates, lies an optimism that is overlooked on antigelastic readings of Plato. Socrates, whether playing a buffoon as in the Euthydemus or a satyr in the *Symposium*, presents us with such a Dionysian optimism. A noteworthy feature of satyr plays was their juxtaposition to tragedies, and their countering of the emotional mood generated by tragedy.[125] Satyr plays are comical renderings of tragedy that end happily. They thus present "a roseate vision of life counterbalancing that of tragedy."[126] We thus find in the *Symposium*, as Usher describes, a new Silenic-Dionysian spirit, a liberation from tragic pessimism to Platonic optimism.[127] It is an optimism drawn in part from how Socrates and Plato have revised comedy and laughter.

For Socrates, laughter is not limited to exposing deficiency. Socrates's myth of Eros's origins offers a critique of Aristophanes's myth as only half right: "what Aristophanes missed was the contribution to the nature of eros by its mythical father Poros (and his own mother Metis). That contribution was the gift of a certain overfullness, resourcefulness, inventiveness, and capacity for a certain rational insight into the nature of things, including ourselves."[128] Aristophanes's myth accounts for humans in terms of our deficiency, hubris, and the eros with which we seek to amend our deficiency. It is Socrates's comical persona, his exemplification of *ponēria*, or the comic resourcefulness typical of comical heroes, that most clearly demonstrates the critique. If Aristophanes's myth offers an account of humans, and human eros, it appears to be a tragic one in which the likelihood of the consummation of eros, or finding one's literal other half, is against all odds. Socrates the mischievous satyr has reversed roles with even Aristophanes, making the comic writer appear tragic, while he himself is comical.

Whether fairly or not, Aristophanes (the character) is depicted by Plato as missing something with which Aristophanes (the playwright) imbues his own characters: resourcefulness. This resourcefulness, or fullness, is *ponēria*, the comical roguery by which comical heroes can transcend their own modest circumstances or animal natures. The potential transcendence posed by comedy is what Hyland calls a "finite transcendence," because "it is always and only a possibility of transcendence, one that will be realized only if we put into play, as it were, our Poros/Metis natures, our capacity for a certain rational insight and rational living."[129] That capacity is a fragile one, dependent on the philosophical consistency among how we understand the world and how we apply that understanding in how we live in the world. Both, in turn, are mediated by logos.

An insight emerging from the earlier discussion of the *Euthydemus* and *Cratylus* can be brought to bear here. Much depends on how we use logos, even when it is used playfully. We can use logos as do Euthydemus and Dionysodorus, as something untethered to anything, and thus representative of nothing. Or, we can use it as Socrates seems to be suggesting we ought, as something tied to a set of preconditions for consistent usage, preconditions that do tether it, but also enable logos potentially to express reality and to improve its users. In the *Republic*, Socrates suggests that the sort of play that prompts philosophy is "a lawful play" (*ennomōterou . . . paidias*) that can make "law-abiding, good men" (*ennomous te kai spoudaious . . . andras*) out of children playing (*Republic* 424e–25a).[130] Alcibiades's comparison of Socrates to a satyr extends to Socrates's *logoi*, after all. Shaggy, ugly, and comical on the outside, they too may contain treasures of unspeakable beauty.

As Socrates suggests in the *Phaedrus*, it is by comparing ourselves to such mythical beasts that we might arrive at a greater understanding of the self. And so, Alcibiades offers to us, the *Symposium*'s participants and audience, the opportunity to compare ourselves to the comical beast-human-god that is Socrates, to ask whether we are more or less like him in body or soul, more or less philosophically courageous, or more or less *sōphrōn*. For Usher, the comparison of Socrates to a satyr represents him as more alien to us, something out of reach, and to some extent this may be true. Satyrs are indeed strange figures, but like us, they and Socrates are also akin to us: flawed, fragmented, but able to rise to the occasion and even, at times, to make that occasion and ourselves transcend the ordinary.

Comparisons to such figures occurs through the medium of logos. The self-knowledge generated by comparison to a mythical figure, or in this case, to Socrates as a satyr, occurs by saying what a soul is *like*, rather than what it *is*. Socrates is *like* a satyr, Alcibiades tells us. Griswold indicates the connection this implies amongst logos, eros, and self-knowledge.[131] There appears to be a way of understanding the self via logos. Socrates's urging Charmides to look inside himself, and his focus on inquiry into psychic goods illustrates this. Logos mediates our access to ourselves as well as to being. If logos is, as Sallis suggests, a gathering together, then perhaps we can be said to gather together the parts of Socrates so as to compare and understand ourselves, a task shown here to be only partially possible.[132]

While complete self-knowledge remains evasive, some steps toward it may still be achieved. Alcibiades's describes Socrates as equally empty or deficient, and full. Rustic and ugly on the outside, what makes Socrates divinely beautiful to Alcibiades are his internal treasures, specifically his virtues of courage and *sōphrosynē* (*Symposium* 219d). The discussions of courage in the *Laches* and *sōphrosynē* in the *Charmides* contrast the external and internal trappings of moderation and courage. If Hyland is right that, in the *Charmides*, Charmides's headache is due to a hangover, he is even less likely to be *sōphrōn*.[133] Stesilaus in the *Laches* demonstrates comical incongruity in his feigning of *andreia* in a mock battle against nobody, wielding complicated weaponry, and yet jumping at the drop of a stone. Both exhibit incongruity between what might be called internal and external displays of virtue.

Laughter's separation and distance from self-knowledge, however, is misleading, for there is also a sense in which laughter renders such self-knowledge possible. It is that possibility in laughter to which the Conclusion now turns. In discussing symposia in the *Laws* 649d9, the Athenian specifies Alcibiades's claim regarding wine and truth in the *Symposium*: "in wine there is both proof of one's character and light-hearted play [*en oinō basanos kai paidia*]."[134] Socrates proves himself a satyr. Such self-knowledge provides a way of accessing higher orders of existence, including the human and, potentially, the divine, much as does Socrates-the-satyr, the attendant of Dionysus.

Conclusion: *Ponēria*, Self-Knowledge, and Comical, Platonic Optimism

At the risk of flogging a dead *Philebus* passage, we can, in conclusion, return once more to 48c, where the nature of the laughable (*to geloion*) is deemed a form of *ponēria*. Rather than translating this morally, I suggest we translate this comically as implying knavery or roguishness, as opposed to moral viciousness. Comedy is not an expression of moral vice for Socrates; it is an expression of resourcefulness, of our Poros natures. As was suggested in the first chapter, Socrates's behavior in the *Apology* might best be characterized as roguish. As the chapters following it suggest, Socrates regularly plays the mischievous, roguish satyr, incongruously alternating between acting the buffoon (or other comical roles) and offering heroic displays of virtue. If this comical, as opposed to moral, translation of *ponēria* holds, several significant points follow regarding self-knowledge and the role of the comical in Platonic dialogues.

If laughter and comedy are more prominent parts of Platonic dialogues than generally thought, a more specific conception of the self emerges. In it are apparent the simultaneous revision and adoption of the comical self. The comical self, as Socrates embodies it, is abundant, overfull, and resourceful, in addition to being, as Aristophanes might suggest, laughable and deficient. As Socrates demonstrates in the *Apology*, no matter how bleak the circumstances or how much public opinion has turned against one, it always remains possible to compare oneself—through *ponēria*—to Achilles, the most admired of epic heroes, and, when that goes over poorly, to retreat to comparison, instead, with a gadfly.[1] The stinging horse fly is a base and crude comparison, outrageous to "dignified" Athenians and itself intended to sting the jury. Like his *logoi*, Socrates is a satyr.

Socrates has been shown here to embody several key characteristics of the comical hero, which justifies taking Alcibiades's simile of Socrates as a satyr seriously. His *ponēria*, like that of Aristophanean heroes, can also be exhibited in a crafty use of *logoi*, such as puns, the elaborate etymologizing of the *Cratylus*, and linguistic jokes such as that as to whether boiling the cook is the cook's business (*Euthydemus* 301d). Beyond his resourcefulness, or *ponēria*, Socrates turns the tables on his opponents, as in his own judging of his jurors, or the true jurors from the "men of Athens," as he refers to those who fail to use logos and vote to convict him, remaining mere "men" in doing so. He exhibits the comical beast-human-divine complex, displaying traits of all three in how he is described by others as well as by himself, and perhaps most apparently, in Alcibiades's comparison of Socrates to the very embodiment of beast and god.

As has been shown, Plato draws from Old Comedy in a number of ways, including employing its formal structure, as in the *Laches*. The formal structure of Old Comedy includes a *parabasis*, in which the audience is addressed directly. An insight emerging from this is that, if the Platonic dialogues bear a closer relationship to such comedy, the relationship between text and audience must be adjusted accordingly. For just as a *parabasis* addresses its audience directly, so too is what will later be called the "fourth wall" far more permeable in comedy. Witness the alleged interplay between Socrates and the masked actor impersonating him at a production of the *Clouds*. If so, we must ask how it is that the dialogues address, involve, or even implicate us.

As has been argued, Greek laughter is prone to excesses, but this very feature makes it particularly suitable for addressing and describing the beings for whom it is a distinguishing feature. Such laughability may be inherent to humans in general. The comical figure is malleable and mutable, and in these shifts—whether actual or potential—lies a fundamental challenge to the achievement of self-knowledge. And yet, in these descriptions lie parameters and limitations that also serve to delimit and thus know oneself, however partially. Laughter in the Platonic dialogues suggests that humans are never far from being laughable, even when dignified and noble. Indeed, the philosopher is repeatedly described by Socrates as laughable, and Socrates has been shown regularly to expose himself as a subject of laughter, playing the fool in the *Cratylus* and *Euthydemus* to enact the absurd consequences of the denial of falsity. While this can be read as an indication of the reform of laughter and comedy in Platonic dialogues wherein laughter is presented as no longer to be feared, there is still more to it than that. When we take laughter and comedy as more than frivolous, it becomes possible to see the ways in which they are appropriate: they expose the incongruities within ourselves as well as the hubristic pretensions to exceed human limitations. They crack open what we take to be one, consistent whole, and expose the beast-human-divine complex within it. We thus may have more in common with Socrates-the-satyr than we might think.

If laughter and comedy play a more significant role within the Platonic dialogues than usually assumed, as I have argued, then we must account for the comical representation of humans. As Freydberg writes of human representation in Aristophanes's plays, "Human vulnerability and human folly belong to who we are . . . The laughter they provoke is the complement of the thoughtful treatment they require."[2] But this cannot only be the laughter of derision. It may be difficult not to laugh derisively at Hippias for proclaiming his "godlike state of mind" to be due to never having "met anyone superior to me in anything," let alone for having Socrates soundly disprove this in practice in the dialogue following (*Lesser Hippias* 364a). It may be irresistible to feel a twinge of smug satisfaction when Critias is brought back down from the dizzying heights of claiming to have knowledge of knowledge in the *Charmides* and, instead, is prompted to admit knowing only *that* he knows, and not *what* he knows at all (*Charmides* 170c). Limiting laughter to such kinds, wherein we may just take ourselves to be somehow superior to the comic butt, precludes us from recognizing larger points being made.

Plato's laughter, as I have argued, is much broader in scope, types, and functions than a superiority theory or, perhaps, than any single theory of comedy can cover. Laughter is applicable to more persons and situations than the egregious Hippias or the arrogant Critias. It may be precisely when we think ourselves invulnerable to laughter that we render ourselves most laughable, and thus most like a Hippias or a Critias. The broader point is, as Freydberg suggests, that such invulnerability eludes us. We may be less like tragic heroes in this and more akin to the heroes of comedy, with Socrates—the satyr—included among them. Like Socrates, we too may be divided within ourselves into incongruous halves. Like Socrates, we may also come to think that being laughed at does not matter, but that lacking self-knowledge does (*Euthyphro* 3c). Laughter need not be a barb aimed just at specific individuals. The lesson of the *Laches* seems to be that it is typical of all humans to see the laughable in others, but to ignore it in oneself.

In both form and content, the dialogues seek to remedy this by turning laughter back on the interlocutors and the audience. In the *Charmides*, the *Protagoras*, and in the *Laches*, Socrates suggests that the inquiry, the logos, or the very idea under investigation is laughing at the interlocutors for failing in their efforts. The composition of the *Laches* borrows its complex structure from Attic Old Comedy, and the second chapter argues that doing so makes use of *parabasis* and the direct address of the audience to let us know that we are implicated. Neither interlocutor nor audience is immune to laughter, particularly if we too are stuck in *aporia*. If being laughable can be generalized in this sense, then a picture of humans more broadly emerges from laughter.

Laughter in the Platonic dialogues marks a self-forgetting—a forgetting of ourselves as physical beings, a forgetting of what our philosophical positions commit us to, and a forgetting of the many ways in which we fall short of embodying a Dorian harmony among our words and deeds. It is a forgetting of how quick we are to presume ourselves better than we are and how slow we can be to realize it. It is a forgetting of how easily we can deceive ourselves, and how dangerous such self-deception can be. Given that contemporary studies[3] regularly reveal that the majority of Americans polled consider themselves to be more moral than the majority of Americans, or as Berke puts it, "the average person considers himself to be better than the average person,"[4] the comic dimensions of the dialogues retain their relevance for us today. But laughter is also an invitation to look into the mirror it holds up and to see ourselves for the vulnerable and limited beings that we are. In this sense, laughter can play a positive role in regard to the Delphic imperative to "know oneself." We see in laughter some of the dimensions in which to do so: namely, through our words as well as our deeds.

Laughter, as presented here, opens us to philosophy if we recognize ourselves as potentially laughable. It does so more specifically in two ways. First, seeing oneself as laughable requires a recognition of one's deficiency, including one's ignorance. It is only from such a position that philosophy can be undertaken, since believing that one knows as, for instance, Critias does, cuts a person off from the chance to remedy one's ignorance. Second, laughter induces wonder, with which philosophy itself begins. Ewegen speculates as to an even more intimate relationship between laughter and wonder: "Perhaps laughter—at least, the right kind of laughter—is nothing other than vocalized wonder, nothing other than the cock-crow of philosophy."[5] Laughter may not itself provide answers, but it has been shown to initiate the sort of wonder with which philosophy begins.

Ridicule and being ridiculous contribute to this same goal of self-awareness. Derisive laughter is aimed by Socrates at those who do not yet recognize themselves as such in part to remedy this lack of self-knowledge. Other forms of laughter are more appropriate for those who already see themselves as laughable, including self-reflective laughter. These forms operate on resourcefulness—our Poros nature, but also on deficiency—our Penia nature. The very persons who arrogantly presume themselves immune from such deficiency are the ones most vulnerable to feeling a loss of status coming from ridicule. As Socrates does for Critias, the blow can be softened by an inclusive, self-reflective laughter. The question is whether Critias, and others like him, can laugh at himself. If he can, he recognizes that he does not know, and so, potentially opens himself up to remedying this through philosophy.

One of the questions cutting across several of the dialogues addressed in this book is to whom one can turn in order to learn?, since, as laughter in the dialogues makes clear, we are all in need of education. An answer is implied by a comical reading. It has been argued that a comical reading shows how Plato's dialogues address the audience more directly, whether by putting the *Apology*'s audience into the position of jurors judging the Athenian jury whom Socrates puts on trial, through a direct address akin to the comical *parabasis* in the *Laches*, by prompting us to laugh and thus to take a position in what is presented in the *Cratylus* and *Euthdemus*, or by holding up Socrates-the-comical-hero of the *Symposium*—a satyr, and asking us to consider whether we are like him. The implication and turn toward the audience is significant, for it shows us what we must do to find the right teacher. As he does for Charmides, Socrates is urging us to "look inside ourselves," and not merely inside our cloaks. The teacher of virtues such as *andreia* and *sōphrosynē*—the educator—can be none other than oneself, even if Clinias, at the end of the *Euthydemus*, does not yet realize this. The mirror that Plato's laughter holds up shows us the way forward.

We can use Socrates qua satyr as he suggests we use mythical figures like Typhon: to inquire into ourselves, to seek self-knowledge. What can we take away from a comparison to Socrates-the-satyr? Like Socrates-the-satyr, humans are both empty and full, and beast, human, and divine simultaneously. We have read too much into our deficiency, and comedy's ability to expose it without taking into account the counterbalance of our resourcefulness, our fullness, our *ponēria*. Humans, like Socrates's mythical genealogy of Eros, thus may have more in common with comical characters, including satyrs. As Sheffield suggests, "Philosophers are . . . those who are in between lack and possession, ignorance and wisdom, the *phaulon* and the *spoudaion*. Philosophers, then, are not fitting subjects of Aristophanic ridicule, but rather call for a genre which can combine the low and the high, the *phaulon* and the *spoudaion*, the comic and the tragic in the presentation of the poverty and the nobility of the philosophical life."[6] Like Socrates, we are the tensions among these polarities, nobly striving to overcome our situation, and yet always falling at least a little short. We are laughable, like Socrates and like philosophers generally.

The adapted, comical self exhibits what Hyland, in a different context, calls a "finite transcendence," which is caught in a tension between wisdom and comedy. It is "a transcendence in that it recognizes, against comedy, that our everyday situation is not satisfactory or acceptable, that it should and can be transcended, that, indeed, the best life can be lived in pursuit of this transcendence toward wisdom. On the other hand, it is finite transcendence, in that it recognizes the impossibility of a complete transcendence to achieved wisdom."[7] Neither passive acceptance of our situation (shown by Lysimachus) nor foolish faith in overcoming it (such as Critias displays) are acceptable. However, comical self-knowledge allows us to move from being blindly ridiculous to being self-consciously laughable. It may be but a humble step up, but it is one entirely fitting with our laughable, human selves.

The difference shown between being ridiculous and being laughable in the Platonic dialogues examined here offers a critical incentive toward doing philosophy. Comedy along the lines of Aristophanes shows us that all are more-or-less equally laughable. The proper reaction to this might be to stop struggling to acquire better understanding or to improve one's circumstances and, instead, to accept things as they are, and all persons for the laughable beings that we are. Clinias faces such a choice in the *Euthydemus*: if philosophers are as ridiculous as the sophistic brothers, neither are preferable to each other nor remotely acceptable as teachers. But this is a big "if." For if philosophers are capable of playful and self-reflective laughter, they illustrate the human form of wisdom discussed in the *Apology*, and this would move them from being ridiculous to merely being laughable. One wonders whether Thales, rubbing his bumps and bruises at the bottom of the well, realized his mistake and chuckled along with the girl. Being the laughable Thales, however sore, is still far preferable to being the servant girl, who appears to laugh without recognizing how she herself is self-ignorant and ridiculous.

In this modest move from being ridiculous to being laughable, and in the significance of comedy and laughter in the dialogues, lies a Platonic optimism that has been overlooked. For among the philosophical tools we have at our disposal are those of the comical hero: *ponēria*, a rustic, roguish, scrappiness and resourcefulness, and a creative and tenacious will toward the impossible—whether that be an all-female political takeover of ancient, patriarchal Athens, turning one's jurors toward a critical, philosophical analysis, or perhaps toward the cultivation of self-knowledge. In this and in the beast-human-divine complex lies the possibility of change, of developing the self along the spectrum. But doing so demands a better understanding of that self, and of the pitfalls to be avoided in improving it. Plato's laughter, in its many forms, can assist in each of these endeavors.

Far from Nietzsche's description of him as a great opponent of Dionysus, Socrates can be seen here to channel a Dionysian (in addition to the acknowledged Apollonian) spirit. Far from causing envy and malice toward Athenians, the emphasis on Socrates's ugliness emphasizes his similarity with Dionysus's attendant satyrs. And far from relying exclusively on detached, disembodied, and unemotional reason to achieve philosophical purposes, Socrates can be seen here to provoke outrage, anger, envy, malice, and other emotions in his audience, as he does in the *Apology*, to make philosophical points (such as the proper basis for arriving at a judgment of someone) and to provoke and invite his audience into doing philosophy. Alcibiades cautions that the very *logoi* of Socrates appear ridiculous, but are of the greatest worth (*Symposium* 222a). In saying this, he gives us the strongest support to *not* throw away what appears ridiculous, foolish, or absurd, and instead open these things up to examine the intelligence in them, much as we also may treat Socrates-the-Silenus, and much as I have attempted to do here with the laughter of Plato's dialogues. Nietzsche may not have heard Plato's laughter, and Diogenes Laertius may have claimed that it never occurred aloud, but it is the hope underlying this book that we, Plato's contemporary audience, might hear such laughter more clearly.

Notes

Introduction

1. Kierkegaard (1989), 261.

2. *Euthyphro* 3c, 3e. Euripides's Medea, for instance, motivates herself to murder her own sons at several points with reminders that she might be laughed at if she were to choose another option. Sophocles's Ajax kills himself in fear of being laughed at by Odysseus for having lost the contest for Achilles's armor. That neither case of anticipated laughter actually occurs is less important than the force with which such anticipation acts on these figures, and what it motivates them to do. Tragic laughter may be sinister, as Dillon (1991) implies, but comic laughter and the laughter of Platonic dialogues need not be dark.

3. Dillon (1991), 348–50.

4. For more on the role that readers play in the dialogues, see Klein (1965), 7–10.

5. I follow Beard (2014) and Halliwell (2008) on this.

6. Attic Old Comedy is contemporaneous with some of the dramatic dating of the dialogues, but not necessarily with the dialogues' written dates. Aristophanes's plays indicate a span from 427 to 385 BCE, presenting the possibility of overlap of the writing of some Platonic dialogues with later Aristophanic comedies. See Lowe (2007) for Aristophanes's dates.

7. Grant (1924), 48.

8. Grant (1924), 49.

9. Aristotle, *Poetics* 1447b7–12.

10. For a more detailed look at the dialogues as themselves mimetic, see Tanner (2010).

11. Quintilian, as cited by Hordern (2004), 113.

12. Cunningham, Introduction to Sophron's *Mimes*, 288.

13. Some indirect support for Aristotle's comical reading might be gleaned from his account of the *megalopsūchos*, described in the

Nicomachean Ethics as one whose characteristic is "greatness in every excellence" (Aristotle, *Nicomachean Ethics* 1123b30–31). Socrates is named as one of five potentially great-souled persons in the *Posterior Analytics*, along with Alcibiades, Lysander, Ajax, and Achilles (97b15–25). Of the five, writes Howland, Socrates's indifference to the turnings of fortune, honor, and dishonor, marks him as "the only one whose soul is free from the potentially tragic tyranny of *thumos*, which manifests itself in anger and in the pursuit of honor and victory" (Howland [2002], 36). *Megalopsūchia*, Aristotle writes in the *Nicomachean Ethics*, "seems to be a sort of crown (*kosmos*) of the virtues . . . and is not found without them." Implied here is that the *megalopsūchos* embodies the virtues, as best as one can, and that the greatness of soul orders or crowns these as an additional embellishment. If we assume that the social virtues are included, then the *megalopsūchos* would seem to embody *eutrapelia*. If Aristotle is right about him, then Socrates's freedom from the "tyranny of *thumos*" and the love of honor further supports this. Not only is Socrates distanced from tragic heroes, then, he is linked with laughter, and as we will see in the first chapter, the freedom from being driven by *thumos* also links Socrates with comical heroes.

14. Cicero, *De Oratore* II.270.

15. Cicero, *De Officiis* I.104.

16. Ewegen (2014), 16.

17. Many philosophers, philologists, and classicists have done important work that recognizes the significance of laughter (or aspects thereof), in Greek antiquity or in Plato specifically, in ways that go far beyond malicious ridicule. See Arieti (1991), Baracchi (2001), Benardete (1993), Bloom (1962), Brock (1990), Clay (1975), DeVries (1985), Freydberg (2008, 1995), Greene (1920), Halliwell (2008, 2005, 1991), Halper (2011), Körte (1914), Michelini (2000), Nussbaum (2009), Rankin (1969), Sallis (1996), Saxonhouse (1978), Sommerstein (2009), Sprague (1994), Strauss (1966), Usher (2002), and Wood (2007). To my knowledge, however, there is no extended examination of the uses and implications of laughter in Platonic dialogues, which is what this book aims to provide.

18. Such a reading also prompts several potential objections. One problem that arises immediately is that if we are to read, say, Socrates in the *Republic*, contra millennia of secondary literature, as humorously rather than seriously, postulating a communistic restructuring of society, it effectively lets Socrates, and perhaps Plato, off the hook. Can we then no

longer criticize the radical and dangerous propositions made by Socrates concerning the city in speech? Of course we can, but we need not attribute these beliefs to either Socrates or Plato in order to do so. What this issue brings to light is the assumption that Plato is writing an exposition of his and/or Socrates's beliefs. For many reasons that I will discuss later, not the least of which is the literary form of the dialogue in which the bulk of extant Platonic writings exist, this is not a justified assumption. I am grateful to Raphael Sassower for calling my attention to this problem.

19. Morreall (1987), 10. Morreall is not a Platonic scholar and in this sense, my criticism of his work is exaggerated. He does, however, represent a line of thinking about Plato and the Greeks that precludes recognizing any positive potential in laughter. Much to Morreall's credit, he does not argue for a derisive view of comedy and laughter, and his work does much to further a much-needed revision within philosophy of the role and signficance of laugher therein.

20. Morreall (2009), 4.

21. Morreall (1987), 14.

22. If the superiority theory can be attributed to Hobbes, why can it not be to Plato? There is a significant difference in their choices of writing media: Hobbes's *Leviathan* is a treatise, whereas Platonic dialogues are dramatic and literary pieces. Taking the latter to express the personal beliefs of their author is, I would argue, a fallacy. Similarly, the attribution to Plato of a Superiority Theory of laughter may be based, aside from the *Philebus* passage, on taking the myth of Gyges as presented by Glaucon in the Republic as *Plato*'s position. If we read the *Republic* carefully, I would argue, not only is there little support for claiming that *Plato* is a Psychological Egoist, as is Hobbes, but there is even little support for attributing this position to Glaucon.

23. Hobbes (2002), 45-46.

24. Freud (2002), 85.

25. Freud (2002), 92.

26. Freud (2002), 110.

27. Freud (2002), 115.

28. Halliwell (2008), 21.

29. Halliwell (2008), 22.

30. Aristotle, *Rhetoric* 1389b11.

31. Halliwell (2008), 221.

32. Hutcheson (1997), 230.

33. Hutcheson (1997), 226.

34. Hutcheson (1997), 230.

35. Hutcheson (1997), 235.

36. Hutcheson (1997), 235.

37. Bergson (2008), 5.

38. Bergson (2008), 21.

39. In a very compelling essay, Howland argues against determining a chronological ordering and the significance with which this is generally credited on the grounds of philological and methodological considerations. By deeming these "traditional" considerations in the arguments for chronology, I do not mean to suggest these to be classical considerations. As Howland suggests, today's orthodoxy in terms of determining chronological ordering does not, in fact, extend through classical antiquity (Howland [1991]).

40. The dialogues' meaning, in such cases, is assumed to hinge on the access they provide to Plato's own doctrine or beliefs. This assumption entirely ignores the form in which they were written: apart from the letters, Plato's extant works are literary, dramatic, and philosophical dialogues, and understanding what *Plato* thought based on what is argued in the dialogues seems as relevant as deducing what, say, Shakespeare thought from an interpretation of *Hamlet*. Although understandably enticing, what Plato believed is not the hermeneutic *telos* of reading the dialogues, nor is it necessarily accessible to us through the dialogues. Fortunately, we need not have such privileged, personal information about Plato to find meaning in the dialogues, any more than we need to understand, say, Shakespeare's own political philosophy before we can find meaning in his works.

41. Arieti takes this one step further by arguing that dramatic considerations take precedence over philosophical argumentation in the dialogues. Although giving the dramatic elements their just attention is of great importance, this strikes me as one step too far in that it nonetheless segments and prioritizes the dramatic and philosophical from one another. This, I contend, we cannot justifiably entirely do (Arieti [1991]).

42. See John Harman, "The Unhappy Philosopher: Plato's 'Republic' as Tragedy," *Polity* 18, no. 4 (1986): 577–94 and Jacob Howland, "Plato's 'Apology' as Tragedy," *Review of Politics* 70, no. 4 (2008): 519–46.

43. Arieti, for instance, asserts this label specifically for several dialogues, including the *Laches*, and describes the dialogues generally as "prose comedies" (Arieti [1991], 151).

44. Clay (2005).

Chapter 1

1. Griswold (1996), 251n18.
2. Critchley (2002).
3. Brann (1968).
4. Howland (2008), 520.
5. Howland (2008), 526.
6. Sallis (2002), 30.
7. Greene (1920), 72.
8. The summary is from Colaiaco (2001), 36.
9. Aristotle *Rhetoric* II 1.1377b25-77b29.
10. Aristotle *Rhetoric* II 1.1377b31-78a3.
11. Aristotle, *Rhetoric* II 3.1380a24-26.
12. See Brann (1978), Sallis (2002).
13. Calogero (1957), Coulter (1964).
14. Coulter (1964), 271.
15. Schmid offers a case for this based on the *Palamedes*'s influence on Antiphon. For this and more on such arguments, see Coulter (1964), 300n2.
16. Calogero (1957), 14-15. The comparison is from Gorgias, *Defense of Palamedes* 30, and Plato, *Apology* 36c.
17. Calogero (1957), 14-15. The comparison is from Gorgias, *Defense of Palamedes* 33, and Plato, *Apology* 34c-35c.
18. Calogero (1957), 14-15. The interruptions begin at Gorgias, *Defense of Palamedes* 22, and Plato, *Apology* 24b.
19. Calogero (1957), 14-15. This comparison is taken from Gorgias, *Defense of Palamedes* 1, and Plato's *Apology* 38c-d, 34e-35c.
20. Calogero (1957), 14-15. This claim is made at Gorgias, *Defense of Palamedes* 3, and Plato, *Apology* 28a.
21. Coulter (1964), 294-95. These are taken from Gorgias, *Defense of Palamedes* 21, and Plato, *Apology* 38a.
22. See Coulter (1964), 269-70.
23. See Coulter (1964), 269-70.
24. Coulter (1964), 270.
25. Coulter (1964), 291.
26. See Plato's *Gorgias* 522c-e, where Socrates says that to die due to lacking powers of flattery is not shameful.
27. See Coulter (1964), 270.
28. Coulter (1964), 296.

29. Gorgias, *Defense of Palamedes* B11a.33.

30. Aristotle, *Rhetoric* II 8.1385b29-86a1.

31. Plutarch *Instituta Laconica* 24.239b.

32. Critias 88 B 44 Diels-Krantz (see Bernd Seidensticker).

33. Pindar, *Pythian Odes* 2.54–56.

34. Aristophanes, *Peace* 1301-04.

35. Clay (2000), 68. Also, see Peter H. von Blanckenhagen, "The Shield of Alcibiades" (1964).

36. Archilochus, fragment 114 West, quoted in Clay (2000), 58.

37. Whitman (1964), 46-47.

38. Whitman (1964), 30.

39. Whitman (1964), 34.

40. Whitman (1964), 50.

41. Whitman (1964), 50.

42. Whitman (1964), 50.

43. Whitman separates comical and tragic imagery too sharply here. Homer uses the lion image to describe not only Achilles's power, strength, and nobility, but to critique his beastlike savagery, articulated best by Achilles himself when he threatens to devour Hector raw *Iliad* XXII.346-48. Achilles can be seen as fluctuating throughout the *Iliad* between beast and god before ultimately discovering himself as a human in the scene with Priam in Book XXIV. The beast human god structure may thus play a yet greater role in Homeric epic than Whitman implies.

44. Aristophanes, *Knights* 149.

45. Aristophanes, *Knights* 573-76.

46. Whitman (1964), 103.

47. Whitman (1964), 58.

48. Whitman (1964), 52.

49. Whitman (1964), 53.

50. Whitman (1964), 55.

51. The reasons behind the moniker are disputed. Cicero claims that Democritus earned it from having written a now lost treatise on laughter, but, as Grant points out, *De Risu* does not occur amongst the titles listed in the *Life* by Diogenes Laertius (Cicero, *De Oratore* II.235). Hippolytus implicitly suggests it due to his personal comportment towards others and all, or most, things.

52. Diels, 360, fragment 20.

53. Horace, *Epistle* II.1.194-201.

54. Juvenal, *Tenth Satire*, lines 29-54.
55. Gerhard, *Phoenix von Kolophon*, cited by Grant, 16.
56. Juvenal, *Tenth Satire*, lines 68-73.
57. Diels, 426, fragment 8.
58. Diels, 405, fragment 15.
59. I am grateful to an anonymous reviewer who suggested this phrase.

Chapter 2

1. The citation is from Socrates, who quotes an unnamed comic poet poking fun at philosophers in the *Republic* (607b).
2. Thucydides, *Peloponnesian War* 5.65-73.
3. Thucydides, *Peloponnesian War* 7.50-55, on the Athenian defeat at Syracuse, and 7.86.2, on Nicias's death at the hands of the Syracusans.
4. Schmid (1992), 51.
5. Schmid (1992), 51.
6. Nails (2002), 48.
7. Emlyn-Jones (1999), 123-24.
8. Emlyn-Jones (1999), 124.
9. Emlyn-Jones (1999), 127.
10. Schmid (1992), 49.
11. Sommerstein (1973), 26-27.
12. Schmid (1992), 48-51.
13. Sommerstein (1973), 26.
14. Tessitore (1994), 123f17.
15. That Laches, Nicias, and Lysimachus appear to act the role of the chorus in the second *parabasis* is not inconsistent with Old Comedy. Sommerstein notes that some comic plays had a second chorus with a different identity. Sommerstein (2000), 12.
16. For more on the *rhesis*, see Sommerstein (2000), 20-21.
17. Lowe (2007), 55.
18. Lowe (2007), 27.
19. The *Clouds*' second *parabasis* occurs at 1113-30.
20. This claim does not ascribe to Plato any awareness or intention that his dialogues would be read several millennia later, any more so than it does to Aristophanes. If the structural comparison is fair, then the same address of audience can be assumed in both cases.

21. Schmid (1992), 49.

22. Schmid (1992), 49.

23. Schmid (1992), 49–50.

24. Hoerber (1968), 97.

25. Hoerber (1968), 100. Shorey writes, "In the *Laches*, Laches insists exclusively on the temperamental aspect of bravery which opposes it to other virtues, Nicias on the cognitive element which identifies it with them." Shorey (1960) 15n41, as cited by Hoerber (1968), 41.

26. Hoerber (1968), 101.

27. Schmid (1992), 38, 89–90.

28. Plutarch alludes to the center as a place of honor. He describes the young Cicero as having established a repute that earns him a privileged space amongst others. Some rude fathers of esteemed sons, Plutarch tells us, were angered to see their sons "walking with Cicero placed in their midst [*meson*] as a mark of honour [*epi time*]" (Plutarch, *Life of Cicero* 2.2–3).

29. Howland (1998), 635.

30. See Schmid's discussion at Schmid (1992), 55–59.

31. For more on the verbal comparison of Lysimachus to Cephalus, both of whom use very similar phrasings, see Emlyn-Jones (1999), 125n8.

32. Emlyn-Jones (1999), 124n6.

33. Emlyn-Jones does not hold this view, but recognizes the strange first impression made by Lysimachus in the beginning of the dialogue. Emlyn-Jones (1999), 124.

34. Emlyn-Jones (1999), 124.

35. Emlyn-Jones (1999), 124n6.

36. More precisely, this is Thucydides reporting a funeral oration by Pericles. Emlyn-Jones (1999), 134, and Thucydides 2.40.

37. Dobbs points this out. Sprague's translation omits the invocation of Hera, but the Greek clearly reads "*eu ge nē tēn Hēran*," Dobbs (1986), 830.

38. Emlyn-Jones writes, "Lysimachus is in some respects a 'Polonius figure' whose elaborate, repetitive syntax and stylistic awkwardness paint a picture of a pedantic, elderly man, anxiously aware of being out of touch with his children's generation and contemporary life generally, to the extent of not even being personally acquainted with Socrates, though a long-standing friend of his father (180c5ff)." Emlyn-Jones (1999), 124.

39. Nichols (1987), 269–70.

40. This leads Emlyn-Jones to write: "Plato is using [Lysimachus] to mark the widening gap between his unchanging perceptions

and the developing positions explored by Socrates and the others," Emlyn-Jones (1999), 125.

41. Although Nicias suggests that he will straighten out some points on the definition of *andreia* with Damon, he fails to acknowledge what the *aporia* reveals—his ignorance. If genuine (and not simply an attempt to save face after Laches's jibes), Nicias's expressed intention to pursue this subject further appears to be for the sake of positioning him to instruct Laches (200b), rather than to know for himself.

42. This claim does imply a written date occurring after Aristophanes's *Birds*, performed in 414 BCE.

43. Cratinus 171, line 73 in Storey (v.1), 355, and Teleclides 44 in Storey (v.3), 305.

44. Phrynichus 23 in Storey (v.3), 61, and Eupolis 193 Storey (v.2), 171-72.

45. Phrynichus 62 in Storey (v.3), 75.

46. Phrynichus 62 in Storey (v.3), 75.

47. Aristophanes, *Birds* 638.

48. Plutarch, *Nicias* 2.4 and 4.1-2.

49. Thucydides, *Peloponnesian War* 7.50.4.

50. Dobbs (1986), 844.

51. O'Brien (1963), 146.

52. Dobbs (1986), 845.

53. Nichols (1987), 277.

54. Nichols (1987), 277.

55. Arieti suggests the image of the generals bickering like schoolboys (Arieti [1991]), 58.

56. See Emlyn-Jones's discussion of the stylistic elements of Nicias's and Laches's epideixeis. Emlyn-Jones (1999), 127.

57. Nails (2002), 273.

58. Nails (2002), 273.

59. See Schmid (1992), 91-92.

60. Aristotle, *Politics* 1340a39-340b1.

61. Aristotle, *Politics* 1340b2-3.

62. One question concerning *andreia* is whether a courageous temper is somehow within us already or whether it can be produced, encouraged, or enhanced. In the discussion in the *Republic* as to whether education is more akin to putting sight into blind eyes, or more like turning the seeing eye around to its proper objects, Socrates says, "Therefore, the other virtues of a soul, as they are called, are probably somewhat close

to those of the body [*sōmatos*]. For they are really not there beforehand and are later produced by habits and exercises, while the virtue of exercising prudence [*phronēsai*] is more than anything somehow more divine [*theioterou*], it seems" (*Republic* 518d–e). Virtuous humans are thus between animals and the divine. If animals can be courageous, as raised by Socrates at *Laches* 196d, then courage is, at least partly, bodily. On the other hand, if the Dorian harmony can encourage courageous imitations, then courage is not entirely derived from a natural temper or disposition. If the Dorian harmony can encourage or even produce courageous behavior, then courage would seem to be something beyond what is endowed in humans by *phūsis*. There is thus a tension between Laches's extolling Dorian harmony, if understood as in any productive of *andreia*, and his defense of courage in wild animals.

63. Hoerber (1968), 100.

64. Hoerber (1968), 100.

65. Nichols (1987), 274.

66. Nails (2002), 181.

67. Nails (2002), 181.

68. Nails (2002), 181.

69. Nails (2002), 181.

70. O'Brien (1963), 146.

71. Tessitore (1994), 125.

72. That this is comical swaggering is suggested explicitly by Alcibiades's quoting of a phrase directly from Aristophanes to describe it (*Symposium* 221a–b).

73. Nichols disagrees. He claims that the drunken Alcibiades describes the difference between Socrates and Laches as one of Socrates's being *emphrōn*, or "in possession of his mind," not as a difference of courage. While this is true, the definition Laches agrees to is that *andreia* is *phronimos karteria*, and if the wise or *phronimos* part is lacking in Laches, so too is courage as he defines it, (Nichols [1987], 278).

74. Dobbs (1986), 829.

75. Dobbs (1986), 848.

76. Sprague's translation, used here, does not place this emphasis on *andreia*'s gender, using the neutral *itself* or *it* instead of *herself* or *her*. It could be argued that Socrates is doing no such thing, and simply using the pronoun appropriate to the Greek noun, but there are repeated references throughout the dialogue to manliness and effeminacy in this discussion

of "manly courage" that constitute pointed references to a subtext of masculinity and what we would today refer to as machismo. Socrates, who describes himself as a midwife and describes learning from women such as Diotima, may be immune to such gender dynamics. Laches and Nicias, however, may not be.

77. *Thumos* may be the very spirit of Laches, whose love of victory seems to push to a malicious form of laughter against his opponents. Nichols stresses Laches's own heroic code as opposed to that of Socrates: "Unlike Laches, Socrates is not moved most deeply by patriotism, love of honor, and fear of shame and ridicule to courageous actions; rather, his courageous actions are made possible by his philosophic thinking" (Nichols [1987], 278–79). If so, then ridicule would indeed be particularly impactful on Laches. For an illuminating discussion of *thumos* in the *Laches*, see Schmid (1992), 111–16.

78. Schmid (1992), 130.

79. Arieti claims that Laches and Nicias "failed in life because they failed philosophically. Laches had insisted that there be a harmony between words and deeds (188c–d). Yet he himself admits that he cannot put into words what he means by courage (194a–b)," (Arieti [1991], 59).

80. See chapter 1 for more on tragic laughter. Key distinctions between tragic and comic laughter will be discussed in chapter 4.

81. Ast, cited in Hoerber (1968), 95.

82. That manliness (and effeminacy) is at issue is further supported by the fact that forms of the word *anēr*, or man, occur twenty-six times within the *Laches*.

83. Tessitore points out that this is the same word (*truphaō*) Socrates uses to denounce Euthyphro when Euthyphro opts out of continuing the search for an understanding of piety (*Euthyphro* 11e–12a). Tessitore (1994), 123f15.

84. Tessitore (1994), 123.

85. Tessitore (1994), 123.

86. Tessitore (1994), 123f17

87. Tessitore (1994), 124.

88. Arieti (1991), 58.

89. Arieti (1991), 56.

90. To a large extent, Schmid's claim seems correct. Where I would object is in any subsuming of comic and tragic elements within the greater heading of irony. Comic and tragic elements can and ought to

receive recognition apart from the irony to which they may contribute. Schmid (1992), 53.

91. See Schmid (1992), 128–31, and Dobbs (1986).

92. Dobbs (1986), 827.

93. Aristotle, *Nicomachean Ethics* 1115a6.

94. Lysimachus's enthusiasm to meet Socrates on the next day so that they could go back to school together is a formally correct response to *aporia*, but, as noted elsewhere, Lysimachus lacks the abilities necessary to philosophy. See *Republic* 485b–86b, and Tessitore (1994), 124.

95. Homer *Odyssey* XVII.353.

Chapter 3

1. Hubbard (1991), 2.

2. Hubbard (1991), 5.

3. Hegel attributes to comical characters an "imperturbable self-assurance" despite their inability to be what it is they project. Hegel, *The Philosophy of Fine Arts* IV, 329, as cited in Hubbard (1991), 6.

4. Griswold (1986), 43.

5. Hyland (1981), 13.

6. Falling down can also be tragic, as even Oedipus can be said to have "fallen." The difference appears to concern the significance of the fall's consequences. Tumbling off a bench with nothing more than a bump may be funny, whereas losing one's kingdom, one's family, and one's sight is not.

7. Aristophanes, *Acharnians* 1178–80.

8. Nietzsche (1990), 117, and Diogenes Laertius, *Lives of the Philosophers*, 3.21.

9. Halper (2011), 321.

10. This is in no way to imply a simple opposition between tragedy and comedy. Schlegel, for instance, describes comedy as "the direct opposite of Tragedy," and particularly in consideration of the Greeks. Schlegel (1846), 146. The relationship of tragedy and comedy is neither exclusive nor hierarchically ranked. For a fuller discussion on their mutual entanglement and implication, see Silk (2000), 42–97.

11. Dillon (1991), 352. Dillon counts twenty-six examples of positive and twenty-nine examples of negative laughter occurring in the extant plays of Aristophanes. Tragic laughter, on the other hand, associates laughter

with mockery, hatred, and madness. Dillon counts twelve examples of such laughter in Aeschylus, twenty-nine in Sophocles, and thirty-nine in Euripides, all of which support this. See Dillon (1991), 345n4.

12. Dillon (1991), 347–48.

13. This supports a reading of Medea as a hero, rather than the embodiment of *akrasia*, as more of the literature on Euripides's *Medea* suggests.

14. Euripides, *Medea* 1362, as cited by Dillon 350. The six lines are: 383, 404, 797, 1355, and 1362.

15. Sophocles, *Ajax* 120.

16. Dillon, (1991), 345n4.

17. Sommerstein counts approximately fifty of the ninety-six occurrences of laughter in Aristophanes's plays as derisive, implied by the uses of *katagelaō*, *katachaskō*, *enchaskō*, and their derivatives (Sommerstein [2009], 107).

18. Sommerstein (2009), 107–10.

19. Sommerstein (2009), 110–12.

20. Sommerstein (2009), 112–14.

21. Sommerstein points out that sexual pleasure involving a young bride, potentially given in marriage without her consent, or a slave-prostitute may not exemplify mutual pleasure, but that the example in question at *Clouds* 1078 involves a seemingly mutual arrangement (Sommerstein [2009], 113 and 113n19).

22. Sommerstein (2009), 114.

23. Sommerstein, as cited by Sommerstein (2009), 114.

24. Sommerstein (2009), 114.

25. Schlegel (1846), 147.

26. Although it might be suspect to attribute to Plato a critique of his own relatives (the Charmides in question likely being his uncle and Critias, his cousin [see Nails (2002), 90–94]), the purported dates are suggestive. The dramatic events portrayed in the dialogue, taking place after the battle of Potidaea (432 BCE) occur before Plato's birth in May 429 BCE [see Nails (2002), 243–51 and 311–12], and the dialogue appears to have been composed approximately in 380 BCE, when popular sentiment was deeply opposed to the Thirty and their affiliates. Both Critias and Charmides were deposed as leaders among the fifty-one and killed in the battle of Munychia in 403 BCE (Nails [2002], 92 and 110). Overthrown by many of the people to whom they denied suffrage, the right to a jury trial, and other rights, they were replaced with a more democratic system.

Rather than merely an attack on Critias and Charmides, the *Charmides* might instead be a defense of Socrates, who was accused of a corrosive influence on young political aspirants such as Alcibiades and Charmides, implied at *Apology* 33d-34a.

27. Desjardins (2002), 116.

28. Socrates does offer an elaboration of his understanding of this formulation of justice at *Republic* 443d-e.

29. Desjardins (2002), 117.

30. *Meno* 97e6-98a4 is cited to support this (Desjardins [2002], 117).

31. More specifically, by "performative contradiction," I mean a contradiction occurring between the form and content of a speech act. For instance, if I say aloud, "I am mute," I directly contradict what I am saying by what I am doing by saying it. In the terminology of John Austin, such performative contradictions involve a tension between locutionary and illocutionary forces that prompts a change in perlocutionary force. Such performative contradictions occur repeatedly in Platonic dialogues, such as in the *Republic*'s own Divided Line image, which warns us of trusting images, and yet constitutes an image itself. The perlocutionary force involves a state of *aporia*, since the more I trust the image itself, the less I can trust what it is telling me. The audience then is denied an authoritative answer, and thus is provoked into active participation in the dialogue. See Tanner (2010).

32. Morreall (2009), 4-15.

33. See also Wood (2007), 79.

34. Benardete (1993), 202.

35. Xenophon, *Memorabilia* 1.2.12.

36. Xenophon, *Hellenica* 2.4.19.

37. The conversation between Socrates and Charmides reported by Xenophon focuses on Socrates's attempts at convincing Charmides to enter politics to benefit the city. Interestingly, Charmides there expresses fear at being ridiculous in doing so, and Socrates exhorts him to investigate himself, much as he begins to do in the *Charmides* (*Memorabilia* 3.7).

38. In this sense, the same author thus can write both comedy and tragedy, as discussed at *Symposium* 223d, namely, Plato. Diskin Clay offers a provocative and compelling argument toward such a claim in his essay "The Tragic and Comic Poet of the *Symposium*" (1975).

39. Qualifications such as "when there's no call for it" and "must contain some new twist" are significant here. The law is not absolute: it

neither restricts doing and saying anything ridiculous, nor does it forbid such buffoonery onstage. The concern and danger seem to be for the actors, much more so than for the audience, otherwise slaves and aliens would be barred, as are citizens. The mimicry in the *Charmides* is not left to slaves and aliens, but is performed by the best and the brightest citizens of Athens. Is there, as per the second qualification, a "new twist" (*kainon*) involved here?

40. Charmides refuses this too. His earlier blushing upon being asked whether he is *sōphrōn* (158c) made him appear a more likely candidate. He later equivocates again as to whether he exemplifies such virtue (176b) and yet demands forcefully that Socrates chants the Thracian charm for him. The charm, for Socrates, is only necessary for those who lack *sōphrosynē* (158b–c), hence Socrates's original question to Charmides as to whether he is *sōphrōn*. Charmides's demand for the charm at the dialogue's end implies a realization that he is not *sōphrōn* (176b). Although this would seem a promising realization, Charmides's refusal truly to "look inside himself," to think for himself, and to turn away from heteronomy undermine this.

41. This may well be evasion on Critias's behalf, as Schmid suggests. Critias's earlier understanding of *sōphrosynē* as minding one's own business has very quickly been shown to lead to an intolerable conclusion (that the *sōphrōn* may not know herself to be *sōphrōn*), and Critias, quickly abandoning his earlier definition, is now seeking to recover by trying on a new answer and reasserting himself to those present with a longer speech rooted in religious tradition, but one that has been radically transformed. Critias claims that this is but a new explanation of what he previously meant, but since that was never explained properly and since he does not now clarify what connects the two, he speaks, as he interestingly says of the god of light's injunction, "very darkly, as a seer would do" ([165a] Schmid [1998], 36).

42. Critias's interpretation of what we might today call the perlocutionary force of the Delphic inscription is significant. Rather than an imperative, Critias claims that "Know thyself" constitutes a greeting from the god, adding, "or so I suppose the man thought who dedicated this inscription" (164e). This addition is striking. Rather than divine revelation, the Delphic inscription is of human origin, but ascribed to a god. Further, reading this as a greeting, rather than a moral imperative, reduces or even eliminates the power differential between gods and mortals. Gods (or humans acting like gods) greet mortals as though they were equals,

and humans pretend to be gods by attributing divine origins to their own words. Critias replaces understanding oneself in one's limitedness in a world divinely ordered, as the Apollonian message is traditionally interpreted to mean, with atheism and hubris. See Schmid's discussion of this in Schmid (1998), 36–38.

43. Schmid (1998), 101.

44. Schmid (1998), 101.

45. Although the accusation of being an *adoleschēs* is more commonly employed by comic poets against Socrates, Plato and philosophers (cf. Eupolis's fragment 386, where Socrates is described as a "babbling beggar [*ptōchon adoleschēn*]," and in Alexis's fragment 185, where one is said to be able to "*adoleschein* privately with Plato"), *lērōn* and cognates are also used, such as in Aristophanes's *Clouds* 359, where Socrates is hailed by the Chorus as the "high priest of the subtlest nonsense [*lērōn hiereu*]," and in Epicrates's fragment 10, where the more ambiguous, but likely pejorative, form *leschais* is used to describe the ridiculous conversations that happen in Plato's Academy. That Socrates was aware of these accusations by comic poets is evidenced in the *Phaedo*, where he says "I do not think . . . that anyone who hears me now, not even a comic poet [*kōmōdopoios*], could say that I am babbling [*adoleschō*] and discussing things that do not concern me . . ." (70c–d). For comic fragments, see Storey (2011).

46. A temporal defense of Hippias might suggest that Hippias's claim was perhaps true up until Socrates showed him up. If so, he might not commit a performative contradiction as such.

47. Socrates's good sportsmanship in this regard is suggested by the anecdote recounted by Aelian that Socrates not only attended the performance of Aristophanes's *The Clouds* in 423 BCE, but when the actor portraying him took to the stage wearing a hideous mask, Socrates stood up from his prominent seat in the theater to show the resemblance (Aelian, *Varia Historia* 2.13).

48. Schmid (1998), 122.

49. Schmid (1998), 123.

50. The same is true of compounded *gelaō* forms such as *epigelaō*.

51. Schmid (1998), 151.

52. In this, it may be possible to discern two different models of a ridiculous person: Critias, who refuses to recognize his limitations and his ridiculousness, and Socrates, who is overtly aware of both.

53. In the *Protagoras*, Socrates personifies the logos, which, "if it had a voice of its own" would mock them (*katagelan*) for their mutually reversed

positions (*Protagoras* 361a). In the *Laches*, Socrates personifies courage as ridiculing the interlocutors, saying, "let us endure, so that courage itself [*hē andreia*] won't make fun of us [*katagelasē*] for not searching for it courageously . . ." (*Laches* 194a).

54. Plato is said to have directed Dionysius of Syracuse to the works of Aristophanes to get a sense of the political situation in Athens. (See Cooper [1922], 38–39.) To Plato is attributed the epitaph, "The Graces, desiring an imperishable shrine, chose the soul of Aristophanes" (from the *Greek Anthology*, Croiset 3.532, cited in Cooper [1922], 39). In the *Life of Plato*, Olympiodorus suggests Plato to have died with a work of Aristophanes under his pillow.

55. For more on self-awareness in the characters of Aristophanes, see Hubbard (1991).

56. Nietzsche, *Birth of Tragedy*, 110.

57. On the connection between honor, virtue, and the central position, see Howland (1998).

58. See Greene (1920), Michelini (2000a), Shelley (2003), and Wood (2007).

59. The attribution of what a character in a dialogue says to Plato himself is a hermeneutically insensitive and highly speculative venture. The fact that characters routinely disagree, or that even within the views offered by one specific character, say, Socrates, are inconsistent. The soul, for instance, in the *Republic* is famously described by Socrates as tripartite, whereas in the *Phaedo*, he seems to suggest that the soul cannot have parts. At the very least, committing what has come to be called the "Plato says" fallacy is hermeneutically sloppy, a seeming shorthand akin to saying that Shakespeare says, "To be, or not to be, that is the question," when one really means Hamlet. As such, it seems innocuous enough, but historically many positions have been attributed—inaccurately—to Plato on the basis of what his characters say. This is where the seemingly innocuous shorthand becomes dangerous.

Chapter 4

1. See also Michelini (2000).

2. The term *protreptic* is used here as broadly construed by Michelini, who defines it as "the exhortation . . . to leave conventional ways of life and care for wisdom and moral virtue" (Michelini [2000], 510).

3. Ewegen sees two different types of lives as possible on this basis. The tragic life is one lived in the lower realm of logos, where logos presents itself as the whole, when it can always only be *part* of the whole, and an ambivalent part at that. Kirkland has argued, "what makes this particular life tragic is not just its immersion in falsity, but the inability of those living it to recognize the essentially dual nature of logos" (quoted by Ewegen [2014], 94). Logos, as we are told in the *Cratylus*, can both conceal and reveal, and so it cannot be taken as straightforward truth, since it can also be false. The comic life, on the other hand, is that which is "oriented toward the upper region while mired decisively in the lower" (Ewegen [2014], 96). It is that which recognizes both possibilities intrinsic to logos: "Such a life as would come to see *logos* as dual-natured would understand that *logos always* brings both concealment and unconcealment with itself as intrinsic possibilities. It is not as if the lower parts could simply be left behind in favor of the upper parts, any more that Pan himself could leave his shaggy goatlegs in order to dwell exclusively in his smooth upper body. To the contrary, that essentially dual nature of *logos* necessitates a belonging together of both parts, of the lower and the upper, the human and the divine" (Ewegen [2014], 96). The comic life is as a satyr, inconsistent with itself, shaggy and smooth.

4. Humans cannot be the measure for logos, according to Ewegen. Rather, logos is the measure of human beings, for it is how we come to understand ourselves. Ewegen (2014), 183.

5. Kirkland, for instance, argues that: ". . . in this principally comic etymology, something nonetheless essential concerning the Platonic conception of language comes to light—that is, the possession of language situates human beings essentially *between* appearances and 'what is' and, thereby, *toward* the immortals' perfect wisdom or grasp of being" (Kirkland [2007], 2).

6. See Halper (2011).

7. Kirkland emphasizes that logos cannot be reduced to the will of its user, that it is an always already existent yoke binding humans to the world, but one that does not necessarily reveal that world with accuracy or consistency (Kirkland [2007].

8. Sallis (1996), 183f1.

9. Liddell and Scott (1889), entry for *onoma*, 560.

10. Euripides, *Helen* 42.

11. Heraclitus, fragment 48 in Diels, cited in Kahn (1979), 201.

12. Homer, *Odyssey* 9.366.
13. Euripides, *Orestes* 409.
14. See Sluiter (1997), especially 168–77.
15. This reading assumes a fairly straightforward interpretation of Heraclitus, a notoriously difficult and complex philosopher. While this chapter will not do justice to several thinkers addressed in it, it is my purpose in this part of it only to suggest that the critique of etymology, and specifically of *onoma*, as trustworthy and accurate transmissions of reality has roots extending well beyond Plato's *Cratylus*.
16. Parmenides, fragment 353 in Kirk, Raven, and Schofield (1984).
17. Arieti (1991), 63. Friedländer suspects that the connection of Hermogenes with Eleaticism may itself be derived from the contrast in the *Cratylus*. For more on the questionable and problematic association of Hermogenes and Cratylus with Parmenides and Heraclitus, respectively, see Sallis (1996), 186–87n3.
18. Arieti claims that the drama of the dialogues is not simply to be used to clarify philosophical difficulties, but rather that the meaning of the dialogues is ultimately located in their dramatic dimensions. As such, he reads the *Cratylus* as about the gullibility and rigidity with which followers devote themselves to the thinking of others, at the expense of their own. A fascinating interpretation and one that takes very seriously the significance of the literary dimensions of the dialogues, Arieti's reading of the *Cratylus* and of Platonic dialogues in general, I would argue, goes one step too far in dismissing the significance of the philosophical specifics of these dramas. If these are no more than sophisticated, cautionary moral tales warning us against, say, blind devotion to a philosopher or philosophy, then there would be little need for readers to work through the philosophical complexities of a dense and difficult work such as the *Cratylus*. Arieti is right to recognize the importance of Plato's choice and invention of philosophical dialogues, but to dismiss their philosophical aspects is as one-sided as dismissing their dramatic and dialogical aspects.
19. Sprague (1962).
20. Sprague (1994), 54n28.
21. Sprague (1994), 54n28.
22. Sluiter (1962), 176.
23. Sluiter (1997), 177.
24. Sallis calls the dialogue "a comedy" (Sallis [1996], 185). Greene writes that the dialogue is "equally comic and equally satirical, but truth

lurks behind the ridiculous even more tantalizingly" (1920), 86. Shorey describes the *Cratylus* as having an "almost farcical humor" (1993), 260. Taylor recognizes the "good-natured satire" of the *Cratylus*, but relinquishes it to the status of a "minor dialogue" (2001), 78. Arieti deems it a "wonderful farce" (1991), 63. Ewegen describes the Cratylus as a "comedy" that "begins with a joke and undertakes an absurd task, pursued in a comical way" (2014), 9.

25. Aristophanes, *Clouds* 394.

26. Diogenes Laertius, 9.52. See also Sluiter (1997), 175.

27. The same word is used by Socrates at 278b, where he describes the inconsequential joking of the brothers as "tripping (other people) up [*huposkelizōn*]" and "overturning [*anatrepōn*] them by means of the distinctions in words." Similarly, at 278c, such charlatans laugh at their victims of such word play when they are "sprawling on their backs" (*huption anatetrammenon*).

28. Diogenes Laertius, 9.51.

29. Ewegen makes a very similar point in regards to Cratylus's position and his predominant silence in the dialogue (2014), 173–74.

30. *Cratylus* 278c, 278d, 283a, 283b, 283c, 288b, 288d, 294b, 300e, 306b, and 307b.

31. Michelini (2000), 517.

32. Michelini (2000), 518.

33. Chance sees the brothers as initiating Clinias into the mysteries of philosophy, a point which brings eristics and dialectic into even greater proximity. For a fuller discussion, see Chance (1992), 55–65. Michelini echoes this, arguing that the images with which Socrates describes the brothers' move from being athletes and entertainers to being those initiating an inductee into the Corybantic mysteries by dancing wildly about the initiate seated in a chair. She further points out that Socrates's simile of the brothers' pulling out a chair from under someone (*Euthydemus* 278b–c) reduces this sacred ritual to a practical joke. See especially Michelini (2000), 518–19.

34. Michelini argues that the result of Socrates's never letting his guard down is that, "the dialogue also constitutes a reflexive critique of ironic technique itself" (2000), 531. Chance finds a similarly reflective form of laughter in the *Euthydemus*: "Plato allows philosophers the rare opportunity to laugh at a grotesque caricature of themselves . . ." (1992), 19–20.

35. Chance (1992), 19.

36. Michelini also notes Socrates's enactment of such a "stock figure of ridicule," namely, the old man who returns to school (2000), 514.

Pickard-Cambridge cites large archeological findings of masks in Sparta and of descriptions by Pollux of the masks of New Comedy to claim that old women, often appearing as nurses or midwives, were frequent characters of Attic comedy throughout its duration. Old men characters, most often depicted as leaning on sticks, are stock characters of New Comedy as well as in Plautus and Terence. While Pickard-Cambridge does not see this tendency as strongly in Aristophanes, Hubbard makes a strong case for it, particularly in his early plays. See Pickard-Cambridge (1927), 254–59.

In his eleven extant plays, Aristophanes prominently features old men such as Dicaeopolis, Strepsiades, Demos, Trygaeus, and Philocleon as main characters; and the old Acharnians and Wasps for choruses. One way or another, Aristophanes's old men all rejuvenate themselves so as, through abandoning existing orthodoxies and reasserting themselves, to cease being old men, to ambivalent effect. Demos, for instance, is boiled in a cauldron to miraculously reattain his youth (*Knights*, 1321). Strepsiades attempts to rejuvenate himself by educating himself as though he were a child, only to be beaten by his own son. Intergenerational conflict is thus a central theme in Aristophanes. See Hubbard (1989). All of these themes are present in the *Euthydemus*.

That the elderly schoolboy was recognized as comic in Platonic dialogues is suggested explicitly in the *Laches*, where Socrates encourages Lysimachus to join him in becoming a student again. Socrates says, "if anyone laughs at us because we think it worthwhile to spend time in school at our age, then I think we should confront him with the saying of Homer, 'Modesty is not a good mate for a needy man' " (*Laches*, 201b). Lysimachus responds by stressing that being even older makes him less weary of appearing laughable: "the fact that I am the oldest makes me the most eager to go to school along with the boys" (*Laches*, 201b).

37. This reference to Socrates as a Cronus (*Euthydemus* 287b3) brings him into relation again with Aristophanes, and particularly the contest between the Unjust and Just *logoi*, as Michelini writes, Socrates's "opponent applies to him the same term of abuse that the Unjust Argument directed against the Just Argument, the representative of traditional education" (2000), 522. Aristophanes, *Clouds* 929, cf. 1070.

38. Aristophanes, *Knights* 1321.

39. For Michelini, Socrates in the *Euthydemus* "becomes a comic hero, at first absurd and foolish, later rejuvenated and triumphant" (2000), 516.

40. Chance (1992), 193.

41. Chance (1992), 192.

42. Michelini (2000), 530.

43. Michelini (2000), 531.

44. This is why, as Michelini writes, "Socrates, with his mock-modest airs, reveals the weaknesses of his opponents more to the external audience, the reader or hearer, than to the internal one . . ." (2000), 530.

45. Halper (2011), 321.

46. Chance cites a rich mixture of tones, textures and philosophical takeaway in the *Euthydemus*: "Unleashing all the forces of his tragic and comic art, his powers of persuasion and dissuasion, his love of irony and satire, and even an impulse to slander and abuse, Plato has created for our inspection that measure of baseness and ugliness in all philosophy, and thereby transformed the brothers into types from which we are to turn" (1992), 19.

47. Baxter estimates that the etymologies take up twenty-four of the fifty-seven pages, as numbered by Stephanus. If so, this convoluted and bizarre section comprises nearly half of the dialogue itself, and as such, it seems hermeneutically unsound to dismiss such a large portion of a dialogue as merely a digression, a small joke, or anything that can be dismissed from a general interpretation of the *Cratylus* (Baxter [1962], ff86).

48. Baxter and V. Goldschmidt, *Essai sur le "Cratyle"* (Paris, 1940), offer two prominent interpretations of the *Cratylus* as satirical. For more on this reading, see Sedley (1998), 140, ff1.

49. Sedley (1998), 141.

50. Sedley (1998), 141.

51. Sedley (1998), 143. On interpreting Platonic dialogues comically, Sedley writes, "The desire to make Plato a philosophical hero exerts a powerful hold on those of us who devote their time to studying him, and understandably so. But Plato is *not* one of us. We should not, without compelling evidence, help ourselves to the assumption that he rose effortlessly above presuppositions endemic to his own culture. Sedley is right to warn us against reading Plato in this way, but this claim is not directed at the interpretation of dialogues as comic. If we read Book V of the *Republic* as fully serious (and indeed a direct expression of the author's viewpoints), for instance, Plato can be read as a progressive feminist. Appealing though

this may be, what may be more likely, especially given the case made by Sallis and others, is that Book V is a comic interlude, patterned after Aristophanes's *Assembly of Women* and not meant in any way to suggest a belief in gender equality, or an actual proscription for coeducation. Reading Plato comically does not elevate him above archaic presuppositions, but it does call these presuppositions into question.

52. Sallis does not need to appeal to authorial intent in the way that Sedley does, as his reading is based on what is in the text itself, rather than what we presume "Plato" to have intended with it. The exception to this is his use of Plato's *Seventh Letter* (1996).

53. The distinction of Sallis's approach to the *Cratylus* from that of, say, Sedley, is yet more nuanced than this, as articulated by Sallis himself, who describes three methods of interpreting the *Cratylus*. The first method that Sallis identifies involves taking the etymologies as serious attempts at investigating the origins of names. A second method reverses this, taking the etymologies as caricatures meant to ridicule Plato's historical contemporaries. This assumes that the function of the dialogue is a polemical one and presents the need to demonstrate the comic character of the dialogue as well as the intended target of the satire. Sedley's would be an example of the first approach, and Baxter's, an example of the second. A third method of interpreting the *Cratylus* "seeks to clarify what it is that the etymological investigations genuinely bring to light in connection with that which they are, in comic fashion, put forth *as* bringing to light" (Sallis [1996], 235). The directive is taken from the philosophical-dramatic context, and what is brought to light, says Sallis, "is precisely the situation of human questioning and speaking" (1996, 234).

54. Comic readings such as those offered by Sallis and Ewegen do not assume a mutual distinction between comedy and seriousness. Instead, Sallis attributes to the comedy of the *Cratylus*, a "peculiar seriousness," the consequences of which he attempts to elucidate (1996), 234. Comedy then takes on a very different role than it is usually accorded in philosophy, where it either is viewed as superficial window-dressing, or as satire, directed (sometimes maliciously) at an opponent one wishes to show as merely ridiculous. For Sallis and Ewegen, it is neither vacuous, nor just a barb aimed at denigrating a philosophical opponent; comedy can bear philosophical content. For Ewegen, comedy brings to light the duality of logos, and makes possible a glimpse at true Being (2014), 147.

55. Sallis (1996), 287.

56. Humpty Dumpty and Alice from Lewis Carroll's *Through the Looking-Glass* have the following exchange: " 'I don't know what you mean by "glory," ' Alice said. Humpty Dumpty smiled contemptuously. 'Of course you don't—till I tell you. I meant "there's a nice knock-down argument for you!" ' 'But "glory" doesn't mean "a nice knock-down argument," ' Alice objected. 'When *I* use a word,' Humpty Dumpty said in rather a scornful tone, 'it means just what I choose it to mean—neither more nor less.' 'The question is,' said Alice, 'whether you *can* make words mean so many different things.' 'The question is,' said Humpty Dumpty, 'which is to be master—that's all.' " For Hermogenes, it is clear that the language-user is master, not the language itself (Carroll, as quoted in Baxter [1962], 18–19).

57. It is difficult to avoid making a connection to what Aristotle tells us of Cratylus at a seemingly much later point in his life, where his Heraclitean commitments seem to have driven him to silence: "[Presocratics] held these views because they saw that all this world of nature is in movement and that about that which changes no true statement can be made; at least, regarding that which everywhere in every respect is changing nothing could truly be affirmed. It was this belief that blossomed into the most extreme of the views above mentioned, that of the professed Heracliteans, such as was held by Cratylus, who finally did not think it right to say anything but only moved his finger, and criticized Heraclitus for saying that it is impossible to step twice into the same river; for *he* thought one could not do it even once" (Aristotle, *Metaphysics* 1010a7–14). Unless the correctness of naming and of speaking more generally can be explained, the only sensible alternative on Cratylus's own theory is silence.

58. Socrates, having just sympathized with Cratylus's position, does the same, calling Hermogenes by name (390d).

If the etymology for Hermes's name from *to hermēneia* (407e1–08b7) can be brought into play here, another reason why Hermogenes may be poorly named as such is suggested by the derivation: Hermogenes is not a good producer of interpretations, explanations, or *logoi*, as Hermogenes himself comments at 408b (Baxter [1962], ff10).

59. That the Euthyphro mentioned in the *Cratylus* is the same as the speaker of the *Euthyphro* is supported by Nails. She suggests him to have been approximately twenty years old in the *Cratylus* and in his mid-forties in the *Euthyphro* (Nails [2002], 152–53).

Euthyphro, in the dialogue of the same name, claims expertise on Uranus, Cronus, and Zeus, and the placement of this claim to Euthyphronic inspiration immediately after the etymologies of these gods suggests this to be the same figure. See also Reeve (1997), ff17, and Sallis (1996), 225–26.

60. In the *Philebus*, Socrates suggests the nature of the ridiculous (*geloion ēntina phusin*) to be, ". . . a kind of vice [*ponēria*] that derives its name from a special disposition; it is, among all the vices, the one with a character that stands in direct opposition [*tounantion*] to the one recommended by the famous inscription at Delphi" (*Philebus* 48c). Comedy would seem, in other words, to obfuscate that most philosophical of imperatives, and the putative origin of Socrates's philosophical mission, to "know thyself." Of the three kinds of self-ignorance resulting—those of one's material goods, of one's bodily goods, and of one's psychic goods—Socrates goes on to say that ". . . an overwhelming number (of people) are mistaken about the third kind . . . and . . . believe that they are superior in virtue, although they are not" (*Philebus* 48e). This is especially true, Socrates claims, of the virtue of wisdom.

61. Taylor (2001), 83.

62. Ewegen offers an excellent reading of the etymologies (2014).

63. Anaxagoras, fragment 529 in Kirk, Raven, and Schofield (1984).

64. Socrates's speech is described as dithyrambic elsewhere. Shortly before his first speech in the *Phaedrus*, Socrates suggests that he has been seized by an unusual fluency, even a madness, and is "on the edge of speaking in dithyrambs" (*Phaedrus* 238d). As he and Phaedrus are analyzing his first speech afterward, Socrates describes how, in his speech, he moved past lyric poetry and into epic (*Phaedrus* 241e). As was traditional for dithyrambs (Pickard-Cambridge, 74), Socrates ends with a prayer at the end of the *Phaedrus* (*Phaedrus* 279c).

65. Proclus, Suidas, Athenaeus, and Plutarch are among the sources Pickard-Cambridge cites. Pickard-Cambridge (1927), 10f6. See Pickard-Cambridge for the dithyramb's probable historical derivation from comic revels and processions.

66. Plutarch, *On the 'E' at Delphi*, 9.6–7. http://penelope.uchicago.edu/misctracts/plutarchE.html. The Greek is from http://www.perseus.tufts.edu (Plutarch *De E*, 389a–b).

67. Sprague (1962), 57.

68. Ewegen (2014), 63.

69. Chance (1992), 13.

Chapter 5

1. Nietzsche (1956), 87.
2. Tanner (2010).
3. Nietzsche (1956), 81.
4. Nietzsche (1956), 82 and 85.
5. Sutton (1980), 162.
6. Sutton (1980), 159.
7. Sutton (1980), 162.
8. It could be argued that including the hiccup remedies as part of the *Symposium* is fallacious, but to this, I would suggest that it is included enough in the dialogue as to be mentioned as being excluded, and thereby, a matter of interest. Much like Socrates's mentioning that he will not parade his family in the courtroom in the *Apology*, and like his dismissal of Xanthippe in the beginning of the *Phaedo*, such delineations are significant enough to be incorporated into the dialogue, when they could, much more easily and economically, have been left out altogether.
9. Taylor (1936), 216.
10. Bury (1909), xvii.
11. Although general laughter ensues Alcibiades's speech (222c), Aristophanes is the only one to be specifically noted as laughing out loud in the dialogue (189b). Laughter is understood here as anticipated or implied, not necessarily named as actually occurring, as is consistent with the use of Greek laughter in other sources. See also chapter 1.
12. Bury (1909), xix.
13. Arieti (1991), 101.
14. Friedländer (1969a), 161.
15. Howland (2007), 21.
16. Clay (2005), 74.
17. Rosen (1999), 91-92. The promotion of the poet's speech is read as Plato's preference for Aristophanes.
18. Guthrie (1975), 382n2.
19. Lowenstam asks, "What would a Platonic dialogue look like if the author inserted a dramatic action every time he wanted to indicate that something was not important?" Lowenstam (1986), 47.
20. As cited in Lowenstam, Gierse suggests that "any comprehensive interpretation must explain both the hiccups and the transposition

of speeches" (1986), 45. A possible explanation for the transposition of speeches on my interpretation of the hiccups will be offered in the conclusion. Rather than reading the speeches as of ascending importance, I will suggest there that the central positions—that which Aristophanes hiccups his way into and that of Agathon—are positions of honor, accorded in this case to the comedian and the tragedian.

21. Arieti (1991), 105.

22. Halper (2011), 321.

23. Plochmann (1963), 9-10.

24. Rüchert, Stephens, and Schwegler are cited among others in Bury (1909), xxii.

25. Aristotle, *Poetics*, 1449a35-7.

26. Arieti suggests that the hiccups might signify either what Aristophanes thinks of Pausanias's speech, or they might be a sign of his violating the agreement not to drink too much. Arieti (1991), 101.

27. Schleiermacher, as cited in Bury (1909), xxii.

28. This etymology is suggested in Lowenstam as going so far back as W. S. Teuffel, cited in Bury. Apelt writes, "Ich finde nirgends angemerkt, dass der Arzt Eryximachos im Gastmahl durch seinem Name schon die Rolle ankündigt, die ihm als 'Schlucksenbekämpfer' zugeteilt wird" (1912), 78n1.

29. Strauss (2001), 99.

30. Most prominently, Ast is cited as holding this view by Bury (1909), xxii.

31. Plochmann (1963) and Cobb (1993) argue for this.

32. Strauss (2001), 96.

33. Bury (1909), xxiii.

34. Rüchert and Bury cited by Lowenstam, 44.

35. Clay (2005), 74.

36. Plutarch, *Quaestiones Conviviales* 7.7.10.

37. Plutarch, *Quaestiones Conviviales* 7.7.10.

38. Plutarch, *Quaestiones Conviviales* 7.7.8. Concerning the mixture of sensory indulgence and restrictions, Plutarch writes: "Those guests of Agatho [*sic*], whose discourse was more sweet than the sound of any pipe in the world, were no good authority in this case; for it was no wonder that in their company the flute-girl was not regarded; but it is strange that, in the midst of the entertainment, the extreme pleasantness of the discourse had not made them forget their meat and drink" (7.7.8). Such

a philosopher who dismisses simple pleasures deserves ridicule: "should not a philosopher that banisheth music from a feast, and is afraid of a musician, and bids his linkboy presently light his link and be gone, be laughed at, since he seems to abominate the most innocent pleasures, as beetles do ointment?" (7.7.12).

Aelius Aristides suggests a similarly benign reading of the hiccups, writing "*all' oimai luzein auton edei, hina eis aplēstian skōphthē.*" Cited in Bury (1909), xxii.

39. Athenaeus, *The Learned Banqueters* 5.186a.

40. Athenaeus, *The Learned Banqueters* 5.187c–d.

41. Olympiodorus, *Life of Plato* 3.

42. Olympiodorus, *Life of Plato* 3.

43. The passage from Olympiodorus reads: "According to Orpheus there were four cosmic reigns. First was the reign of Uranus, then Cronus received the kingship, having cut off his father's genitals. Zeus ruled after Cronus, having cast his father into Tartarus. Next, Dionysus succeeded Zeus. They say that through Hera's treachery, the Titans who were around Dionysus tore him to pieces and ate his flesh. And Zeus, being angry at this, struck the Titans with thunderbolts, and from the soot of the vapors that arose from [the incinerated Titans] came the matter from which humanity came into existence. Therefore, we must not commit suicide—not because, as [Socrates] seems to say, we are in our body as if in a prison, since that is obvious and [Socrates] would not call such an idea secret, but rather because our bodies are Dionysiac. We are, indeed, part of Dionysus if we are composed from the soot of the Titans who ate Dionysus' flesh" (Olympiodorus, commentary on Plato's *Phaedo*, cited in Johnston [2007], 66).

44. Plochmann (1963) and Cobb (1993) both suggest this.

45. Halper (2011), 321.

46. Sallis (1996), 374.

47. See Howland (2007), 21. For more on the comic use of anachronism, see Dover (1966), 45.

48. Bury (1909), xxiv.

49. Sheffield (2001), 202.

50. The crown of violets is simultaneously a sign of Aphrodite, a crown worn by Muses, and a symbol of the city of Athens, suggests Nussbaum (2001), 193. The significance of the latter will be explored particularly in conjunction the sort of reversal and antitype that Socrates-as-satyr represents.

51. A wide variety of evaluations exist in the literature on Alcibiades's speech. See also Sheffield (2001).

52. Usher (2002), 216.

53. Xenophon, *Symposium* 5.5.

54. Xenophon, *Symposium* 4.19.

55. Xenophon, *Symposium* 5.8.

56. Amelung (1927), 285.

57. Aelian *VH* 2.13, as cited in Usher (2002), 213.

58. Clay (1972), 53–54n2. It is also of note that, in the passage just cited, Alcibiades appears to confirm the authenticity of such *logoi* by Socrates.

59. In the most extensive evaluation of the comparison, Sheffield (2001) comments on the general satyric tone of the speech, but does not mention these inverse satyrical characteristics attributed to Socrates.

60. An exception may lie in Marsyas, who is associated with wisdom and sexual abstinence, and who thus becomes a better comparison for Socrates (Sheffield [2001], 204).

61. The comparison to Silenus falls short particularly at military courage. Usher points out that Hyginus suggests that the reason Silenus ends up asleep in Midas's rose garden is that he has abandoned a military excursion (Usher [2002], 208).

62. Lissarrague (1990), 236.

63. Lissarrague (1990), 235.

64. Seaford (1984), 32.

65. Seaford (1984), 7.

66. Herodotus, 8.138.

67. Dobrov (2007), 260.

68. Satyr drama is said in the Suda to have originated with the Dorians, like comedy, and invented by Pratinas of Phlius (Grant [1924], 51). When Pratinas immigrated to Athens, the older Dionysiac choruses somehow merged with Attic tragedy, thus begetting the satyr drama (Grant [1924], 52). At the City Dionysia during the Classical period, satyr plays seem to have been performed after each set of three tragedies (Seaford [1984], 2). Neither comedies nor tragedies, satyr plays combine elements of both. The only satyr play surviving in its entirety is Euripides's *Cyclops*, a play whose otherwise tragic themes, such as implied cannibalism and rape, are treated in an oddly humorous fashion. Rape is a theme common to ancient comedies as well, and mythology more broadly. While it is generally not cast as a tremendous violation when it is performed against women, except inasmuch

as it involves violation of male property, the suggestions in the *Cyclops* are of violating the satyrs in the play, including Silenus himself. Although such a distinction rightly offends us today, the violation of a free male was of a different legal and social status than that of women and slaves.

Approximately half of Sophocles's *Ichneutai*, or "The Trackers," was discovered in the twentieth century (Seaford [1984], 1). Evidence concerning satyr drama otherwise derives from titles, fragments, comments, and visual evidence from Athenian vase-painting.

Aristotle describes the satyr play as consisting of short stories composed of comical diction (*lexeōs geloias*) with a strong connection to dancing (Aristotle, *Poetics* 1449a19–23). Horace describes satyr drama at length in the *Ars Poetica*.

> The poet who in tragic song first competed for a paltry goat soon also brought on unclad the woodland Satyrs, and with no loss of dignity roughly essayed jesting, for only the lure and charm of novelty could hold the spectator, who, after observance of the rites, was well drunken and in lawless [*exlex*] mood. But it will be fitting so to seek favour for your laughing, bantering Satyrs, so to pass from grave to gay [*ita vertere seria ludo*], that no god, no hero, who shall be brought upon the stage, and whom we have just beheld in royal gold and purple, shall shift with vulgar speech into dingy hovels, or, while shunning the ground, catch at clouds and emptiness. Tragedy, scorning to babble trivial verses, will, like a matron bidden to dance on festal days, take her place in the saucy Satyrs' circle with some little shame . . . such [is] the beauty that may crown the commonplace. When the Fauns are brought from the forest, they should, methinks, beware of behaving as though born at the crossways and almost as dwelling in the Forum, playing at times the young bloods with their mawkish verses, or cracking their bawdy and shameless jokes. For some take offence—knights, free-born, and men of substance—nor do they greet with kindly feelings or reward with a crown everything which the buyers of roasted beans and chestnuts approve. (220–51)

The spectators of satyr drama, Horace tells us, had just come from ritual observation, having drunk much, and being in a "lawless" mood, and satyr plays indulge this. From Horace's description, it seems that the

Satyr drama, "though often course and excessive, was essentially good natured" (Grant [1924], 52). But Horace also suggests it to be drama of the "commonplace" and approved of by the "buyers of roasted beans and chestnuts," but offensive to "men of substance." He describes its language, not simply as *geloias*, as does Aristotle, but as "vulgar," "trivial," "mawkish," "bawdy," and "shameless." Horace further advises the seeking of "favour" lest the gods take offense, having just been worshiped in their finery, at now being represented in "dingy hovels."

The purpose and function of satyr plays are disputed. Horace, in the passage quoted above, suggests the function of satyr drama to have been detaining the drunken and disorderly spectator. Schlegel says it is "mental relaxation after the engrossing severity of tragedy" (Schlegel [1846], 142, also cited in Seaford [1984], 26). Seaford rejects both previous claims, and argues instead that Satyric drama was instituted to preserve explicit connections to Dionysus otherwise lost in the development of tragedy. In *De Elocutione*, Demetrius describes satyric drama as *tragōdia paidzousa*, or playful tragedy (as cited by Dobrov [2007], 251–52). Linked expressly to tragedy in content, what such "playful tragedy" is for remains a matter of dispute, but any or all of these may be accurate.

69. Nietzsche (1956), 52–53.

70. Nietzsche (1956), 54. François Lissarague claims, to the contrary, that the Satyr play is defined in part by its strictly fictional presentation in which it "stays at one remove from the audience, which observes without being called into account" (as cited by Dobrov, 252).

71. Nietzsche (1956), 54.

72. Nietzsche (1956), 55.

73. Seaford (1984), 7.

74. Seaford (1984), 9.

75. For more on the equation between these questions, see Sallis (1996), especially 6–12.

76. Nussbaum (2001), 198.

77. Nussbaum (2001), 198.

78. The Socrates of the *Charmides*, responding physically to his peek inside Charmides's cloak, is a different figure—affected by bodily eros, even if able to withstand its pull.

79. Such internal division is also characteristic of Greek heroes, who are typically at odds with themselves, being both godlike and animalistic.

See for instance, descriptions of Achilles as seeming divine and as akin to a lion (e.g., *Iliad* XXIX.570, 671).

80. See Sutton (1980), 149–50.

81. Sutton (1980), 122.

82. Sutton (1980), 150.

83. Alcibiades only presumes this was the case, as he was not yet present when the seating occurred. It is actually Agathon who insists that Socrates recline next to him so "that by touching you I may gain the benefit of the wisdom that came to you on the porch" (175c–e). Nonetheless, it is significant that Alcibiades assumes this involved scheming on Socrates's part to sit next to Agathon.

84. Sheffield (2001), 195.

85. The quote is from Aristophanes, *Clouds* 362.

86. Vlastos critiques Diotima's position (which he attributes, I believe unjustifiedly, to Plato) for ignoring the personal dimension of love in favor of an abstract and partial representation of the person in terms of ideals or qualities. The position, for Vlastos, "does not provide for love of whole persons, but only love of that abstract version of persons which consists of the complex of their best qualities" (as cited in Nussbaum [2001], 166).

Nussbaum describes Alcibiades's speech as possibly tragic-comic (Nussbaum [2001], 171).

87. Belfiore, despite the subtitle of her piece ("Socrates as Silenus"), says very little about what it means for Socrates to be compared to satyrs in this way. Instead, she focuses on how the sort of enchantment that Socrates the satyr brings about is one that pacifies strong emotion to work in tandem with reason, rather than, as "deceitful magicians" do, purposefully stoking and manipulating strong emotions to override reason (1980).

88. Lissarrague (1990), 235.

89. In the *Phaedrus*, Socrates tells Phaedrus that there are two sorts of ruling principles in us, at times in accord with one another, and at other times, at odds with one another. He says that, "When judgment guides us by reason toward what is best and is strong enough to prevail, we call that judiciousness [*sōphrosunē*] When desire rules in us and drags us toward pleasure in a manner contrary to reason, its rule is called *hubris*" (*Phaedrus* 237e–38a).

90. Bury writes: ". . . when the subject of the verb *hubrizein* is an adult male and the object a woman or boy, hubris implies, unless the context gives a clear indication to the contrary, that the offense is the commission

of sexual or homosexual assault" Bury (1989), 36. Dover echoes this verbatim in Edmonds (2000), 275. Henderson supports this as well, writing that *hubrizein* "meant 'rape' in the legal jargon of Athens (LSJ s.v. II.3); in comedy it means 'to treat roughly during the sex act' or 'be virile' " Henderson (1975), 159n249. Gagarin and Sheffield note this implication as well, but in the literature, the term *hubris* is otherwise largely taken in a moral sense, as "arrogance" or "excessiveness" on Socrates's behalf. Translating *hubris* morally entirely overlooks Alcibiades's joke (Gagarin [1977], 32–33, and Sheffield [2001], 202).

91. Plutarch draws from this that Socrates is hubristic only on the outside (*Cato Maior* 7.1, as cited in Gagarin [1977], 32n44. Gagarin counters that it is Socrates's inside—his virtue–that supports the accusation of hubris, and argues that Alcibiades mistakes Socrates-the-midwife for a lover, thus fundamentally miscalculating their relationship (1977).

92. Usher (2002), 221.

93. Bury (1989), 36.

94. Bury (1989), 37.

95. Sommerstein describes such *para prosdokian* in Aristophanes, where "the speaker makes us quite sure what we are going to hear next—and then says something quite different. After completing his list of theatrical joys and sorrows, Dikaiopolis goes on, 'Seriously, though—in all the years I've'—and we expect to hear something like, 'In all the years I've lived, I have never been so distressed as I am now.' What Dikaiopolis actually says is, 'In all the years I've washed, I've never had so much soap in my eyes as—yow!—as I have now' " (1973, 34–35).

96. Halper (2011), 322.

97. Edmonds (2000), 275.

98. The reversal of roles once again makes Socrates play that of the passive beloved, who is a stock joke in Aristophanic comedy. See Bury (1989).

99. The authenticity of the *Alcibiades Major* remains questionable, but the grounds given for claiming its spuriousness include that it is too hermeneutically straightforward to be included in an authentic Platonic canon, as noted by D. S. Hutchinson in Cooper (1997), 557–58. Such a line of reasoning seems particularly suspicious as grounds for deeming a dialogue inauthentic, and particularly so if the claims of this book are taken seriously. For if they are, the alleged simplicity of some passages

and even some dialogues may not be so simple after all. Regardless, the occurrence of the reversal of pedagogical roles in the *Alcibiades Major*, either attests to the recurrence of such reversals in Plato's work, or the perception by a close associate that such reversals were frequent enough in Plato's work to merit duplication in an inauthentic work. Both possibilities support my point.

100. Demetrius *De Eloctuione* 169, as cited in Seaford (1984), 5.

101. Lissarrague (1990), 236.

102. Sutton (1980), 122.

103. Sophocles's *Dictyulci*, and Sutton (1980), 153, as cited by Sheffield (2001), 209n25.

104. Sheffield (2001), 200-02.

105. Sheffield (2001), 201.

106. For more on Dionysus as the judge and how this echoes Aristophanes's *Frogs*, see Strauss (2001), 34 and 257.

107. Usher (2002), 214f41.

108. Sheffield (2001), 200.

109. Aristotle, *Nicomachean Ethics* 1108a18-23.

110. Aristotle, *Eudemian Ethics* 1233b39-34a4.

111. Theophrastus, *Characters* 1.1.

112. Theophrastus, *Characters* 1.4f3.

113. Theophrastus, *Characters* 1.7.

114. Vlastos (1987).

115. See Sheffield (2001), 205.

116. See also Clay (2005), 74.

117. Halper (2011), 322.

118. Halper (2011), 322.

119. Halper (2011), 321.

120. Halper (2011), 322.

121. Howland (2007), 20.

122. Griswold (1986), 43.

123. Hyland (2015), 198

124. Hyland (2015), 204.

125. Sutton notes how common this sort of juxtaposition is in Roman theater, where tragedies were followed by *exodia*, in Japanese No plays, which were followed by *Kyogen*, and in Elizabethan tragedies, followed as they were by jigs (1989, 94).

126. Sutton (1989), 101.

127. Usher (2002).
128. Hyland (2015), 204.
129. Hyland (2015), 204.
130. See also Sallis (1996), 22.
131. Griswold (1986), 9.
132. Sallis (1996).
133. Hyland (1981), 35–43.
134. Usher (2002), 226.

Conclusion

1. I am grateful to Allison Postell for pointing this out in conversation.
2. Freydberg (2008), 197.
3. Alicke (1985); Allison, Messick, and Goethals (1989); Dunning, Meyerowitz, and Holzberg (1989); and Goethals, Messick, and Allison (1991), as cited by Epley and Dunning (2000).
4. Berke (1998), 4.1, as cited by Epley and Dunning (2000).
5. Ewegen (2014), 15.
6. Sheffield (2001), 206.
7. Hyland (1995), 137.

Works Consulted

Adam, James. *The Republic of Plato.* Cambridge, UK: Cambridge University Press, 1902.

Aelian. *Historical Miscellany.* Translated by Nigel G. Wilson. Cambridge, MA: Harvard University Press, 1997.

Amelung, W. "Notes on Representations of Socrates and of Diogenes and Other Cynics." *American Journal of Archeology* 31, no. 3 (1927): 281-96.

Apelt, Otto. *Platonische Aufsätze.* Leipzig: B. G. Teubner, 1912.

Ardley, Gavin. "The Role of Play in the Philosophy of Plato." *Philosophy* 42, no. 161 (1967): 226-44.

Arieti, James. *Interpreting Plato: the Dialogues as Drama.* Savage, MD: Rowman & Littlefield, 1991.

Aristophanes. *The Complete Plays of Aristophanes.* Translated by Moses Hadas. New York: Bantam Books, 1962.

Aristotle. *The Complete Works of Aristotle*, vols. 1 and 2. Edited by Jonathan Barnes. Princeton, NJ: Princeton University Press, 1984.

Athenaeus. *The Learned Banqueters* 8-10.420e. Translated by S. Douglas Olson. Cambridge, MA: Harvard University Press, 2008.

———. *The Learned Banqueters* III.106e-V. Translated by S. Douglas Olson. Cambridge, MA: Harvard University Press, 2006.

Atkinson, J. E. "Curbing the Comedians: Cleon versus Aristophanes and Syracosius' Decree." *Classical Quarterly* 42, no. 1 (1992): 56-64.

Austin, J. L. *How to Do Things with Words* (2nd ed.). Edited by J. O. Urmson and Marina Sbisà. Cambridge, MA: Harvard University Press, 1962.

Bakhtin, Mikhail. *Rabelais and His World.* Translated by Hélène Iswolsky. Bloomington, IN: Indiana University Press, 1984.

Baracchi, Claudia. *Of Myth, Life, and War in Plato's* Republic. Bloomington: Indiana University Press, 2002.

———. "Beyond the Comedy and Tragedy of Authority: The Invisible Father in Plato's 'Republic.'" *Philosophy and Rhetoric* 34, no. 2 (2001): 151–76.

Barker, Sir Ernest. *Greek Political Theory*. London: Methuen & Co., 1918.

Barnes, Hazel E. "Greek Tragicomedy." *Classical Journal* 60, no. 3 (1964): 125–31.

Barney, Rachel. "Plato on Conventionalism." *Phronesis* 42, no. 2 (1997): 143–62.

Bassett, Samuel E. "Wit and Humor in Xenophon." *Classical Journal* 12, no. 9 (1917): 565–74.

Baudelaire, Charles. *Essence of Laughter and Other Essays, Journals and Love Letters*. Edited by Peter Quennell. New York: Meridian Books, 1956.

Baxter, Timothy M. S. *The* Cratylus*: Plato's Critique of Naming*. Leiden (The Netherlands): E. J. Brill, 1962.

Beard, Mary. *Laughter in Ancient Rome: On Joking, Tickling, and Cracking Up*. Oakland: University of California Press, 2014.

Bell, Jeremy, and Michael Naas, eds. *Plato's Animals*. Bloomington: Indiana University Press, 2015.

Benardete, Seth. *Plato's "Laws": The Discovery of Being*. Chicago: University of Chicago Press, 2000.

———. *The Tragedy and Comedy of Life: Plato's* Philebus. Translated with commentary by Seth Benardete. Chicago: University of Chicago Press, 1993.

———. *Socrates' Second Sailing: On Plato's* Republic. Chicago: University of Chicago Press, 1989.

Berger, Peter L. *Redeeming Laughter*. Berlin: Walter de Gruyter & Co, 1997.

Bergson, Henri. *Laughter: An Essay on the Meaning of the Comic*. Translated by Cloudesly Brereton and Fred Rothwell. Lexington, KY: Wildside Press, 2008.

Bestor, Thomas Wheaton. "Plato's Semantics and Plato's 'Cratylus.'" *Phronesis* 25, no. 3 (1980): 306–30.

Blondell, Ruby. *The Play of Character in Plato's Dialogues*. Cambridge, UK: Cambridge University Press, 2002.

Bloom, Allan. Commentary on Plato's *Symposium*. Chicago: University of Chicago Press, 2001.

———. Interpretive Essay in *The* Republic *of Plato*. New York: Basic Books, 1962, 307–472.

———. Response to Hall. *Political Theory* 5, no. 3 (Aug. 1977): 315–30.

Brann, Eva. "The Offense of Socrates: A Re-Reading of Plato's *Apology*." *Interpretation*, 7/2 (1978): 1–21.

Brickhouse, Thomas C., and Nicholas D. Smith. *Socrates on Trial*. Oxford: Clarendon Press, 1989.

Brisson, Luc. *Plato the Myth Maker*. Translated by Gerard Naddaf. Chicago: University of Chicago Press, 1998.

Brock, Roger. "Plato and Comedy." In *'Owls to Athens': Essays on Classical Subjects*. Edited by E. M. Craik. Oxford: Clarendon Press, 1990, 39–49.

Buckley, F. H. *The Morality of Laughter*. Ann Arbor: University of Michigan Press, 2003.

Butler, Samuel. *The Humor of Homer, and Other Essays*. Freeport, NY: Books for Libraries Press, 1914.

Bury, R. G. Introduction to *The Symposium of Plato*. Cambridge, UK: W. Heffer and Sons, 1909.

Calogero, Guido. Gorgias and the Socratic Principle Nemo Sua Sponte Piccat. *Journal of Hellenic Studies* 77 (1957): 12–17.

Chen, Ludwig C. H. "Onomatopoeia in the Cratylus." *Apeiron* 16, no. 2 (1982): 86–101.

Cicero. *De Oratore*, v. I (Books I and II). Translated by W. W. Sutton. Cambridge, MA: Harvard University Press, 1945.

———. *De Officiis*. Translated by Walter Miller. Cambridge, MA: Harvard University Press, 1913.

Clay, Diskin. "The Tragic and Comic Poet of the *Symposium*." *Arion* 2, no. 2 (1975): 238–61.

———. "Socrates' Mulishness and Heroism." *Phronesis* 17, no. 1 (1972): 53–60.

Colaiaco, James A. *Socrates against Athens*. New York: Routledge, 2001.

Cooper, John M. *Pursuits of Wisdom: Six Ways of Life in Ancient Philosophy from Socrates to Plotinus*. Princeton, NJ: Princeton University Press, 2012.

Cornford, Francis Macdonald. "The Doctrine of Eros in Plato's *Symposium*." In *The Unwritten Philosophy and Other Essays*, Cambridge, UK: (1950): 68–80.

———. *The Origin of Attic Comedy*. Cambridge, UK: Cambridge University Press, 1934.

Corrigan, Kevin, and Elena Glazov-Corrigan. *Plato's Dialectic at Play.* University Park: Pennsylvania State University Press, 2004.

Coulter, James A. "The Relation of the *Apology of Socrates* to Gorgias' *Defense of Palamedes* and Plato's Critique of Gorgianic Rhetoric." *Harvard Studies in Classical Philology* 68 (1964): 269–303.

Craik, E. M., ed. *'Owls to Athens': Essays on Classical Subjects.* Oxford: Clarendon Press, 1990.

Critchley, Simon. *On Humour.* London: Routledge, 2004.

Csapo, Eric, and William J. Slater. *The Context of Ancient Drama.* Ann Arbor: University of Michigan Press, 1995.

———. "From Aristophanes to Menander? Genre Transformation in Greek Comedy." In *Matrices of Genre.* Cambridge, MA: Harvard University Press (2000), 115–33.

Demetrius, "On Style," in *Aristotle 'The Poetics,' 'Longinus' 'On the Sublime,' and Demetrius 'On Style.'* Edited by E. Capps, T. E. Paige, and W. H. D. Rouse. Translated by W. Hamilton Fyfe. London: William Heinemann, 1947.

Depew, Mary, and Dirk Obbink. *Matrices of Genre: Authors, Canons, and Society.* Cambridge, MA: Harvard University Press, 2000.

Desclos, Marie-Laurence. *Le rire des Grecs: Anthopologie du rire en Grèce ancienne.* Grenoble: Millon, 2000.

Desjardins, Rosemary. "Why Dialogues? Plato's Serious Play." In *Platonic Writings, Platonic Readings.* University Park: Pennsylvania State University Press (2002), 110–25.

DeVries, G. J. "Laughter in Plato's Writings." *Mnemosyne* 38 (1985): 378–81.

———. *Spel Bij Plato.* Amsterdam: Noord-Hollandsche Uitgevers Mij, 1949.

Diels, Hermann, and Walther Kranz. *Die Fragmente Der Vorsokratiker* (vols. 1–3). Dublin: Weidmann, 1966.

Dillon, Matthew. "Tragic Laughter." *Classical World* 84, no. 5 (1991): 345–55.

Diogenes Laertius. *Lives of the Philosophers* 1 and 2. Translated by R. D. Hicks. Cambridge, MA: Harvard University Press, 1972.

Dobbs, Darrell. "For Lack of Wisdom: Courage and Inquiry in Plato's *Laches.*" *Journal of Politics* 48, no. 4 (1986): 825–49.

Dobrov, Gregory W. "Comedy and the Satyr-Chorus." *Classical World* 100, no. 3 (2007): 251–65.

Dorter, Kenneth. "The Significance of the Speeches in Plato's *Symposium.*" *Philosophy and Rhetoric* 2, no. 4 (1969): 215–34.

Douglas, Mary. "The Social Control of Cognition: Some Factors in Joke Perception." *Man* 3, no. 3 (1968): 361–76.

Dover, K. J. "Aristophanes' Speech in Plato's *Symposium*." *Journal of Hellenic Studies* 86 (1966): 41–50.

Edmonds, Radcliffe G. "Socrates the Beautiful: Role-Reversal and Midwifery in Plato's *Symposium*." *Transactions of the American Philological Association* 130 (2000): 261–85.

Elliott, Robert. *The Power of Satire*. Princeton, NJ: Princeton University Press, 1960.

Epley, Nicholas, and David Dunning. "Feeling 'Holier Than Thou': Are Self-Serving Assessments Produced by Errors in Self- or Social Prediction?" *Journal of Personality and Social Psychology* 79, no. 6 (2000): 861–75. http://docs.google.com/viewer?a=v&q=cache:I_fVFLs-2HMJ:faculty.chicagobooth.edu/nicholas.epley/EpleyandDunning2001.pdf.

Euripides. *Euripides: Ten Plays*. Translated by Paul Roche. New York: Penguin, 1998.

Ewegen, S. Montgomery. *Plato's* Cratylus*: The Comedy of Language*. Bloomington: Indiana University Press, 2014.

Fideler, David, ed. *The Pythagorean Sourcebook and Library*. Translated by Kenneth Sylvan Guthrie. Grand Rapids, MI: Phanes Press, 1987.

Fine, Gail. "Plato on Naming." *Philosophical Quarterly* 27, no. 109 (1977): 289–301.

Flashar, Hellmut. "Aristoteles, Das Lachen und die Alte Komödie." In *Laughter Down the Centuries* 1. Edited by Siegfried Jäkel and Asko Timonen. Turku, Finland: Turn Yliopisto, 1994, 59–70.

Fortenbaugh, William W., ed. *Theophrastus of Eresus: Sources for his Life, Writings, Thought and Influence*, vols. 1 and 2. Leiden (The Netherlands): E. J. Brill, 1992.

———. "Aristotle and the Questionable Mean-Dispositions." *Transactions and Proceedings of the American Philological Association* 99 (1968): 203–31.

Freeman, Kathleen. *Ancilla to the Pre-Socratic Philosophers: A Complete Translation of the Fragments in Diels'* Fragmente der Vorsokratiker. Cambridge, MA: Harvard University Press, 1966.

Freud, Sigmund. *The Joke and Its Relation to the Unconscious*. Translated by Joyce Crick. New York: Penguin, 2002.

Freydberg, Bernard D. "Comedy and Measure in Sallis." In *The Path of Archaic Thinking; Unfolding the Work of John Sallis*. Albany: State University of New York Press (1995): 157–67.

———. *The Play of the Platonic Dialogues*. New York: Peter Lang Publishing, 1997.

———. *Philosophy and Comedy: Aristophanes, Logos, and Eros*. Bloomington: Indiana University Press, 2008.

Friedländer, Paul. *Plato* I, 2nd ed. Princeton, NJ: Princeton University Press, 1969a.

———. *Plato 3: The Dialogues, Second and Third Periods*. Princeton, NJ: Princeton University Press, 1969b.

Frye, Northrop. *Anatomy of Criticism*. Princeton, NJ: Princeton University Press, 1957.

Garland, Robert. "The Mockery of the Deformed and Disabled in Graeco-Roman Culture." In *Laughter Down the Centuries* 1. Edited by Siegfried Jäkel and Asko Timonen. Turku, Finland: Turn Yliopisto, 1994: 71–84.

Gay, Robert. "Courage and *Thumos*." *Philosophy* 63 244 (1988): 255–65.

Gordon, Jill. *Turning toward Philosophy: Literary Device and Dramatic Structure in Plato's Dialogues*. University Park: Pennsylvania State University Press, 1999.

———. "Against Vlastos on Complex Irony." *Classical Quarterly* 46, no. 1 (1996): 131–37.

Gould, Carol S. "Socratic Intellectualism and the Problem of Courage: An Interpretation of Plato's *Laches*." *History of Philosophy Quarterly* 4, no. 3 (1987): 265–79.

Grant, Mary A. *Ancient Rhetorical Theories of the Laughable: Greek Rhetoricians and Cicero*. Madison: University of Wisconsin Press, 1924.

Greenberg, N. A. "Socrates' Choice in the *Crito*." *Harvard Studies in Classical Philology*, vol. 70 (1965): 45–82.

Greene, William Chase. "The Spirit of Comedy in Plato." *Harvard Studies in Classical Philology* 31 (1920): 63–123.

Griswold, Charles, ed. *Platonic Writings/Platonic Readings*. University Park: Pennsylvania State University Press, 2002.

———. *Self-Knowledge in Plato's Phaedrus*. University Park: Pennsylvania State University Press, 1996.

Gunter, Pete A. "Nietzschean Laughter." *Sewanee Review* 76, no. 3 (1968): 493–506.

Gurewitch, Morton. *Comedy: The Irrational Vision*. Ithaca, NY: Cornell University Press, 1975.

Guthrie, W. K. C. *A History of Greek Philosophy IV: Plato*. Cambridge, UK: Cambridge University Press, 1975.

Hackforth, R. *Plato's Examination of Pleasure*. Cambridge, UK: Cambridge University Press, 1945.

Hall, Dale. "The *Republic* and the 'Limits of Politics.'" *Political Theory* 5, no. 3 (Aug. 1977): 293–313.

Hall, Edith. *Greek Tragedy: Suffering Under the Sun*. Oxford: Oxford University Press, 2010.

Halliwell, Stephen. *Greek Laughter: A Study of Cultural Psychology from Homer to Early Christianity*. Cambridge, UK: Cambridge University Press, 2008.

———. "Greek Laughter and the Problem of the Absurd." *Arion* 13, no. 2 (2005): 121–46.

———. "The Uses of Laughter in Greek Culture." *Classical Quarterly* 41, no. 2 (1991a): 279–96.

———. "Comic Satire and Freedom of Speech in Classical Athens." *Journal of Hellenic Studies* 111 (1991b): 48–70.

Halper, Edward C. "Humor, Dialectic, and Human Nature in Plato." *Epoché* 15, no. 2 (Spring 2011): 319–30.

Harvey, A. E. "The Classification of Greek Lyric Poetry." *Classical Quarterly* 5, no. 3/4 (1955): 157–75.

Heath, Malcolm. "Aristotelian Comedy." *Classical Quarterly* 39, no. 2 (1989): 344–54.

Heller, Agnes. *Immortal Comedy: The Comic Phenomenon in Art, Literature, and Life*. Lanham, MD: Lexington Books, 2005.

Henderson, Jeffrey. *The Maculate Muse: Obscene Language in Attic Comedy*. New Haven, CT: Yale University Press, 1975.

Herodotus. *The History*. Translated by David Grene. Chicago: University of Chicago Press, 1987.

Hobbes, Thomas. *Leviathan*. Edited by A. P. Martinich. Toronto: Broadview, 2002.

Hoerber, Robert G. "Plato's *Laches*." *Classical Philology* 63, no. 2 (1968): 95–105.

Høffding, Harald. *Humor als Lebensgefühl (Der Grosse Humor)*. Leipzig: B. G. Teubner, 1918.

Hokenson, Jan Walsh. *The Idea of Comedy: History, Theory, Critique*. Madison, WI and Teaneck, NJ: Fairleigh Dickinson University Press, 2006.

Homer. *The Iliad* and *The Odyssey*. Translated by Robert Fagles. New York: Penguin, 1996.

Horace. *Satires, Epistles, Ars Poetica*. Translated by H. R. Fairclough. Cambridge, MA: Harvard University Press, 2005.

Hordern. J. H. *Sophron's Mimes: Text, Translation, and Commentary*. Oxford: Oxford University Press, 2004.

Howland, Jacob. "Plato's Dionysian Music? A Reading of the *Symposium*." *Epoché* 12, no. 1 (Sept. 2007): 17–47.

———. "Aristotle's Great-Souled Man." *Review of Politics* 64, no. 1 (2002): 27–56.

———. "The *Republic*'s Third Wave and the Paradox of Political Philosophy." *Review of Metaphysics* 51, no. 3 (March 1998): 633–57.

———. "Re-Reading Plato: The Problem of Platonic Chronology." *Phoenix* 45, no. 3 (1991): 189–214.

Hubbard, Thomas K. *The Mask of Comedy: Aristophanes and the Intertextual Parabasis*. Ithaca, NY: Cornell University Press, 1991.

———. "Old Men in the Youthful Plays of Aristophanes." In *Old Age in Greek and Latin Literature*. Edited by Thomas M. Falkner and Judith de Luce. Albany: State University of New York Press (1989), 90–113.

Huizinga, J. *Homo Ludens: A Study of the Play-Element in Culture*. Boston: Beacon Press, 1950.

Huss, Bernhard. "The Dancing Socrates and the Laughing Xenophon, or the Other 'Symposium.'" *American Journal of Philology* 120, no. 3 (1999): 381–409.

Hutcheson, Francis. "Laughter and Self-Love." *The Scottish Enlightenment: An Anthology*. Edited by Alexander Broadie. Edinburgh: Canongate Books, 1997: 224–42.

Hyland, Drew. "The Animals That Therefore We Were?: Aristophanes' Double-Creatures and the Question of Origins." *Plato's Animals: Gadflies, Horses, Swans, and Other Philosophical Beasts*. Edited by Jeremy Bell and Michael Naas. Bloomington: Indiana University Press (2015): 193–205.

———. *Plato and the Question of Beauty*. Bloomington: Indiana University Press, 2008.

———. *Questioning Platonism: Continental Interpretations of Plato*. Albany: State University of New York Press, 2004.

———. *Finitude and Transcendence in the Platonic Dialogues*. Albany: State University of New York Press, 1995.

———. "Taking the Longer Road: The Irony of Plato's 'Republic.' " *Revue de Métaphysique et de Morale* 93, no. 3 (1988): 317–35.

———. *The Virtue of Philosophy*. Athens: Ohio University Press, 1981.

Jäkel, Siegfried. "The Phenomenon of Laughter in the *Iliad*." *Laughter Down the Centuries* 1. Edited by Siegfried Jäkel and Asko Timonen. Turku: Turn Yliopisto, 1994, 23–28.

Janko, Richard. *Aristotle on Comedy: Towards a Reconstruction of Poetics II*. London: Duckworth, 2002.

Johnston, Sarah Iles. "The Myth of Dionysius." In *Ritual Texts for the Afterlife: Orpheus and the Bacchic Gold Tablets*. Edited by Fritz Graf and Sarah Iles Johnston. Oxon, UK: Routledge (2007), 66–93.

Joubert, Laurent. *Treatise on Laughter*. Translated by Gregory de Rocher. Tuscaloosa: University of Alabama Press, 1980.

Juvenal. *Juvenal and Persius*. Translated by Susanna Morton Braund. Cambridge, MA: Harvard University Press, 2004.

———. *The Satires*. Translated by Rolfe Humpfries. Bloomington: Indiana University Press, 1958.

Kahn, Charles. "Plato's *Charmides* and the Proleptic Reading of Socratic Dialogues." *Journal of Philosophy* 85, no. 10 (October 1988): 541–49.

———. *The Art and Thought of Heraclitus*. Cambridge, UK: Cambridge University Press, 1979.

Keller, Simon. "An Interpretation of Plato's 'Cratylus.' " *Phronesis* 45, no. 4 (November 2000): 284–305.

Kierkegaard, Søren. *Concluding Unscientific Postscript*. Edited and translated by Alastair Hannay. Cambridge, UK: Cambridge University Press, 2009.

———. *The Concept of Irony with Continual Reference to Socrates*. Edited and translated by Howard V. Hong and Edna H. Hong. Princeton, NJ: Princeton University Press, 1989.

Kirk, G. S., J. E. Raven, and M. Schofield, eds. The Presocratic Philosophers (2nd ed.). Cambridge, UK: Cambridge University Press, 1984.

Klein, Jacob. *A Commentary on Plato's Meno*. Chicago: University of Chicago Press, 1965.

Konstan, David. *Greek Comedy and Ideology*. New York: Oxford University Press, 1995.

Körte, Alfred. *Die Griechische Komödie*. Leipzig: Teubner, 1914.

Koziak, Barbara. *Retrieving Political Emotion: Thumos, Aristotle, and Gender*. University Park: Pennsylvania State University Press, 2000.

———. "Homeric *Thumos*: The Early History of Gender, Emotion, and Politics." *Journal of Politics* 61, no. 4 (1999): 1068–91.

Krämer, Hans Joachim. *Plato and the Foundations of Metaphysics*. Translated and edited by John R. Catan. Albany: State University of New York Press, 1990.

Kretzmann, Norman. "Plato on the Correctness of Names." *American Philosophical Quarterly* 8, no. 2 (1971): 126–38.

Lauter, Paul (ed.), *Theories of Comedy*. New York: Anchor Books, 1964.

Leibowitz, David. *The Ironic Defense of Socrates: Plato's Apology*. Cambridge, UK: Cambridge University Press, 2010.

Lee, Edward N. " 'Hoist with His Own Petard': Ironic and Comic Elements in Plato's Critique of Protagoras (*Tht.* 161–71)." In *Exegesis and Argument*. Edited by E. N. Lee, A. P. D. Mourelatos, and R. M. Rorty. New York: Humanities Press, 1973.

Levinson, Ronald B. *In Defense of Plato*. Cambridge, MA: Harvard University Press, 1953.

Liddell, H. G., and Robert Scott. Greek-English Lexicon (7th ed.). Oxford: Clarendon Press, 1889.

Lissarrague, François. "Why Satyrs Are Good to Represent." In *Nothing to Do with Dionysos?: Athenian Drama in Its Social Context*. Edited by John J. Winkler and Froma I. Zeitlin. Princeton, NJ: Princeton University Press, 1990.

Lowe, N. J. *Comedy*. Cambridge, UK: Cambridge University Press, 2008.

Lowenstam, Steven. "Aristophanes' Hiccups." *Greek, Roman, and Byzantine Studies* 7 (1986): 43–56.

Lucian. *Selected Satires of Lucian*. Edited and translated by Lionel Casson. Chicago: Aldine Publishing Company, 1962.

Major, Wilfred E. *The Court of Comedy: Aristophanes, Rhetoric, and Democracy in Fifth Century Athens*. Columbus, OH: Ohio State University Press, 2013.

Meredith, George. *An Essay on Comedy and the Uses of the Comic Spirit.* Edited by Lane Cooper. New York: Charles Scribner's Sons, 1918.

Michelini, Ann N. "Socrates Plays the Buffoon: Cautionary Protreptic in 'Euthydemus.'" *American Journal of Philology* 121, no. 4 (Winter 2000a): 509–35.

———. "The Search for the King: Reflexive Irony in Plato's *Politicus*." *Classical Antiquity* 19, no. 1 (2000b): 180–204.

Miralles, Carles. "Laughter in the *Odyssey*." *Laughter Down the Centuries* 1. Edited by Siegfried Jäkel and Asko Timonen. Turku: Turn Yliopisto (1994): 15–22.

Morreall, John. *Comic Relief: A Comprehensive Philosophy of Humor.* Oxford, UK: Wiley-Blackwell, 2009.

———, ed. *The Philosophy of Laughter and Humor.* Albany: State University of New York Press, 1987.

———. *Taking Laughter Seriously.* Albany: State University of New York Press, 1983.

Morrison, Donald R., ed. *The Cambridge Companion to Socrates.* Cambridge, UK: Cambridge University Press, 2011.

Müller, Reimar. "Demokrit—der 'lachende Philosoph.'" *Laughter Down the Centuries* 1. Edited by Siegfried Jäkel and Asko Timonen. Turku, Finland: Turn Yliopisto, 1994): 39–52.

Murphy, Charles T. "Aristophanes and the Art of Rhetoric." *Harvard Studies in Classical Philology* 49 (1938): 69–113.

Myers, Henry Alonzo. "The Analysis of Laughter." *Sewanee Review* 43, no. 4 (1935): 452–63.

Nails, Debra. *The People of Plato.* Indianapolis, IN: Hackett, 2002.

———. "The Dramatic Date of Plato's Republic." *Classical Journal* 93, no. 4 (1998): 383–96.

Newell, Walter. *Ruling Passion: The Erotics of Statecraft in Platonic Political Philosophy.* Lanham, MD: Rowman and Littlefield, 2000.

Nichols, James H. "Introduction to the *Laches*." In *The Roots of Political Philosophy: Ten Forgotten Socratic Dialogues.* Edited by Thomas L. Pangle. Ithaca, NY: Cornell University Press (1987): 269–80.

Nietzsche, Friedrich. *The Gay Science.* Translated by Walter Kaufmann. New York: Vintage Books, 1974.

———. *Twilight of the Idols and the Anti-Christ* (2nd ed.). Translated by R. J. Hollingdale. London: Penguin, 1990.

———. *The Birth of Tragedy and the Genealogy of Morals*. Translated by Francis Golffing. New York: Anchor Books, 1956.

Norwood, Gilbert. *Greek Comedy*. London: Methuen & Co., 1931.

Nussbaum, Martha. "Stoic Laughter: A Reading of Seneca's *Apocolocyntosis*." *Seneca and the Self*. Edited by Shadi Bartsch and David Wray. Cambridge, UK: Cambridge University Press, 2009, 84–114.

———. *Upheavals of Thought: The Intelligence of Emotions*. Cambridge, UK: Cambridge University Press, 2001.

O'Brien, Michael J. "The Unity of the *Laches*." *Yale Classical Studies* 18 (1963): 133–47.

Olson, S. Douglas, ed. *Broken Laughter*. Oxford: Oxford University Press, 3007.

Otto, Walter F. *Dionysus: Myth and Cult*. Translated by Robert B. Palmer. Bloomington: Indiana University Press, 1965.

Patterson, Richard. "The Platonic Art of Comedy and Tragedy." *Philosophy and Literature* 6 (1982): 76–93.

Pickard-Cambridge, Sir Arthur. *Dithyramb, Tragedy and Comedy* (2nd ed.). London: Oxford University Press, 1962.

Pindar. *The Odes*. Translated by C. M. Bowra. London: Penguin, 1969.

Plato. *Plato: Complete Works*. Edited by John M. Cooper. Indianapolis: Hackett, 1997.

———. *The Republic* (2nd ed.). Translated by Allan Bloom. New York: Basic Books, 1962.

Plochmann, George. "Hiccups and Hangovers in the *Symposium*." *Bucknell Review* 11 (1963): 1–18.

Plutarch. *Moralia* VI. Translated by W. C. Helmbold. Cambridge, MA: Harvard University Press, 2005.

———. Plutarch's Lives. Translated by Bernadotte Perrin. Cambridge, MA: Harvard University Press, 1913.

Popper, Karl. *The Open Society and Its Enemies: The Spell of Plato* (5th ed.). Princeton, NJ: Princeton University Press, 1962.

Proclus. *On Plato's* Cratylus. Translated by Brian Duvick. Ithaca, NY: Cornell University Press, 2007.

Quintilian. *The Orator's Education* (Books 6–8). Edited and translated by Donald A. Russell. Cambridge, MA: Harvard University Press, 2001.

Rankin, H. D. "Laughter, Humour and Related Topics in Plato." *Classica et Mediaevalia* 28, no. 1–2 (1969): 186–214.

———. *Plato and the Individual*. New York: Barnes & Noble, 1964.

Reich, Hermann. *Der Mimus: Ein Litterar-Entwickelungsgeschichtlicher Versuch*. Berlin: Weidmannsche Buchhandlung, 1903.

Reeve, C. D. C. *Socrates in the Apology*. Indianapolis: Hackett, 1989.

Richardson, Mary. "True and False Names in the 'Cratylus.'" *Phronesis* 21, no. 2 (1976): 135–45.

Robinson, Richard. "A Criticism of Plato's Cratylus." *Philosophical Review* 65, no. 3 (1956): 324-41.

Robinson, Thomas M., and Luc Brisson, eds. Plato: *Euthydemus, Lysis, Charmides*. Proceedings of the V *Symposium Platonicum*. Sankt Augustin, Germany: Academia Verglag, 2000.

Rose, Margaret A. *Parody: Ancient, Modern, and Post-Modern*. Cambridge, UK: Cambridge University Press, 1993.

Rosen, Stanley. *The Quarrel Between Philosophy and Poetry*. London: Routledge, 1993.

———. *Plato's Symposium* (2nd ed.). New Haven, CT: Yale University Press, 1987.

Rowe, Christopher. *Plato and the Art of Philosophical Writing*. Cambridge, UK: Cambridge University Press, 2007.

Rusten, Jeffrey. "Who 'Invented' Comedy?: The Ancient Candidates for the Origins of Comedy and the Visual Evidence." *American Journal of Philology* 127, no. 1 (Spring 2006): 37–66.

Saxonhouse, Arlene. "Comedy in Callipolis: Animal Imagery in the *Republic*." *American Political Science Review* 72 (1978): 888–901.

Sallis, John. *Being and Logos: Reading the Platonic Dialogues* (3rd ed.). Bloomington: Indiana University Press, 1996.

———. *Chorology*. Bloomington: Indiana University Press, 1999.

———. *Platonic Legacies*. Albany: State University of New York Press, 2004.

———. *Transfigurements: On the True Sense of Art*. Chicago: University of Chicago Press, 2008.

Schlegel, Augustus William. *Lectures on Dramatic Art and Literature*. Translated by John Black. London: Henry G. Bohn, 1846.

Schmid, W. Thomas. *Plato's Charmides and the Socratic Ideal of Rationality*. Albany: State University of New York Press, 1998.

———. *On Manly Courage: A Study of Plato's* Laches. Southern Illinois University Press, 1992.

Schmidt, Dennis. "Anything but a Series of Footnotes: Some Comments on John Sallis's *Platonic Legacies*." *Epoché* 11, no. 1 (2006): 275–86.

Scruton, Roger, and Peter Jones. "Laughter." *Proceedings of the Aristotelian Society* 56 (1982): 197–228.

Seaford, Richard. *Euripides'* Cyclops. Oxford, UK: Clarendon Press, 1984.

Sedley, David. "The Etymologies in Plato's *Cratylus*." *Journal of Hellenic Studies* 118 (1998): 140–54.

Segal, Erich. *The Death of Comedy*. Cambridge, MA: Harvard University Press, 2001.

———. "The *Phusis* of Comedy." *Harvard Studies in Classical Philology* 77 (1973): 129–36.

Seidensticker, Bernd. "Dithyramb, Comedy, and Satyr Play." *A Companion to Greek Tragedy*. Edited by Justina Gregory. Cambridge, UK: Blackwell, 2005, 38–54.

———. "Archilochus and Oedipus." *Greek, Roman, and Byzantine Studies* 14 (1978): 5–22.

Seneca. *Moral Essays* I and II. Edited and translated by John W. Basore. London: William Heinemann, 1932.

Shelley, Cameron. "Plato on the Psychology of Humor." *Humor* 16, no. 4 (2003): 351–67.

Shaftesbury, Anthony, Earl of. "*Sensus Communis*; an Essay on the Freedom of Wit and Humour." *Characteristics of Men, Manners, Opinions, Times*, vol. 1–2. New York: Bobbs-Merrill, 1964.

Shorey, Paul. *The Unity of Plato's Thought*. Chicago: University of Chicago Press, 1903.

———. *What Plato Said*. Chicago: University of Chicago Press, 1933.

Sinclair, T. A. "Plato's Philosophic Dog (*Republic* ii.375a–76c)." *Classical Review* 62, no. 2 (September 1948): 61–62.

Sluiter, Ineke, "The Greek Tradition." In *The Emergence of Semantics in Four Linguistic Traditions, Hebrew, Sanskrit, Greek, Arabic*. Edited by Wout van Bekkum, Jan Houben, Ineke Sluiter and Kees Versteegh. Amsterdam,1997, 147–224.

Sommerstein, Alan H. *Talking about Laughter and Other Studies in Greek Comedy*. Oxford: Oxford University Press, 2009.

———. *Greek Drama and Dramatists*. London: Routledge, 2000.

———. Ed. *Tragedy, Comedy and the Polis*. Bari, Italy: Levante Editori-Bari, 1993.

———. Introduction to *Aristophanes'* Acharnians, Clouds, *and* Lysistrata. London: Penguin, 1973.

Sophocles. *The Complete Plays of Sophocles.* Translated by Sir Richard Claverhouse Jebb. New York: Bantam Books, 1982.

Sophron. *Sophron and Other Mime Fragments.* Edited and translated by Jeffrey Rusten and I. C. Cunningham. Cambridge, MA: Harvard University Press, 2002.

Sprague, Rosamond Kent. "Platonic Jokes with Philosophical Points." In *Laughter Down the Centuries* vol. 1. Edited by Siegfried Jäkel and Asko Timonen. Turku, Finland: Turn Yliopisto (1994), 53-58.

———. *Plato's Use of Fallacy.* London: Routledge, 1962.

Stewart, Zeph. "Laughter and the Greek Philosophers: A Sketch." In *Laughter Down the Centuries* vol. 1. Edited by Siegfried Jäkel and Asko Timonen. Turku, Finland: Turn Yliopisto, 1994), 29-38.

Stimilli, Davide. "Daimon and Nemesis." *RES: Anthropology and Aesthetics* 44 (Autumn, 2003): 99-112.

Stone, I. F. *The Trial of Socrates.* London: Mackays of Chatham Plc., 1988.

Storey, Ian. Ed. and trans. *Fragments of Old Comedy*, vols. 1-3. Cambridge, MA: Harvard University Press, 2011.

———. and Arlene Allan. *A Guide to Ancient Greek Drama.* Malden, MA: Blackwell Publishing, 2005.

Strauss, Leo. *On Plato's Symposium.* Edited by Seth Benardete. Chicago: University of Chicago Press, 2001.

———. *Persecution and the Art of Writing.* Chicago: University of Chicago Press, 1988.

———. *Studies in Platonic Political Philosophy.* Chicago: University of Chicago Press, 1983.

———. *Socrates and Aristophanes.* Chicago: University of Chicago Press, 1966.

———. *The City and Man.* Chicago: University of Chicago Press, 1964.

Sutton, Dana F. *The Greek Satyr Play.* Meisenheim am Glan, Germany: Verlag Anton Hain, 1980.

———. *The Catharsis of Comedy.* Lanham, MD: Rowman and Littlefield, 1994.

Swabey, Marie Collins. *Comic Laughter: A Philosophical Essay.* New Haven, CT: Yale University Press, 1961.

Swift, L. A. "Archilochus the 'Anti-Hero': Heroism, Flight and Values in Homer and the New Archilochus Fragment (LXIX 4708)." *Journal of Hellenic Studies* 132 (November 2012): 139-55.

Szlezák, Thomas A. *Reading Plato*. Translated by Graham Zanker. London: Routledge, 1993.

Tanner, Sonja. *In Praise of Plato's Poetic Imagination*. Lanham, MD: Lexington Books, 2010.

———. "Pitiful Dramatics and the Feminine Framing of the *Phaedo*." *Dianoia* 12 (November 2007): 43–56.

Tarrant, Dorothy. "Style and Thought in Plato's Dialogues." *Classical Quarterly* 42, no. 1/2 (1948): 28–34.

———. "Imagery in Plato's Republic." *Classical Quarterly* 40, no 1/2 (1946): 27–34.

Taylor, A. E. *Plato: The Man and His Work*. Mineola, NY: Dover, 2001.

Theophrastus. *Characters*. Edited and Translated by Jeffrey Rusten and I. C. Cunningham. Cambridge, MA: Harvard University Press, 2002.

Thucydides. *The Peloponnesian War*. London: J. M. Dent, 1910.

———. *History of the Peloponnesian War*. Translated by Thomas Hobbes. London: Bohn, 1843.

Tuana, Nancy, ed. *Feminist Interpretations of Plato*. University Park: Pennsylvania University Press, 1994.

Tuckey, T. G. *Plato's* Charmides. Cambridge, UK: Cambridge University Press, 1951.

Umphrey, Stewart. "Plato's *Laches* on Courage." *Apeiron* 10, no. 2 (1976): 14–22.

Usher, M. D. "Satyr Play in Plato's Symposium." *American Journal of Philology* 123, no. 2 (2002): 205–28.

Viljamaa, Toivo. "Quintilian's Theory of Wit." In *Laughter Down the Centuries* 1. Edited by Siegfried Jäkel and Asko Timonen. Turku, Finland: Turn Yliopisto, 1994, 85–94.

Vlastos, Gregory. "Socratic Irony." *Classical Quarterly* 37, no. 1 (1987): 79–96.

Weingartner, Rudolph H. "Making Sense of the 'Cratylus.'" *Phronesis* 15, no. 1 (1970): 5–25.

Weitz, Eric. *The Cambridge Introduction to Comedy*. Cambridge, UK: Cambridge University Press, 2009.

Wilson, J. R. S. "Thrasymachus and the *Thumos*: A Further Case of *Prolepsis* in *Republic* I." *Classical Quarterly* 45, no. 1 (1995): 58–67.

Wolfsdorf, David. "The Irony of Socrates." *Journal of Aesthetics and Art Criticism* 65, no. 2 (2007): 175–87.

Wood, James. "Comedy, Malice, and Philosophy in Plato's *Philebus*." *Ancient Philosophy* 27, no. 1 (2007): 77–94.

Xenophon. *Memorabilia*. Translated by Amy L. Bonnette. Ithaca, NY: Cornell University Press, 1994.

———. *Conversations of Socrates*. Translated by Hugh Tredennick and Robin Waterfield. London: Penguin, 1990.

———. *Cyropaedia* (vols. 1-2). Translated by Walter Miller. London: William Heinemann, 1925.

Index

Aelian, 130, 174n47
Aeschylus, 108
Agathon, 119, 122, 125, 128, 136, 141
agōnēs
  in *Clouds*, 28
  hoplomachia and, 28, 30, 31, 39
  in *Laches*, 26, 28–31, 39
  nature of, 28
  parabasis and, 27, 29
  Socrates and, 28, 43
  in *Symposium*, 43
Alcaeus, 13
Alcibiades, xxviii, 122, 130–32, 134–39, 141, 190n83. *See also under* hubris and
  accused Socrates of hubris, xxviii, 117, 119, 128–30, 137, 138, 144, 145
  accused Socrates of scheming, 135–36
  Aristophanes and, 119, 124, 127–28, 139, 141, 168n72, 184n11
  arrival/entrance, 119, 127–28, 141
  character and (lack of) moral integrity, 134
  characterizations of, 160n13
  claim regarding wine and truth, 150
  courage and, 14
  describing Socrates's arguments as ridiculous, 75–76
  Dionysus and, 128, 136, 141
  eros and, 114, 138–39, 141, 145
  joke, 144, 145, 191n90
  Laches and, 42, 168n73
  life saved by Socrates, 14
  love and, 121, 136
  love for and attraction to Socrates, 127, 134, 136–40, 144–45, 149–50, 191n91
    attempts at seduction, 137
  Penia and, 141
  on the retreat from Delium, 42
  self-description, 136
  Silenus and, 125, 129, 140, 142, 157
  on Socrates, 56, 59, 113–17, 125, 128–29, 132–34
    description of Socrates, 127, 132–35, 146, 149
  Socrates alleging the corruption of, 66
  Socrates and, 128, 140–46, 149, 152, 157, 168n73, 172n26, 187n58, 190n83, 191n91
  and Socrates as hero, 15, 114
  on Socrates as mythical beast, 115, 152

Alcibiades (*continued*)
- and Socrates as satyr, xxviii, 56, 113–17, 127–46, 149, 152
- and Socrates changing roles, 138–40
- Socrates contrasted with, 15, 134–35
- Socrates's courage and, 15, 42, 59
- Socratic *logoi* and, 128, 130–31, 142, 143, 149, 157
- *sōphrosynē* and, 59, 138, 149–50
- speech about Socrates, 116, 117, 121, 128–32, 136, 139–41, 144, 145, 184n11, 190n86. *See also* satyr(s)

Alcibiades Major, 140
- authenticity of, 191n99

ambiguity. *See also* uncertainty
- in comical heroes, 16
- in names, and laughter, 112
- of satyrs, 133–34
- use of, 95–97, 99
  - Socrates and, 3, 83, 96, 97

Amelung, W., 130

Anacreon, 13

Anaxagoras, xxv, 107–8

andreia, 25. *See also* courage
- *aporia* and, 25, 42, 44, 47, 48, 167n41
- applying/demonstrating/embodying, 25, 32, 35, 37, 38, 42–44, 47, 49, 51
- comedy and, 25
- courageous temper and, 167n62
- cultivating, 28
- defining, 25, 28, 32, 35, 36, 41, 42, 47, 167n41, 168n73
- feigning, 150
- gender, 43, 168n76
- *hoplomachia* and, 31, 48
- importance, 24
- Laches and, 35–37, 41–44, 48, 51, 53, 168n62, 168n73
- *Laches* and, 24, 25, 33, 48, 53, 150. *See also Laches*
- laughter and, 44, 49, 51, 53
- learning, 155, 167n62
- learning and, 48
- Lysimachus and, 32
- *Meno* and, 48
- Nicias and, 35–37, 48, 51, 167n41
- *Republic* and, 44
- Socrates and, 28, 31, 35, 36, 44, 47, 168n76
- understanding, 25, 28, 36, 37, 41, 47, 48

Apollo and Dionysus, 3, 21, 56–57, 78, 108, 115

Apollodorus, 119

Apology of Socrates (Plato), 8–10, 12, 85, 98, 131, 151
- blame that Socrates casts on comedy, 101
- as comical, 1, 3–8, 15, 21, 24, 57, 64, 85, 98, 101, 129, 131, 157
- *Defense of Palamedes* (Gorgias) and, 8–11, 13, 18, 21
- more-than-human wisdom, 1, 24, 72, 74, 106, 110
- self-knowledge in, 1, 2, 57
- Socrates's jury, 3–12, 15, 17, 85, 131, 137, 152, 155
- Socrates's unattachment to life in, 18
- tragedy and, 5, 8, 21, 24

aporia, 37, 46, 48, 71, 72, 75, 154, 172n31

Laches and, 42, 44, 50, 52–53, 167n41
learning and, 48
Nicias and, 36, 42, 50, 52–53, 167n41
ontological, 56
Socrates and, 25, 47, 50, 52, 70–71, 170n94
Archilochus, xxvi, 13, 14–15, 18
Arieti, James, 47, 119, 121, 162n41, 162n43, 177n18, 185n26
Aristides, 26
Aristophanes, 56, 124, 179n36
Alcibiades and, 119, 124, 127–28, 139, 141, 168n72, 184n11
eros and, 114, 120, 126–28, 141, 144, 145, 147, 148
Eryximachus and, 121–23
Laches and, 35, 52
Nicias and, 35, 52
Plato and, 57, 73, 84, 121, 124, 125, 148, 175n54, 184n17
plays of
Assembly of Women, 181n51
beast-human-god structure in the, 17
The Birds, 57
The Clouds, 27–30, 46, 91, 118, 136, 174n45, 174n47
human representation in the, 153
influence of the, 23
laughter in the, xiii, xv, 23, 60, 61, 144, 156, 170n11, 171n17, 184n11
love in the, 124–27
Old Comedy(ies), xiii, 23, 52, 78, 191n98
para prosdokian in the, 191n95
Peace, 14, 57
resourcefulness in the characters of the, 148
themes and motifs in the, 57
as tragic, 148
The Wasps, 26, 41–42
wobbly characters in the, 57
ridicule and, xiii, 144
Socrates and, xxvi, 15, 20, 27, 73, 84, 91, 99, 101, 118, 119, 122, 127–28, 135, 136, 139, 148, 174n47, 179n37
speech, 118–20, 122–24, 139, 144
Aristophanes's hiccups, xii, xxviii, 114, 117–28, 144–45, 184n20, 185n26
ridicule and, 121, 122, 124–25
Aristophanes's myth, 117, 126, 141, 147, 148
Aristotelian tragic heroes, 12, 13
Aristotle, xiv, 159n13
andreia and, 49
on Cratylus, 182n57
on fallacy of equivocation, 96
on harmony and character, 40
laughter and, xxi, xxii
on the liberal and illiberal jest, 62
logos and, xiv, 6
on modes of persuasion, 6–7
Plato and, xiv
on satyr plays, 188n68
Socrates and, xiv–xv, 7, 12–13, 142, 160n13
on tragic heroes, 12–13
on words vs. actions and truth, 142–43
Athenaeus, 124–25

atopos, 72–74, 139
Socrates as, 74, 84
Austin, John L., 90

beast-man-god composite, the self as a, 114
beast-man-god structure, 16, 17, 114, 152, 153, 157
in Homeric epic, 164n43
Socrates and, 112–16, 131, 147, 149, 152, 156
beastly and the divine, satyrical tension between the, 116
Belfiore, 190n87
Bergson, Henri, xxiii
Berke, 154
Birds, The (Aristophanes), 57
Birth of Tragedy, The (Nietzsche), 114–15
body
and bodily functions, 127. *See also* Aristophanes's hiccups
Dionysus and the, 119, 122, 126, 186n43
eros and the, xxvii–xxviii, 114, 117, 119–21, 123, 127, 128, 135, 138, 141, 145, 189n78
laughter and the, 145
Bury, Henri Blaze de, 119, 124, 128, 138, 190n90

Callias, 106
Callicles, 76
Carroll, Lewis, 182n56
certitude, 51, 52. *See also* uncertainty
Chance, 112, 178nn33–34, 180n46
Charmides, 58–59, 66, 74, 171n26, 173n40
Critias and, 58–59, 66, 80
headache, 150
Socrates and, 58, 71, 74, 80, 81, 95, 138, 147, 149, 155, 172n26, 172n37, 173n40
eroticism between, 59, 71–72, 80, 147
sōphrosynē and, 58, 59, 63, 66, 71, 74, 138, 147, 173n40
Charmides (Plato), xiv, 56, 64, 66, 73, 77, 78, 150, 153
bench scene, xii, xiv, 58–59, 62, 67, 75, 80, 81
Critias in, 66–68, 114, 131
as a defense of Socrates, 172n26
laughter in, xii, xiv, xxvii, 58–59, 68, 73, 78, 79, 154
tragic and comic, 59–67
types of, xxvii, 62, 64
mimicry in, 173n39
Socrates in, xxvii, 57, 58, 67, 68, 73, 74, 76, 78, 131, 154
sōphrosynē in, 63, 64, 66, 67, 73, 78, 150
Socratic vs. Critian, 67–77
tragic ending, 66
Cicero, xiv, xv
Clay, Diskin, xxx, 119
Cleon, 41, 42
Clinias, 66, 94, 96–98, 101, 147
Clouds, The (Aristophanes), 27–30, 46, 91, 118, 136, 174n45, 174n47
comedy. *See also specific topics*
inserts distance between audience and characters, 101
comical hero, 148, 157
Socrates as, xxv–xxvi, 4, 12, 15, 16, 18, 20, 21, 25, 57, 113, 114, 152, 155, 160n13

traits, 15–18, 148
consequential laughter
nature of, xxi
playful laughter and, xxi–xxii, 48, 56, 62
contradiction (*antilegoi*), 93, 94. *See also* performative contradictions
comedy and, 103–4
conceptions of, 94
Dionysodorus and, 92–94
logos and, 47–48
nonexistence/impossibility of, 93–95, 100
Socrates and, 47–48, 91–94, 124
Coulter, James A., 8–9
courage, 27, 187n61. *See also andreia*
aspects of soul are involved in, 31
Laches and, 14, 31, 35, 45–52, 166n25, 168n62, 168n73, 169nn76–77, 169n79
Nicias and, 31, 35–36, 42, 45, 47, 48, 51–52, 166n25
ridicule and, 37, 43, 48
Socrates's, 15, 42, 59
Stesilaus and, 31, 39, 41, 42
uncertainty and, 36, 42, 51, 52
Cratylus, xxvii, 86, 88, 89, 91–92, 100, 102, 104–6, 110–11, 182n57. *See also under* performative contradictions
Aristotle on, 182n57
contradictions, 91–92
Hermogenes and, 86, 88, 89, 91, 92, 102, 104–6, 109–11, 182n58
Cratylus (Plato), 181n53. *See also under* logos
hubris and, 102, 106–11
laughter and logos in, 86–92
logoi in, 92, 102
logos and the satirical, 102–12
Critchley, Simon, 4
Critias, xxvii, 13, 56, 58–59, 62–64, 66–75, 79, 80–81, 114, 131, 153, 155, 156
in *Charmides*, 66–68, 114, 131
Charmides and, 58–59, 66, 80
hubris and, 62, 63, 68–70, 72, 75
performative contradictions, 68, 73
ridiculousness and, 63, 66, 69, 174n52
self-knowledge and, 67–69, 71, 73
sōphrosynē and, 58, 59, 66–71, 73, 75, 173n41
Thomas Schmid and, 71, 173n41
Crito, 85
educating his sons, 95, 99, 100
Euthydemus, Dionysodorus, and, 94, 98–101
on philosophy, 98
Socrates and, 7, 83–84, 95, 98, 99, 101
Critobulus, 129
Ctesippus, 94, 95, 98

Damon, 41, 44
Defense of Palamedes (Gorgias), 8–12, 18, 21, 90
Demetrius, 140
Democritus, xxv, xxvi, 19–20
derision (*katagelatai*), 60, 76. *See also* ridicule
derisive comedy, 14
derisive laughter (Type 1 laughter), 1, 44, 49, 53, 56, 60, 61, 97. *See also* malicious laughter

derisive laughter (*continued*)
Aristophanes's hiccups as, 122
of the feminine, 43
Plato and, xi, xvi, xvii
in the plays of Aristophanes, 60, 61, 153, 171n17
vs. self-reflective laughter, 147
of Socrates, 53, 155
purpose of the, 155
terminology, 60, 75
tragic laughter as, xxvi, 62
derisive view of comedy, 60
Desjardins, Rosemary, 63, 78
difference, conceptions of, 94
Dikaiopolis, 191n95
Dillon, Matthew, 60–62, 170n11
Diogenes Laertius, xiv, 57, 88, 92–93, 158
Dionysodorus
Euthydemus and, 93–95, 98–103. *See also* sophistic brothers
logos used by, 94–95, 147–49
mistakes, falsities, contradictions, and, 92–94, 102–3
performative contradictions, 102–3
Protagoras and, 93
Socrates and, 93, 94, 96–101, 143, 147
use of ambiguity, 96, 97, 99
Dionysus, 3, 21, 61, 108, 125–26. *See also* satyrs
Alcibiades and, 128, 136, 141
Apollo and, 3, 21, 56–57, 78, 108, 115
and the body, 119, 122, 126, 186n43
laughter and, 56–57
satyr drama and, 187n68
Silenus and, 140, 141
Socrates and, xvi, 3, 21, 114, 115, 126, 141, 143–44, 146–50, 157
Symposium and, 122, 124, 127, 140, 144, 146, 147
Diotima, 43, 121, 123, 127, 134–35, 143
dithyrambs, 108, 183nn64–65
Dobbs, Darrell, 42
Dorian harmony, 43
Dover, K. J., 138
duality, 92
in logos, 85, 86, 92, 112, 176n3, 181n54

Edmonds, Radcliffe G., 139
eirōneia, 142–43
elenchos, 26, 30
Emlyn-Jones, Chris, 26, 32, 166n38, 166n40
epideixis, 38
equivocation, fallacy of, 96
erastēs (lover), 136, 138, 140
erga (actions/deeds), 31, 42. *See also logoi:* (in)consistency vs. actions (*erga*) and
eristics, 100
erōmenos (beloved), 136, 138–40
eros, 119, 123
Alcibiades and, 114, 138–39, 141, 145
Aristophanes and, 114, 120, 126–28, 141, 144, 145, 147, 148
and the body, xxvii–xxviii, 114, 117, 119–21, 123, 127, 128, 135, 138, 141, 145, 189n78
defined, 120

laughter and, 114, 117
logos and, 114, 147
nature of, 127
self-forgetting and, 114, 117
Socrates and, 59, 67, 80, 114, 117, 134–35, 189n78
Eros, 14
Socrates's myth of the origin of, 140, 148, 156
eroticism. *See also* sexuality
between Charmides and Socrates, 59, 71–72, 80, 147
Eryximachus, 118, 121–23, 126, 128, 144
ethos, 6, 10, 88
etymologies, 103
absurdity, 91
Aristophanes and, 91
comedy and, 107, 108
comic/comical, 84–85, 91, 108, 176n5
and knowledge, 109, 110
logos and, 85
of names, 110, 152, 181n53, 182n58
critique of, 177n15
of names of gods, 111, 182–83nn158–159
Plato and, 103
as ridiculous, 91, 103, 107
Socrates and, 83–86, 91, 100, 106–10
laughter and, 86, 106
Euelpides, 61
Euripides, 60, 87, 135, 138
Euthydemus, 81, 98, 147
Dionysodorus and, 93–95, 98–103. *See also* sophistic brothers
logos used by, 102–3, 106, 147–49
mistakes, falsities, contradictions, and, 93, 102–3
performative contradictions, 92, 94, 95, 100, 102–3
Protagoras and, 93
Socrates and, xiii, 10, 93, 94, 96–101, 143, 147–49
use of ambiguity, 96, 97
Euthydemus (Plato)
laughter and false speaking in, 92–102
logoi in, 85, 87, 92, 93, 102
Euthyphro, 72–74, 105–7, 182n59
Euthyphro (Plato), 53, 72, 105–6, 159n2, 169n83, 182n59
eutrapelia, xxi, 160, 160n13
Ewegen, S. Montgomery, xvi, 155, 176nn3–4, 178n24, 181n54
exodos, 27, 29, 30

falling down, 170n6
"false" names, 88–90. *See also* names: veracity; naming: truth and falsity in
falsity. *See also under* contradiction; Dionysodorus; Euthydemus; Hermogenes; self-knowledge
Euthydemus's denial of, 93
logos, truth, and, 92, 95, 102
ridicule exposing, 75
fear
of being ridiculous, 37, 68, 72, 172n37
of malicious laughter, 45
of pretense, 80
of ridicule, 34, 48, 52–53, 169n77
of self-deception, 68, 69, 78, 80, 106

fear (*continued*)
of self-ignorance, 52, 68, 78, 106
finite transcendence, 114, 148, 156
forgetting. *See* self-forgetting
Frede, Dorothea, 79
Freud, Sigmund, xx–xxi
Freydberg, Bernard D., 153
Friedlander, Paul, 119, 177n17

Gagarin, 191nn90–91
gelaō, xvi, 60–62, 75. *See also* laughter
gender dynamics, 40, 43, 46, 168n76
Socrates and, 40, 43–44
Gerhard, Gustav Adolf, 19
"godlike state of mind," 72, 153
Gorgias, *Defense of Palamedes*, 8–12, 18, 21, 90
Greene, William Chase, 5, 177n24
Griswold, Charles, 56, 149
Guthrie, W. K. C., 119–20

Halliwell, Stephen, xxi–xxii, 62
Halper, Edward C., 59, 85, 101, 121, 139, 144–45
Hegel, Georg Wilhelm Friedrich, 55
Henry, 150
Heraclitus, 87–90, 109–10, 182n57
Hermogenes and, 88, 89, 109
Hermogenes, 110, 177n17
contradictions, falsity and, 91–92, 104–5
Cratylus and, 86, 88, 89, 91, 92, 102, 104–6, 109–11, 182n58
Heraclitus and, 88, 89, 109
language and, 182n56
logos/*logoi* and, 109, 182n58
names/*onomata* and, 86, 88, 89, 91, 92, 104, 105, 107–11, 182n58
Parmenides and, 88, 89, 109
Socrates and, 106–11, 182n58
Hippias, 72–74, 81, 106, 153
Hippolytus, 19
Hobbes, Thomas, xx, xxii, 64, 161n22
Hobbesian laughter, xx
Hoerber, Robert G., 31, 40–41
Homer, 13, 16, 73, 119
Homeric hero, Socrates and the, 8–18
honor (*timē*), 6, 14, 31, 32, 45, 53, 60, 160n13
vs. dishonor, xxvi, 14, 39, 45, 53, 137–39, 160n13
hoplomachia, 46
agōnēs and, 28, 30, 31, 39
andreia and, 31, 48
Laches and, 30, 32, 37–38, 41, 46, 48
Nicias and, 28, 32, 37, 38, 46, 48
Socrates and, 31
study of, 37, 46
teachers of, 38, 41, 46
Horace, 13, 19, 133, 188n68
Howland, Jacob, xxv, 5, 31, 119, 146, 162n39
Hubbard, Thomas K., 55
hubris, xxi, 1, 49, 74–75
Alcibiades's, 139
Aristophanes and, 148
Bury on, 138, 190n90
Cratylus and, 102, 106–11
Critias and, 62, 63, 68–70, 72, 75
meanings and connotations of the term, 138, 190nn89–90

nature of, 138, 190n90
sexual assault and, 190–91n90
Socrates accused of, 136, 138, 139, 142, 143, 191n91
by Alcibiades, xxviii, 117, 119, 128–30, 137, 138, 144, 145, 191n91
hubristēs, 138–39
humility
laughter and, xii
self-aware, 20
vs. self-importance, xvii
Humpty Dumpty theory of language, 104, 182n56
Hutcheson, Francis, xxii–xxiii
Hyland, Drew, 56, 147, 148, 156

ignorance. *See also* self-ignorance
recognition of one's, 20
incongruity theory of laughter, xxii–xxiv
incongruity(ies), 55
and laughter, xiii, 117. *See also* incongruity theory of laughter
philosophical, xxviii
of Socrates, 105–6, 108, 128, 131, 146, 151, 153–54
between words and actions/deeds, 64, 105–6, 110. *See also logoi*: (in)consistency between actions (*erga*) and; performative contradictions
Aristotle on truth and, 142–43
incongruous laughter, 144–46. *See also* incongruity(ies): and laughter
in *Symposium*, xxviii, 146
innocuous vs. tendentious jokes, xx–xxi

jest, types of, xv
jokes
Freud on, xx–xxi
types of, xx–xxi
Juvenal, 19

katagelaō, xvi, 60, 62, 75. *See also* ridicule
katagelasen, 74, 75
Kierkegaard, Søren, xii
Kirkland, 176n3, 176n5, 176n7
"know thyself," xvi, xxviii, 2, 65, 173n42, 183n60. *See also* self-knowledge; *sōphrosynē*

Laches, 14, 24–32, 36, 37–39, 45, 46, 48–53, 169n77
agōnēs, 28, 31
Alcibiades and, 42, 168n73
andreia and, 24–25, 28, 35–37, 41–44, 48, 51, 53, 168n62, 168n73
aporia and, 42, 44, 50, 52–53, 167n41
Aristophanes and, 35, 52
characterizations of, 53
as comical figure, 39–45
courage and, 14, 31, 35, 45–52, 166n25, 168n62, 168n73, 169nn76–77, 169n79
ergon and, 35, 41
failure, 169n79
failure in logos, 41–42, 45
gender dynamics and, 169n76
hamartia and self-blindness, 24–25

Laches (*continued*)
hoplomachia and, 30, 32, 37–38, 41, 46, 48
logoi and, 31, 35, 39
Lysimachus and, 27–30, 32, 46, 49, 50, 165n15
Melesias and, 46, 50
Nicias and, xxvii, 24–32, 35–38, 41, 42, 44–46, 48, 49, 51–53, 165n15, 166n25, 167n41, 169n76, 169n79
Old Comedy and, 53, 165n15
performative contradictions, 43, 44
personality, 169n77
poverty and, 53
ridicule and, 43–45, 48, 52–53, 169n77
self-knowledge and, 45–50, 53
Socrates and, 14
Socrates contrasted with, 25, 53, 168n73, 169nn76–77
Sophist and, 36
Stesilaus and, 32, 38, 39, 42, 44
Thomas Schmid and, 29, 40
thumos, 44, 160n13, 169n77
Laches (Plato). *See also specific topics*
andreia and, 24, 25, 33, 48, 53, 150
comical structure, 26–32
courage, laughter, and self-knowledge, 45–51
logoi in, 31, 35, 39, 52
parabasis in, 23, 27, 29, 30, 32, 52, 152, 154, 155, 165n15
tragedy and, 24, 25, 30, 41, 45, 47, 48, 53
laughability
being blindly vs. self-consciously laughable, 156
as fundamental human characteristic, 23
humanity as laughable, 18–21
recognizing oneself as laughable, 27
laughter (*gelaō*)
as an ambivalent force, 49
on the bench. *See Charmides*: bench scene
inserts distance between audience and characters, 101
Plato and Socrates's novel conception of, 20
Plato's revision of, 78
pleasure of, xx–xxi
purposes/goals, 25
Socrates on being laughed at, xii
terminology, xvi, 60–62, 74–76
that exposes the limitations of the laugher, xxvi
types of, xxi–xxii, 60–64. *See also specific types of laughter*
undergoes a philosophical change in Plato, xii
Lissarrague, Francois, 132, 140, 189n70
lofty, the, 73
logoi, 93, 103, 119
Aristophanes and, 179n37
in *Clouds*, 28
(in)consistency between actions (*erga*) and, 31, 35, 39–41, 52, 85. *See also* incongruity(ies): between words and actions/deeds; performative contradictions
in *Cratylus*, 92, 102

in *Euthydemus*, 85, 87, 92, 93, 102
failure to use, 92
Hermogenes and, 109, 182n58
in *Laches*, 31, 35, 39, 52
Laches and, 31, 35, 39
of Nicias, 35
in *Republic*, 29
restrictions on use of, 87, 93
and ridicule, 142
Socrates and, 93, 94
Socratic, 116, 128, 131, 141–43, 187n58
Alcibiades and, 128, 130–31, 142, 143, 149, 157
as comical, xiv
key to understanding, 142
ponēria and, 152
as satyr-like, 131
Socratic, and Alcibiades, 128, 130–31, 142, 143, 149, 157
in *Symposium*, 29
Unjust vs. Just, 179n37
logos, 43, 77, 79, 83, 85, 94, 119, 147–49
Aristophanes's hiccups and, 126
Aristotle and, xiv, 6
comedy and, 75, 86, 102, 110, 181n54
comic, 86, 87, 103, 109, 111
contradictions and, 47–48
Cratylus and, 176n3
Dionysodorus's use of, 94–96, 100, 147–49
duality in, 85, 86, 92, 112, 176n3, 181n54
eros and, 114, 147
Euthydemus's use of, 95, 96, 100, 102–3, 106, 147–49
gap between words and, 102
Hermogenes and, 109, 182n58
Laches and, 41–43, 45
laughter and, xxvi, 47–48, 75, 78, 102, 111, 147
in *Cratylus*, 86–92
limits/limitations of, 6, 10, 17, 21, 85–87, 92, 111
names, naming, and, 85, 89, 90, 102
nature of, 85, 148–49, 176n4, 176n7
dual, 85, 86, 92, 112, 176n3, 181n54
Nicias and, 35, 41
pathos/pathē and, 6, 7, 12
performative contradictions and, 78, 86, 89–90, 102–3
and the satirical *Cratylus*, 102–12
self-knowledge and, 110–12, 149
sensible use of, 86, 92, 93
Socrates and, xiv, 6, 7, 10, 12, 17, 18, 21, 41, 43, 45, 78, 83, 85–87, 92–94, 96, 100, 103, 109–12, 147, 149, 152, 154, 174n53
Thomas Schmid on, 75
truth, falsity, and, 92, 95, 102
will and, 176n7
love, xxii. *See also* Alcibiades; *erastēs*; *erōmenos*
Aristophanes's plays, 124–27
Lowenstam, Steven, 120, 184n19
Lysimachus, 165n15, 170n94, 179n36
agōnēs and, 31
Cephalus and, 166n31
characterizations of, 32–34, 166n38

Lysimachus (*continued*)
Chris Emlyn-Jones on, 166n38
as comical figure, 32–34
compared with Strepsiades, 27
education and, 27–30, 32, 33, 37, 46, 48–50, 179n36
family, 26–30, 32, 33, 46, 48–50
Laches and, 27–30, 32, 46, 49, 50, 165n15
laughing at, 52
mediocrity, 25
Melesias and, 25, 27–30, 32–34, 46, 48–50
Nicias and, 27–30, 32, 37, 46, 49
personality, 32–34, 46, 50, 53, 156, 166n38
Plato and, 166n40
ridicule and, 34, 52
Socrates and, 26–34, 37, 46, 52, 166n38, 166n40, 170n94, 179n36
Stesilaus and, 27, 39

malice (*phthonos*), 65, 99, 124, 157
Socrates and, xviii, 66
malicious, Aristophanes's hiccups as, 124
malicious comedy, 65
malicious laughter, xv–xvii, xix, xx, 60, 66, 169n77. *See also* derisive laughter
fear of, 45
Socrates and, xviii–xix
tragic laughter and, 53
malicious ridicule (*katagelasta*) vs. playful laughter (*geloion*), 144
megalopsūchos, 159n13
Melesias, 25, 32–33
education and, 27–29, 33, 48–50
family, 27–29, 32, 33, 46, 48–49
Laches and, 46, 50
Lysimachus and, 25, 27–30, 32–34, 46, 48–50
Nicias and, 46, 50
personality, 25, 30, 32–34, 46
Socrates and, 27–29, 33, 34, 50
Stesilaus and, 27, 29
Meno (Plato), 33, 42, 48
Michelini, Ann N., 96, 101, 175n2, 178nn33–34, 179nn36–37, 180n39, 180n44
Midas, 130, 133, 137
Mimes, Sophronic, xiv
moderation. *See sōphrosynē*
Morr, 9
Morreall, John, xvii, xix, 161n19

Nails, Debra, 38–39, 41
names, 107–9. *See also* etymologies; *onomata*
ambiguities in, and laughter, 112
changing, 104
"false," 88–90
Hermogenes and, 86, 88, 89, 91, 92, 104, 105, 107–11, 182n58
nature of, 88, 104, 105, 109–10
problems with and limitations of, 88, 109
puns on, 119, 123
Socrates and, 108, 109
terminology, 87
veracity, 88, 104, 105, 108–11. *See also* Hermogenes: names/*onomata* and; naming: truth and falsity in

naming (*onomazein*), 88, 112
the impossibility of correctly, 89
logos and, 89, 102
and refusals to name, 87
truth and falsity in, 89–91, 104–5. *See also* Hermogenes: names/*onomata* and; names: veracity
Nichols, James H., 33, 36, 41
Nicias, 28, 35
agōnēs, 28, 31
andreia and, 24–25, 28, 35–37, 48, 51, 167n41
anxiety about future events, 36
aporia and, 36, 42, 50, 52–53, 167n41
Aristophanes and, 35, 52
as comical figure, xxvii, 34–37, 49–50, 52–53
contradiction between the claims and actions of, 35
courage and, 31, 35–36, 42, 45, 47, 48, 51–52, 166n25
death, 24, 165n3
failure and defeat, 24, 34–35, 169n79
hamartia and self-blindness, 24–25, 36
hoplomachia and, 28, 32, 37, 38, 46, 48
Laches and, xxvii, 24–32, 35–38, 41, 42, 44–46, 48, 49, 51–53, 165n15, 166n25, 167n41, 169n76, 169n79
logos and, 35, 41
Lysimachus and, 27–30, 32, 37, 46, 49
Melesias and, 32
Old Comedy and, 35, 41
Plutarch and, 35
Socrates and, 25, 27–29, 35–37, 41, 44, 45, 47, 50
Sophist and, 36
as teacher, 37, 50
Thucydides and, 35
Nietzsche, Friedrich Wilhelm, 57, 114–15, 133–34, 157, 158
Nussbaum, 134–35

O'Brien, Michael J., 35
Old Comedy, xv, 34, 35, 39, 129
Aristophanes and, xiii, 23, 52, 78, 191n98
Attic, 41, 127, 154, 159n6
heroes of, 17
Socrates compared with, xxvi, 15–16, 83–84
initial scene (prologue) in, 27
Laches and, 53, 165n15
laughter and, xiii, 23, 84
Nicias and, 35, 41
parabasis and, 23, 27, 30, 84, 152, 154, 165n15
structure, 29–30, 152, 154
Olympiodorus, 125–26, 186n43
onoma, 87–88, 104
translations and uses of the term, 87
onomata, 88–90, 92–93, 96, 104, 109, 110. *See also* names; naming
optimism, 114, 147
Platonic, 113, 148, 157
Socratic culture as rooted in, 79
optimistic spirit, 114

Palamedes. *See Defense of Palamedes*
Pan, 111–12

parabasis
  agōnēs and, 27, 29
  in *Clouds*, 29
  definition and nature of, 28, 152
  in *Laches*, 23, 27, 29, 30, 32, 52, 152, 154, 155, 165n15
  Old Comedy and, 23, 27, 30, 84, 152, 154, 165n15
  Socrates and, 29, 155
Parmenides, 88–90, 109–10
parodos, 27, 28
Pausanias, 119, 121–24
pederasty, 138
performative contradictions, 91–92, 110, 172n31. *See also* incongruity(ies): between words and actions/deeds; *logoi:* (in) consistency between actions (*erga*) and
  of Cratylus, 86, 92, 105
  in Cratylus's joke, 78, 86
  of Critias, 68, 73
  defined, xvi, 64, 73, 172n31
  of Dionysodorus, 92, 95, 100, 102–3
  of Euthydemus, 92, 94, 95, 100, 102–3
  of Euthyphro, 53, 73
  of Hermogenes, 92, 105
  of Hippias, 73
  of Laches, 43, 44
  and laughter, 43, 44, 64, 90
  logos and, 78, 86, 89–90, 102–3
  Socrates and, 44
Pericles, 33
persuasion, modes of, 6–7. *See also* *ethos*; *logoi*
Phaedo (Plato), 125, 174n45, 175n59
Phaedrus, 121, 124, 126
Phaedrus (Plato), 3, 115–16, 183n64, 190n89
Pheidippides, 27–28
Philebus (Plato), xviii–xx, 2, 65, 79, 124, 146, 151, 183n60
philosophers
  Presocratic, 19, 87–89, 182n57
  as ridiculous, 74–76
  as "the refined thinkers who are really poor," 53, 54
philosophy. *See also specific topics*
  comedy and, 63, 84
Phrynichus, 35
Pickard-Cambridge, Arthur, 179n36
Pindar, 14
Plato. *See also specific topics*
  antigelastic readings of, xiv, 58, 79, 147
  gelastic reading of, xiv, xv
  laughter and, xi
"Plato says" fallacy, xix, 175
playful comedy, 124, 125
playful laughter (*geloion*), xvi, 44, 56, 62, 64
  consequential laughter and, xxi–xxii, 48, 56, 62
  expressing superiority, xxii
  nature of, xxi
  vs. ridicule, 144, 157
  slapstick and, 62. *See also* slapstick
  wisdom and, 1, 157
playful tragedy, 140, 189n68
playfulness, Socrates and, 95, 100, 107, 108
pleasures, shared
  laughter arising from, 61

Plochmann, George, 126
Plutarch, 13, 35, 108, 124, 166n28, 185n38, 186n38, 191n91
Poetics (Aristotle), xxii, 188n68
poetry, 13, 14, 87
  Plato on, 115, 125
poets, 87, 119, 188n68
  comic, 53, 72, 119, 126, 174n45
  Plato and, 124
political jokes, 26
ponēria, 17, 151, 156
  comic heroes and, xxvi, 16, 17, 148, 152, 157
  nature of, 16, 79, 148, 157
  Old Comedy and, xxvi
  Socrates and, xxvi, 2, 17, 65, 148, 151–52, 183n60
  translations of the term, 79, 151
ponēria roguery, xxvi
Presocratic philosophers, 19, 87–89, 182n57
pretense, fear of, 80
pretensions, laughter as exposing, 64, 121
Proclus, 103
Prodicus, 106
Protagoras, 10, 47, 85, 92–93
Protagoras (Plato), 47–48, 174n53
Protarchus, xviii
psychoanalytic perspective on jokes and humor, xx–xxi

Quintilian, xiv

rape, 138, 187n68, 191n90
renaming, 104
Republic (Plato), 29, 31, 40, 75, 124, 149, 161n22, 167n62
ridicule (*katagelaō*), xiii, 19, 43, 46, 142. *See also* derisive laughter
  andreia and, 38, 41, 43
  Aristophanes and, xiii, 122, 144
  Aristophanes's hiccups and, 121, 122, 124–25
  courage and, 37, 43, 48
  exposing falsity, 75
  fear of, 34, 48, 52–53, 169n77
  Hobbes and, xxii
  and honor, 45
  Laches and, 38, 41, 43–45, 48, 52–53, 169n77
  laughter and, xiii, xiv, xvi, xvii, xxi–xxii, 32, 44–46
  laughter of, 39
  Lysimachus and, 34
  Nicias and, 35, 44, 52–53
  Odysseus and, 59, 61
  Plato and, 125
  ridiculer becoming the one ridiculed, 44
  and self-awareness, 155
  self-blindness and, 48
  self-knowledge, self-ignorance, and, 53
  Socrates and, 37, 43–44, 48, 52–53, 74, 75, 122, 179n36
  Stesilaus and, 38, 39, 44
ridiculousness, xviii, xxiii, 66–67, 74, 77
  Aristophanes and, 144
  Aristotle and, 122
  awareness of one's, 174n52
  Critias and, 63, 66, 69, 174n52
  etymologies as ridiculous, 91, 103, 107

ridiculousness (*continued*)
fear of being ridiculous, 37, 68, 72, 172n37
goal of not looking ridiculous, 143
Laches and, 37, 41
vs. laughability, 156–57
laughter and, 66, 73
Lysimachus and, 34
nature of, 2, 65–66
of philosophers, 74–76
self-certainty and, 69
self-knowledge, self-ignorance, and, xviii, 2, 3, 20, 37, 48, 64–66, 155
Socrates and, xviii, 2, 3, 7, 18, 43–44, 65, 66, 68, 72, 79, 115–16, 130, 143, 146, 174n52
Socrates on the nature of the ridiculous, 183n60
Stesilaus and, 41, 47
Rosen, Stanley, 119
Rückert, Frédéric, 124

Sallis, John, 5, 149, 177n24, 181nn51–54
satyr plays. *See also* tragicomedy
Aristotle on, 188n68
satyric drama, 133, 136, 187–89n68. *See also* Alcibiades: speech about Socrates
satyric humor, 117
satyrical behavior, 138
satyrical characteristics attributed to Socrates, 187n59
satyrical imagery, 128, 139, 145
satyrical laughter in *Symposium*, 117, 145–46
satyrical speech. *See* Alcibiades: speech about Socrates
satyr(s)
ambiguity of, 133, 134
Silenus as a, 129, 130, 133, 135, 140
Socrates as a, xxviii, 56, 113–17, 127–45
Alcibiades and, xxviii, 56, 113–17, 127–46, 149, 152
Schlegel, Augustus William, 62, 170n10, 189n68
Schleiermacher, Friedrich, 123
Schmid, W. Thomas
on *andreia*, 44
Critias and, 71, 173n41
harmony and, 40
irony and, 47
and comic and tragic elements, 169n90
on *Laches*, 26, 27, 29, 30, 47
Laches and, 29, 40
on logos, 75
on over-inflation of self-concept, 74
Socrates and, 40
on *sōphrosynē*, 74
Seaford, Richard, 133, 134, 189n68
Second, 106–7
Sedley, David, 91, 103, 180n51
self-awareness, 20
comedy and, xvi
self-blindness, 20, 49, 52. *See also* self-ignorance; self-knowledge: lack of
andreia and, 49

courage to face, 48
failure to recognize one's, 24
of Laches and Nicias, 24–25
laughter and, 25, 51
overcoming, 27
and ridicule, 48
self-certainty, 58, 69, 70
basis of, 69–70
lack of, 69
laughter and, 68
and ridiculousness, 69
sōphrosynē and, 58, 69–70
self-concept, overinflated, 74
self-consciousness, 55. *See also* self-knowledge
vs. the comical, 56
laughter and, 78–80, 156
of one's being laughable, 76
of Socrates, 78, 113
self-control. *See sōphrosynē*
self-deception (*exapatasthai auton*), 40, 49, 109, 111
fear of, 68, 69, 78, 80, 106
laughter and, 51, 68, 109
laughter preventing/remedying, 78
laughter revealing, 106
overcoming, 51
Socrates and, 67, 68, 78
Socrates on, 109
as the "worst thing of all," 109
self-directed laughter, 18–21, 44
vs. other-directed laughter, 4
self-forgetting, 37, 44, 49–50, 70, 117, 127
comedy as, 103, 110, 111
eros and, 114, 117
hazards of, 154
laughter and, 49, 111, 154
nature of, 154
self-identity, 111
self-ignorance, 19, 58, 59, 65, 157. *See also* self-knowledge: lack of
fear of, 52, 68, 78, 106
laughing at, xvii
laughter expressing, 77
laughter preventing/remedying, 78
laughter revealing, 106
power and, 66
ridiculousness and, 65–66
Socrates on, 68, 78, 183n60
types of, 65, 183n60
self-ignorant persons' power to affect others, 66
self-knowledge, 3, 111, 151. *See also* "know thyself"; *sōphrosynē*
achievement of, 110–11
challenges to the, 152
steps toward the, 149–50
Apology and, 1
assessment of one's, 48
assuming oneself falsely in possession of, 1, 23
comedy and, 1, 27, 56, 65, 102
comical, 156
and the comical, xvi, 55–56, 78
of comical figures, 146–47
Critias and, 68, 71
Critias on, 67–69, 73
eros and, 149
impossibility of achieving (complete), 23, 56, 69, 113, 116, 146–47, 149

self-knowledge (*continued*)
  Laches and, 45–50, 53
  lack of, xii, 20, 37, 53, 55, 64, 65, 77, 154, 155. *See also* self-ignorance
    fear of, 52
    wisdom of aware of vs. ignorance of one's, 1, 3–4, 20, 23, 24, 64–66
  laughter and, xii, 1–4, 20, 23, 24, 27, 48, 53, 55–57, 64, 77, 111, 150, 154, 155
  logos and, 110–12, 149
  nature of, 20, 56, 67
  performative contradictions and, 64
  in *Philebus*, 2, 65
  Plato and, 56
  pursuit of, 3, 4, 24, 27, 116
    Socrates's, 116
  requires a precise measure of one's goods, 66
  Socrates and, xvi, 20, 37, 56, 57, 67–69, 113
  Socrates lacking, 1, 3–4, 116
  Socrates on, xii, 1, 3, 66, 112, 113, 116, 154–56
  Socrates possessing, 1–3
  sōphrosynē and, 55, 56, 58, 65, 67
  superiority and, 71, 77
  use of mythical creatures to seek, 116, 149, 156
  virtue and, 113
  what constitutes, 20, 67
self-love as motivation for all human action, xxii
self-perception, the comical as a function of, 55
self-possession (*emphrōn*), 42
self-recognition, comic, xvii
self-reflection, 69, 70
  laughter and, xii, 86
  by Socrates, 59, 71–72
self-reflective laughter, xxvi, 80, 84, 121, 157
  vs. derisive laughter, 147, 155
  effects of, 101–2, 121, 155
  nature of, 78–79
  of Socrates, 78, 84–86, 97, 147, 155
self-reflexiveness, 1
self-sufficient, Socrates as, 135
semantics. *See* names; naming
sexual assault, 190–91n90. *See also* rape
sexuality, 29, 61, 120, 126, 138, 139, 171n21, 191n90. *See also* eros; eroticism
shared pleasures, laughter arising from, 61
Sheffield, 142, 156
Silenus, 135
  Alcibiades and, 125, 129, 140, 142, 157
  Dionysus and, 140, 141
  Midas and, 130, 133, 137
  military courage and, 187n61
  as satyr, 129, 130, 133, 135, 140
  Socrates and, 115, 116, 125–26, 129, 130, 140–42, 157, 190n87
slapstick, xi, 39, 58, 62, 117, 118, 144, 146
Socrates. *See also specific topics*
  characterizations of, xxvi, 143. *See also* comical hero: Socrates as

as great-souled person, 160n13
as satyr, xxviii, 56, 113–17, 127–45
as self-conscious hero, 57, 113
and the Homeric hero, 8–18
as laughable, 49
personality, xxvi, 143
unattachment to life, 18
physical description, 129
self-description, 147
self-reflection, 59, 71–72
and traits of comical heroes, 15–18
Sommerstein, Alan, 61–62, 191n95
Sophist (Plato), 36–37
sophistic brothers, 85, 92, 93, 96, 99, 102, 157. *See also* Dionysodorus; Euthydemus
sophistry, 100
sophists, 10, 38, 95–97, 99, 100
Sophocles, 60, 135
Sophron, xiv
Sophronic Mimes, xiv
sōphrosynē, 55
Alcibiades and, 59, 138, 149–50
in *Charmides*, 64, 66, 73, 78, 150
Charmides and, 58, 59, 63, 66, 71, 74, 138, 147, 173n40
comedy and, 56, 65
Critias and, 58, 59, 66–71, 73, 75, 173n41
definitions, 67, 70
vs. hubris, 138
laughter and, 55–57, 64, 67, 75, 78, 80
nature of, 70, 71, 73, 80, 173n41
of Socrates, 59, 66, 138, 149–50
Socrates and, 71–74
Socrates on, 56, 67–69, 80, 173n40
translations of the term, 55
Sprague, Rosamond Kent, 88, 90, 110
Stesilaus, 46
in combat, 31, 32, 38–39, 42, 46, 150
as a comical figure, 37–39, 42, 44, 47
courage and, 31, 39, 41, 42
Laches and, 32, 38, 39, 42, 44
ridicule and, 38, 39, 44
teaching Athenian youth, 27, 29, 30
Strepsiades, 27–28, 46–47, 61, 99, 130, 179n36
superiority, 71–73, 76, 106, 153
comedy as based on feelings of, 124
playful warning against thinking oneself superior, 62
self-knowledge and, 71, 77
of Socrates, 41
Socrates on, 65
superiority theory of laughter, xiii, xxi–xxii, 75, 77, 97, 153, 161n22
arguments against, xviii–xix, xxi–xxiv, xxvii, 20, 58, 59, 62–65, 77–81
attributed to Plato, xv–xix, xxiv–xxv, 63–65
Charmides bench scene and, 59
limitations, xix–xx
overview, xvii–xxi
slapstick and, 58
Socrates and, xviii, xxiv, 20, 64, 65
Sutton, Dana F., 117, 135, 140

Symposium (Plato), 29, 43. *See also* Alcibiades
Dionysus and, 122, 124, 127, 140, 144, 146, 147
incongruous laughter in, xxviii, 146
satyrical laughter in, 117, 145–46

Taylor, A. E., 107, 118–19, 178n24
temperance, 55, 72–73. *See also* *sōphrosynē*
tendentious vs. innocuous jokes, xx–xxi
Terence, 47
Tessitore, 27, 42, 46, 47, 169n83
Thales, 43, 44, 49, 76–77, 81, 127, 157
Theaetetus (Plato), 43–44, 76, 96, 129
Theodorus, 129
Theophrastus, 143
Thucydides, 24, 35
thumos, Laches's, 44, 160n13, 169n77
tragedy, xxix, 24, 148, 187–89n68. *See also Birth of Tragedy*
Alcibiades and, 136
Apology and, 5, 8, 21, 24
Charmides ending as a, 66
comedy and, xvi, xvii, xxix–xxx, 28–29, 144, 146, 170n10
Laches and, 24, 25, 30, 41, 45, 47, 48, 53
laughter and, xii, 24, 25, 30, 48, 62, 147. *See also* tragic laughter
playful, 140, 189n68
vs. satyry plays, 135
Socrates and, xvi, xvii, 5, 8, 12, 13, 21, 24, 139, 144
Socrates on, 136, 146
tragic, the satyr as, 146
tragic elements, 47
in *Apology*, 5
and comic elements in plays, 47, 146
tragic figures, 23
being laughed at, xii
tragic heroes, 17, 53
Aristotelian, 12, 13
tragic laughter, 41, 45, 53
vs. comic laughter, xxvi, 56, 59–67, 78, 159n2, 170n11
courage and, 41
as derisive laughter, xxvi, 62
tragic pessimism vs. comical, Platonic optimism, 113
tragic poetry, Plato's alleged hostility toward, 115
tragic vs. comic imagery, 164n43
tragic vs. comic life, 176n3
tragicomedy, 112. *See also* satyr plays
transcendence, 17, 113, 114, 147–48, 156
trial of Socrates. *See Apology of Socrates*
Trygaeus, 14, 57

uncertainty, 47, 51. *See also* ambiguity
courage and, 36, 42, 51, 52
Usher, M. D., 129, 130, 148–49, 187n61

vice. *See ponēria*
Vlastos, Gregory, 143, 190n86
vulgarity, xiii, 16, 73, 117, 133, 188–89n68

Whitman, Cedric, 16, 17, 164n43
wisdom, 1. *See also* self-knowledge
  human, 2, 18, 24, 106
    defined, 24
  more-than-human/greater-than-human, 1, 2, 4, 18, 24, 72, 74, 106, 110
  of the recognition of one's lack of self-knowledge, 1, 3, 23, 24
  Socrates on, 24
  superhuman, 105, 106, 132

Xenarchus, xiv
Xenophon, 9, 66, 129, 130